SOME PART
OF MYSELF

J. FRANK DOBIE

1888–

SOME PART OF MYSELF

UNIVERSITY OF TEXAS PRESS
AUSTIN AND LONDON

To
Fannie, Elrich, and Martha
and the memory of
Lee and Henry

"The Unveiling of a Self-Portrait" originally appeared in slightly different form in *The New York Times*'s Book Review Section. © 1956 by The New York Times Company. Reprinted by permission.

"How My Life Took Its Turn" originally appeared in slightly different form in *Wings*, published by The Literary Guild of America, Inc., February, 1931, under the title "How I Became a Hunter of Legends." It is reprinted here by permission.

"Storytellers I Have Known" was originally published in slightly different form by The Texas Folklore Society. Copyright © 1961 by The Texas Folklore Society. Reprinted by permission.

International Standard Book Number 0-292-77558-X
Library of Congress Catalog Card Number 79-67708

Printed in the United States of America

First University of Texas Press Printing, 1980
Reprinted by arrangement with Little, Brown and Company, Inc.

Foreword

IN a letter written December 9, 1963, to his friend Edward Welbourne, Master of Emmanuel College, Cambridge University, Frank Dobie wrote, "I don't know if I'll ever get an autobiography completed. All I have of it is many scraps — some long, some short." It is out of these "scraps" and the Sunday "pieces" — articles appearing in a few Texas newspapers without interruption for twenty-five years — that this book has been made. For some time Frank had cast into an "autobiographical box" a copy of whatever he wrote about himself, not limited in the box as in the book to early life, and also recollections scribbled on a used envelope, a blank check, a hotel menu or any other handy bit of paper; newspaper interviews; short accounts of his life prepared to be sent out upon request; letters, particularly correspondence with Miss Ruth Dodson, who wrote about the country and the families he had known as a boy; a diary kept intermittently over about two years of young manhood; and much else. There are several versions of "The Life of a Writer in the Southwest," which in one form or another Frank had read before three audiences: a writers' conference at Corpus Christi; the Texas Institute of Letters in session at Houston; and a University of Texas audience in Batts Hall on the campus. Portions have gone into chapters of this book.

"Scraps" is not altogether the right word. Several of these autobiographical sketches appeared in magazines and other publications: *Southwest Review*, a proving ground for much of Frank's writing; *Atlantic;* publications of the Texas Folklore Society; the Literary Guild's *Wings*, and the *New York Times Book Review*. Yet he did not consider these essays finished — or any writing of his until it was stored between hard covers, after which time he never looked at it again. For example, a manuscript on college years, published in *Southwest Review* (Winter 1957) has this annotation, "Fully corrected after lecture and S.W. Review editing." It has many alterations in longhand as the writer continued to search for the exact word, some added material, and a few subtractions with the note: "In preceding chapter." He was editing for his autobiography.

The newspaper pieces are short and have required welding, to use Frank's word. Even into the long essays I have inserted some material that seems to me to belong, my criterion being Frank's own of interest. Some notes had to be left in the box because they consisted of only a word or phrase jotted down as reminder. One such is "head in a hornet's nest." Another is "Jim Alexander's corpse." Still another is "trapping quail."

Frank read a chapter of his projected autobiography before his club, Town and Gown, on December 6, 1956. In introductory remarks he said, "If what I write is not interesting in itself — entirely removed from any acquaintance with me, liking for me or disliking of me — then I shall not have succeeded in this essay at autobiography." This is an admirable statement, but I do not agree with it. If I did, I should not have used as a chapter "Along Lake George," which was written in 1913. I have included it in the belief that those who, long after, knew Frank Dobie will find interesting something of him from the time he was young as well as what, having become a practiced writer, he recalled in prose. Some readers may be amused to find how much Dobie young resembled Dobie old.

I should like to express thanks to Wilson Hudson for the

gentle proddings that had something to do with Frank's putting down personal recollections and for his encouragement to me. "Wilson Hudson thinks I have written enough chapters of autobiography to make a book. Perhaps I have," Frank wrote in his will. Lon Tinkle, book critic for the Dallas *News*, has read parts of the manuscript with helpful comment. I am deeply grateful to Willie Belle Coker, who has been much more than typist to me, as she was to Frank.

BERTHA McKEE DOBIE

On Waller Creek
Austin, Texas

Contents

Only a few hints, a few diffused
faint clews and indirections
I seek for my own use to trace
out here.

— Walt Whitman

SOME PART
OF MYSELF

CHAPTER ONE

Unveiling of a Self-Portrait

No autobiography is as good as the best biography. Perhaps the strongest impression I retain from any straightout autobiographical narrative is from Benvenuto Cellini's, though more than forty years have passed since it enthralled me. It is a minor work compared with Boswell's life of Johnson; so is the best known and also the best American autobiography — Benjamin Franklin's.

The supreme character revelations in literature have not been by either biographers or autobiographers. Both of these come to big spots, vast areas, in their subjects that they do not comprehend and, therefore, cannot reveal. The creator of Huckleberry Finn made a botch of an autobiography. "Know thyself" is a fine adage, but no self-portrait in literature is so strong, so deep and wide, so rich in both complexities and simplicities, so full and yet so cleared of dross as the created character of Hamlet.

In his recollections *My Childhood*, *In the World*, and *My Universities*, Maxim Gorky is a supreme narrator, conversation and incident revealing the insides of a stream of characters who had entered his life. The work is truth but probably is not historical fact. All first-class biographies and autobiographies transcend fact.

I don't know that the truth, all the truth available, about

anybody would sum up justice. Perhaps the best things and the worst things too lie too deep in a being ever to come out. Aside from the impossibility of arriving at justice through truth, nobody, for various other reasons, wants all the truth about himself published. Nobody wants justice either. "God's bodykins, man . . . use every man after his desert, and who should 'scape whipping?" Truth is one thing, justice is another; no autobiography has ever been written that was either.

Montaigne was never the kind of philosopher who evolves a systematic explanation of the universe. Instead of knowing, he was all the time aware of not knowing. "There is scarcely anything I am sure of knowing," he said. His autobiographical essays show him unadmiring of self; yet his passion for expressing his own mind, tastes, values, and desires was boundless. He did not write, strictly speaking, an autobiography, but everything he wrote is autobiographical. Only deference to convention checked him from extending his honesty to those literally naked experiences for confessing which Rousseau had a genius. "If you intend," acidulous Carlyle wrote, "to interest readers — that is to say, idle neighbors and fellow creatures in need of gossip — there is nothing like unveiling yourself." But with all of his unveiling, Rousseau is not — to me — as honest as Montaigne or as human. In this country the demand for *I Confess* and *True Confessions* kind of writing has led to a great deal of tawdry fiction and no outstanding autobiography of which I am aware. I don't pretend, however, to keep up in reading. I'd be satisfied to read Montaigne over every time a new autobiography is offered. I'm never, of course, satisfied.

Unless a person attaches a good deal of importance to himself, he or she would never attempt an autobiography. Even if a writer never talks directly about himself but only about what he has observed, he has a good opinion of himself as observer and cannot possibly avoid revealing his sense of values, which may be the most important asset that any human being possesses. If voting were limited to individuals with a just sense of values and if enough — don't ask me to define *enough* — voters were left after the delimiting process had been accomplished, the nations would be transmuted into utopias.

Autobiography is not nearly so specialized a form of writing as is generally taken for granted. The author of the most banal textbook in Education, spelled with a Capital E, reveals unconsciously the life-killing mediocrity of his own mind. "O that he were here to write me down an ass," Dogberry cried. Every person who writes anything on any subject at all writes down the degree of his own asininity. Nobody, you know, has an absolute minus in that attribute; the gradations are in pluses. Some never hear, as in Barrie's *Rosalind*, "the still small voice saying, 'Ass, Charles, ass.' "

A writer, whether he is sincere or hypocritical, churlish or generous, humorous or humorless, sensuous, sensual or insensate, whether led by fleeting beauty to the doorway of the dead or stagnating in obtuseness to it — any and every writer is always writing himself down, is constantly giving out what he has fed on. This would not be so true of a writer in some strict field of science or even of science fiction as of writers in general; yet even mathematicians have to express themselves.

Autobiography is frequently regarded as a kind of personal monument, self-erected. Some autobiographies seem to have been written on the principle followed by Shanghai Pierce in having a life-size marble statue of himself carved — by a tombstone maker — and set up overlooking his ranch. Somebody asked him why he put it up. "I knew damn well nobody else would do it if I didn't," he said.

The best novels are written to say something about life — in fiction form. The greatest plays say something about life in dramatic form — and I am positive without being able to prove it that *Hamlet* reveals the innerness of Shakespeare as no biography based on ten thousand documented facts, if they existed, could reveal it. The great poems say something about life in poetry forms. The great biographies and autobiographies say about life in their forms.

The autobiographical medium permits considerable saying about life ruled out by other mediums of writing. Thus Somerset Maugham explains his reason for writing *The Summing Up* — the wisest modern book I know on life and writing. It is a book of ideas, not of reminiscences, though plenty of experience enters into it. It ends with a quotation from Fray Luis de León: "The beauty of life is nothing but this, that each should act in conformity with his nature and his business." Unless an autobiography is written in conformity with the writer's nature and business, it will not be valid. Yet that statement is so vague that it is valueless.

Here I am a writer with some interest — not overpowering; not nearly so overpowering as was my interest in *The Longhorns* and then in *The Mustangs* — in writing about and out from myself. The main trouble is a very old one — what to select. One part of me goes in the path set by W. H. Hudson's *Far Away and Long Ago.* In this autobiographical classic the harsh world is forgotten in the distilled innocence of a vanished life. It is a pleasure to me to recollect another vanished life that is a part of me — soon to vanish also. Yet I am not vain enough to imagine that anything I might write will stay the vanishing. The wild flowers of a rainy spring and the grasses of a showery summer are good and beautiful and sufficient even though they vanish.

I have come to value liberated minds as the supreme good of life on earth. The subject is very complex and proliferates into many areas of living. I should not be satisfied with an autobiography that did not bear witness to my passionate belief in freedom of thought. Anybody with intellectual perspective who exercises freedom of thought becomes a freethinker

— a thinker unbound by custom or creed; he is a skeptic. Any time that anybody in this period of excessive religiosity — generally as alien to the spiritual as the grossest materialism and the rankest obscenity — evidences skepticism, he arouses controversy and is charged with being an "atheistic communist." More times than not controversy defeats its own aims.

Shall I write of the Far Away and Long Ago as a thing apart or infuse into it some of the stubborn questionings that arise from Now? Those questionings will dispel the aura that is art and delightfulness. I crave to be an artist and nobody values more highly than I the delightful in literature. Nearly all controversial writing is dull to me, even when I am on the side of the controversialist. A writer is forever debating with himself not only choice of detail but what truth to leave out in the interest of another truth.

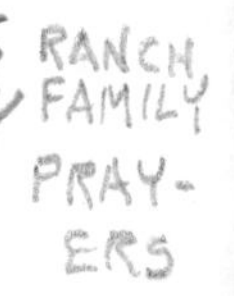

When I remember my father's unwavering sincerity, my mother's absolute goodness blended finely with brightness, the fireplace burning in the rock room of whitewashed walls where we had family prayers, my father reading a chapter in the Bible beside a kerosene lamp on a little pine table, then saying, "Let us pray," and praying aloud while we all knelt at our chairs, I could in some moods attempt a Texas Cotter's Saturday Night. One night after listening to the chapter ending with Daniel's interpretation of the handwriting on the wall, I saw very plainly in imagination, while my father prayed, a detached human hand tracing upon the whitewashed wall high up against the ceiling those tremendous words: MENE, MENE, TEKEL, UPHARSIN. My father had a clear, well-timbred voice, and I can hear him reading the interpretations of the words now: "MENE; God hath numbered thy kingdom, and finished it. TEKEL; Thou art weighed in the balances, and art found wanting. PERES; Thy kingdom is divided, and given to the Medes and Persians." . . . And "in that night was Belshazzar the king of the Chaldeans slain."

Very few climaxes in the literature of the world come up to the handwriting on the wall chapter. It is burned into me in association with family prayers. Yet so far as religion goes the prayers gave me nothing enduring. To tell the truth, they generally bored me, and prayers and table blessings that I unavoidably listen to every once in a while in these latter years seem to me mummery, except for the respect I always feel toward sincerity and true reverence. I know very well that wishing for high and beautiful things is good for the soul, but advising the Author of the Universe, as my father often denominated the All-High, seems to me an insult to intelligence.

My father was a ranchman, but I doubt if he ever prayed for rain; it would hardly have been in character for him to have so prayed, but I associate cow people, drouths, ranch country and prayers for rain with family prayers. When a few years ago Governor Allan Shivers of Texas proclaimed a day for prayers to break the drouth, I wondered why he as a very astute real estate trader did not corner — for a song — a big block of fertile land west of the Pecos, take along a colony of believers, and lead them in prayer to God to change the climate. The climate of the Sahara or of the North Pole is as susceptible to prayers as the climate of Texas.

The late Cap Molesworth, who used to ranch in Uvalde County, delighted in telling of a ranchman out there who believed in prayer. He would not eat anywhere without a blessing that, if he gave it, often got prolonged into a regular prayer. One day, during one of the usual drouths of the country, he came by a ranch about dinnertime and was asked to give thanks at the table. His prayer — as remembered by Cap Molesworth and then by me — went something like this:

"O Lord, we are very appreciative of all Thy mercies and gifts to Thy sinful children, but I would respectfully call Your attention to the drouth that is now burning up this country. If we don't get rain purty soon, our cattle are going to perish. As a matter of fact, as You've probably noticed, we've already started skinning. Now, Lord, when You cause it to rain, we don't want one of those mizzle-pizzle mists that sift down all day and don't put out enough moisture to wet a saddle blanket. What this country needs is a series of gully-washers and fence-lifters, rain that will soak down as deep as any mesquite root runs, put water out in every creek hole, and make the frogs holler 'Hallelujah!'

"And now while I think of it, O God, this morning I sent Juan Largo out in Chapote Pasture to find a white-faced cow that has got a brown spot on her left jaw. I saw her about a week ago and know that by now she's got a calf. Dry as it is, the blowflies and screwworms are plenty bad, and if Juan Largo don't put some screwworm medicine in that calf's navel today, I'm apt to lose it. The cow is probably in the brush with her calf, and I wish You'd kindly direct Juan Largo to the right thicket. Receive now our humble thanks and Amen."

I could write a whole chapter of anecdotes on praying for rain, but look where we've traveled to from the family prayers on a ranch that, measured by change, is only a little less remote from these machined times than is Belshazzar's feast. I had no skepticism then, though I think I quit the "Now I lay me down to sleep" formula about the time I could go to bed by myself.

The chief recollection I have of praying a personal prayer unto God goes back to about the age of ten. My father sent me horseback to a Mexican house on the ranch a half mile or so away to get scales for weighing cotton and then to carry the scales to a field some distance off. I got the scales and also the weights, tying the weights to my saddle strings and carrying the balance in my hand. About the time I reached the field gate I noticed that I had lost the big hundred-pound weight. No cotton could be weighed without it. I was a very conscientious boy and felt deeply troubled. A good part of the distance I had traveled was across pastureland studded with trees and bushes, not on a road. Weeds and grass, particularly broomweeds, were high. I did not have much confidence in my ability to backtrail myself and see the weight in the vegetation. I prayed God fervently to help me find it. I did not get down from the saddle and onto my knees as was proper but prayed as I rode slowly back the way I had come. Before long I found the weight — and straightway forgot all about God.

As an autobiographer I'd like to sketch several characters — one or two not out of love. In Daudet's story "The Pope's Mule," the mule saves a kick for seven years until he gets a fine chance to deliver it. I save a kick or two — not that I have the outlook of the man who was writing a book on "The Sons-of-Bitches of Boone County As I Have Known Them." Somebody asked him when he was going to finish it. "Every time I think I'm through," he answered, "I discover another one."

An ideal autobiography would be the cream of the whole jest of life — the "immortal residue" — but how to distill and refine until only that kind of residue were left?

CHAPTER TWO

A Plot of Earth

ON the twenty-sixth day of September, 1888, I was born in a three-room whitewashed rock house on the ranch of my parents in southern Live Oak County, Texas, in the Brush Country west of the Nueces River. Ramirenia Creek and Long Hollow coursed through the ranch. My father owned the land before he and my mother were married. They added to it and added to the house while rearing six children, I being the oldest. As ranches went at the beginning of this century, it was small, approximately seven thousand acres. Not long before my father died in 1920, he sold off three thousand acres to an adjoining landholder. My mother kept the remainder until her death, November 22, 1948.

A little while ago as one of six heirs I signed a piece of paper passing ownership of the inheritance to alien hands. Time with its unending changes may see another human being on this plot of earth with roots into it as deep as mine, but not soon, I think. No one of the six men who bought it has any idea of living upon it. They are oil men, not ranchers; they bought it as a hunting place and as an investment. It has become a piece of property and little more. Before long I shall become a clod of earth. Until then, no matter who holds title to the ground, my roots into it will be ineradicable.

In a way I feel that for a piece of money I have betrayed the soil that nurtured me, though the purchasers, with means and with modern ideas of conservation, will probably do more to restore it than my family did. As a matter of fact, we did absolutely nothing to restore it. For nearly thirty years it has been leased to individuals concerned, through circumstances and inherited attitudes, only with wringing a season-by-season profit from it.

After 1906 we were absentee owners. In that year my family moved to the town of Beeville, twenty-seven horse miles over a weary road to the east, where we used to trade. That fall I left for college, never to reside again in the region. Nevertheless, for years after I left, I spent summers on the ranch, and have never ceased returning to it with eagerness. It has been a place where I belonged both in imagination and in reality, a place on which I felt free in the way that one can feel only on his own piece of earth. It has said more to me than any person I have known or any writer I have read, though only through association with fine minds and spirits have I come to realize its sayings.

It is not a rich land. Caliche hills and thorned brush make a section of it forbidding. The remainder is sandyish. Yet sweep of hills and valleys, wooded Ramirenia Creek, and liveoak trees scattered singly and clustered into groves make the ranch gracious. One of the liveoaks has the largest spread in all that part of Texas. Chiltipiquines, the little round, red Mexican peppers, grow wild under it. It is near what used to be called Alligator Waterhole; alligators lived there before I was born. Some of the mesquites along Ramirenia Creek are noble in girth and spread. In a seasonable spring all the land is beautiful with growing grass, fresh leaves on the trees and brush, wine-burnished hollyhocks and baby-blue-eyes in the valleys, Mexican primroses, pink phlox and Indian paintbrushes on the slopes, splashes and stretches of the lupines called bluebonnets, and scores of other kinds of wild flowers everywhere. All wild flowers are beautiful, but I may be a little fonder of the pink Mexican primrose than of the bluebonnet. The yellow-and-orange-flowered lantana bush and the gray-leaved ceniza (ashes), with lavender flowers after rain, bloomed in summer.

I did not know it at the time, but I began listening to this piece of land talk while I was the merest child. When my father settled on it, as he used to tell, Ramirenia Creek ran clear water the year round. When I was a youth, it held lasting waterholes that supplied the cattle in two pastures. Then the waterholes filled with sand and we had to bore wells and put up windmills. For a third of a century now the creek has been bone dry except after rains. Erosion.

Yet I stick up for the old ranch as a ranch. Cattle thrive there if it is not overstocked and if drouths are not too prolonged. As a result of popular ideas on game conservation, it has more deer and wild turkeys than it had a generation ago. A widow named Polan and her two sons and daughter lived on an overgrazed half-section of land joining us. At times they must have subsisted mainly on wild meat and cornbread. They had a milch cow or two. One son, Andrew, was a constant hunter, and one year killed about twenty deer on our ranch. In time few were left to kill. When I was not more than six years old, my father rode in one day with a wild gobbler tied to his saddle. He had roped it on a prairie. By the time I was grown no turkeys were left at all and most of the prairie land had grown up in brush.

One day, while Papa and I were waiting in the Primm pasture for another rider, I got down off my horse and looked around to see what I could see. I picked up a rounded stick, sharp at one end with a groove cut in it just below the head. Papa said it was a "stake pin." Some rider had staked his horse on the prairie, not a bush in sight to tie his horse to. A person would have a hard time now finding in that area a spot of land open enough to stake a horse. This taking of the land by brush has gone on over tens of millions of acres in southern Texas, a result of grazing off and trampling down the turf.

When my father began ranching, he raised horses, traded horses, and drove a herd or two to Kansas. I used to hear talk by him and other men about mares trailed northeastward from our country to Arkansas or some other faraway land that showed up in the spring to have their colts on ground where they had been raised and had raised colts of their own — to their querencia. This was before barbed wire fenced the country. The instinct in me is the instinct that was in those homing mares. But for all that I can think and use words beyond horse power, words do not make clear what I feel. I am unable to make something clear to myself, much less to others. It is not sentimentality, not even sentiment, that I feel. Something of instinct, strengthened perhaps by cultivated sensitivity, lies beyond rationalization. The Brush Country of southwest Texas is my querencia.

I do not wish to go back there to live. The summers are scorching; for nine months of the year the air is enervating. Clouds drift up from the Gulf of Mexico, barely fifty miles away and not more than a hundred feet lower, but they seldom drop rain. One can waste his heart out there vainly hoping for rain, and during the frequent drouths the unyielding land is a desolation. If I were wealthy, I should buy the ranch, modernize the house, and live there during the hunting season with books, typewriter, some pictures and mesquite furniture beside the fireplace in the room where I was born. The fire in that fireplace would talk to me as no fire in any other fireplace can talk.

The richest days of my life have not been spent on this ranch, not at all. The hymn-singing we had on Sundays at home gives me a depressed feeling to this day. I was afraid of

Dobie ranch house in ruin and the tree that gave it gracious shade dead from drouth

Ten years old

God, prayed Him to help me find a lost pocketknife, and found out that we did not have much in common. In time the personal God of my forefathers became for me as mythical as Jupiter and not nearly so plausible as Venus. Itinerant preachers were favored in our home above all other company. They specialized in eating fried chicken, potato salad and lemon pie, long blessings at the table, longer prayers in the evening.

There were two or three youths in the country with whom I felt congenial, but I remember little from my boy schoolmates but vulgarities and stupidities. Puberty brought wretchedness — the payment for adult Puritan refusal to face physiology. I was too tame.

But no play world could have been happier than ours. With pegs, twine and sticks we built big pastures and stocked them with spools, from which my mother's sewing machine had used the thread, for horses; with tips of cattle horns, sawed off in the branding chute in the ranch corrals, for cattle; and with oak galls for sheep and dried snail shells for goats. The goats could not be branded, but we branded the other stock with pieces of baling wire heated red-hot. We made long trains of flat, rectangular sardine cans to haul the stock from one ranch to another. For wagon and team we snared green lizards with a horsetail hair and hitched them to a sardine can or — better, because lighter to pull — a matchbox. We traded "cattle" for "dollars" molded in the bottoms of round wooden bluing boxes out of lead melted from solder on tin cans and from bullets that had been shot for practice into oak trees. When it rained enough to make the creek run, we made waterwheels with my father's help and had a fine time with them while the water lasted. One of our entertainments at night was to make shadows on the wall with our hands, simulating bird beaks, ears that worked, and the heads of outlandish animals.

Every boy had a "frog sticker," as he sometimes called his pocketknife. He bragged:

Buffalo handle and barlow blade,
Best old knife that ever was made.

We played a game in which we threw a knife at a big prickly pear leaf. The object was to make the knife go through the prickly pear pad into the ground and stand up straight. Often the ground was too hard for the knife to penetrate and occasionally too soft to hold it.

Small inverted cone-shaped bowls made by doodlebugs in the sand fascinated us. A child would get down over a hole and chant, "Doodlebug, doodlebug, your house is on fire. Come on out!" I never knew a doodlebug to come out, but sometimes it stirred, and when it stirred at the bottom of the hole, the even flow of the sand downward was beautiful to see.

On one occasion I led my sister Fannie and three younger brothers and two or three cousins on a cave-digging excursion. We were digging out a cave to live in, under the creek bluff. We had been excavating maybe two hundred yards from the house. A little before sundown we climbed up the bluff to go home. I pointed across the valley to a dead, whitened tree on the hillside and told the others it was a giant coming to get us. I made them see the giant's long, naked arms. "Look, he is waving his arms at us!" I cried. I got my little band to believing that he was striding toward us like the giant that Jack the Giant-Killer killed. I became more thoroughly convinced than any other child in the pack, and with a yell led the race to home and Mama.

When older, I was a knight in the image of Ivanhoe and with my brother Elrich set up a tournament course. The course had three posts in a line a hundred yards apart. Each post had an arm of wood about three feet long. Hanging from this arm was a metal ring about two inches in diameter, held by a spring clasp so that it could easily be disengaged. The horseback runner would run lickety-split down the line of rings, trying to spear them with the "tournament pole" held in his right hand. Riding my horse Buck, I became good at spearing rings.

Tennyson's *Idylls of the King* put me into a world where for months wan lights flickered on plains farther away than Troy. I had read of the music of the spheres, and one starlit Sunday night while I was riding home on horseback alone after all-day church service, the other members of the family traveling in a hack, I heard what I took to be the music of the spheres. After that I would go out at night to listen to it until I discovered that the sound was made by a variety of katydid. Nevertheless, a certain pulsation of night has continued to seem to come down from the stars rather than up from the earth.

Our ranch house, the main part of which still stands, is in an extensive grove of liveoaks on a kind of plateau overlooking the valley of Long Hollow. For most of its distance this hollow used to be a mere drainage way, its bottom grassed over in places, carrying water only after hard rains, though it could get on a boom then. Now it is a deep, wide gulch of waste. Erosion. When I first knew it, the valley was a cornfield. Then it was turned out as a part of what we called the horse pasture, where the milch cows as well as saddle horses were kept. That old field is now a dense thicket of mesquites and huisaches. The huisache came to our land not more than twenty-five years ago. It is beautiful in bloom and beautiful, too, in its grace of green, but it usurps soil without paying anything at all to it or to the livers upon it.

Thousands of times I have looked across that valley, and something from those vistas remains deep inside me. In the early morning wild turkeys now and then gobbled from the woods on the far side, and the cheerio call of the bobwhite came from every direction. On the slope coming down the valley, about half a mile away, stood a hollow, whitened liveoak in which buzzards raised their young every year. "Puke like a buzzard" was a common expression of the country, and I used to ride my horse up close to the tree to observe the young white birds, frightened and unable to fly, verify the saying. Every day nearly I watched buzzards sail. Nothing in the sky is more serenely graceful. Whenever I see a buzzard sailing now, the sight takes me back to the sky over our ranch. One spring the bluebonnets on Long Hollow were up to my stirrups. They bloom that high inside me every spring. In my study hangs a little watercolor of Mexican primroses. It speaks to me of the Mexican primroses I knew as a child.

In spring and early summer I often awoke hearing the quick, bright cry made by diving scissortail flycatchers. They nested in mesquites in the calf pasture just north of the house, Long Hollow being to the south. Countless times in these later years a glimpse of the salmon-hued underpart of a flying scissortail has brought back to me those morning awakenings.

The house had a paling fence around it, and in the yard were more flowers — roses, chrysanthemums, cannas, violets especially — than any other ranch in that part of Texas had. The "garden," very prolific, was where vegetables grew. They and the flowers were irrigated from a cypress cistern and a supplementary dirt tank into which a windmill, just back of the kitchen, pumped water. The yard was bare of grass, in the pioneer tradition that guarded against snakes. Now and then a rattlesnake was killed in it. At the corner of a wide L-shaped gallery to the house — "porch" being a literary word that I never heard spoken — grew a cape jasmine. It happened that at the close of school one year I received as a prize a copy of Owen Meredith's *Lucile* with *Il Trovatore* appended.

> *And I swear as I thought of her thus in that hour*
> *And how, after all, old things are best,*

I smelt the smell of that jasmine flower
Which she used to wear in her breast.

When I read those lines in *Il Trovatore*, the jasmine by our gallery became affixed to them. Its aroma has never left me.

My mother had some sort of help a good part of the time but often none. With or without help, she was too busy cooking, sewing, raising children and keeping house to garden. My father tended the flowers as well as the vegetables. He set out orange trees, which never bore. He laid out a croquet ground in the shade of oaks. He could do anything from repairing a windmill to making a coffin for a Mexican child that died on the ranch and lining it with the bleached domestic my mother kept on hand. He was *patrón* for some Mexicans who did not live on the ranch, sometimes going security for them at the store where they bought food and other supplies. He hoped his eldest son would choose a career better than ranching — that of a clean-collared banker perhaps. He paid eight and ten per cent to his banker and liked him.

Back of the house was a rock smokehouse, long ago crumbled down, for the rock was caliche, not true stone. Every winter my father, aided by Mexicans, killed hogs and cut them up for curing. Occasionally he killed a calf. The meat he butchered was all the meat we had. It was ample. The Mexicans cut the long, strong-fibered leaves of bear grass (a yucca), heated them lightly over a fire to make them more pliable, and then used them to tie the hams, shoulders, and side bacon to poles across the smokehouse. The meats were cured by smoke from a fire of corncobs kept smoldering for days on the dirt floor. We had no hickory, needed none. Bear grass will always for me mean homemade hemp, also thatches for Mexican huts.

Hams and bacon were nothing to us children compared to the bladders of the slain hogs and cattle. They were the only balloons we knew. No child could ask for better. The way we made a bladder expand was to warm it slowly by a fire, gradually blowing air into it through the quill of a turkey feather, until the walls became so thin that it would have floated away had it not been restrained. At last, yielding to temptation, somebody gave it a pommel and it burst with a wonderful sound. Nobody wanted to part with his balloon, but nobody could resist that grand explosion. We got a weak, very weak, explosive effect by holding the broad petal of a wild prickly poppy, which we called thistle, across the lips and blowing it to smithereens, but this was pallid play compared with smashing an expanded hog bladder.

Beyond the smokehouse was a big stable combined with corncrib, hayloft and rooms for tools, saddles and buggies. Along the near end of it grew a row of pomegranates, so hardy that after fifty years and through the recent drouth that killed many oaks, one still exists. Their fruit was a treat. Near them a stout mustang grapevine twined up into the Coon Tree, an oak out of which a chicken-stealing coon had been shot. High up across its branches, we children had a platform — the "house in the Coon Tree," we called it — to which we ascended by the grapevine and on which we spent golden hours reading books or playing and in season drinking (without ice, of course) pomegranateade. The pomegranates in Solomon's anatomization of his love were — and still are — a great deal clearer to me than the idea that this love was "the church." Great numbers of jackdaws built nests in the Coon Tree and adjacent oaks.

Back of the Coon Tree, next to the barn, were a shed and three pens. The smallest pen was for the milch calves; the largest for driving the saddle horses into and for the milch cows. The third pen held hayricks and fronted the horse stalls, but only the buggy horses and work teams were fed. Before daylight somebody — and in time that job was mine —

caught the night horse out of the little pasture in front of the house and rode to bring in the remuda from the horse pasture. Many a morning I walked stooping over to the ground every few steps trying to skylight a night horse taking his sleep standing up. He always had a drag-rope around his neck, and I would try to get hold of it before he would wake.

One dewy morning while I was hunting the saddle horses, the cobwebs were so thick between all the mesquite bushes that I had to keep brushing them away in order to see. The phenomenon came back to me when long afterwards I read Gilbert White's account (in *The Natural History of Selborne*) of a shower of cobwebs. Master Cobweb in *A Midsummer Night's Dream* also belongs to the cobwebs in the horse pasture. Cobweb was our remedy for staunching the flow of blood from a cut or a jab in boy or horse. The remedy was common when Shakespeare wrote. "If I cut my finger, I shall make bold with you," Bottom says to Cobweb.

The sandy ground in front of the stalls for buggy, hack, tools, harness, and saddles had been paved with caliche. Red ants bored through the caliche and colonized below. They are very plentiful in that country and during warm weather work night and day. They have a vicious sting, the pain of which is alleviated by application of wet soda. We saddled our horses on the caliche or close to it. While we were saddling, the horses would stamp the caliche in order to knock off the red ants crawling above their hoofs. When we were running cattle, as the phrase for working cattle went, we ate breakfast, saddled, rode away from the house with the men, and waited for daylight to see by. For several years after I went off to college I half-awakened before daylight every morning to the sound of those horses stamping their feet on the caliche. I could hear the low voices of Mexicans saying indistinguishable words, the popping down of saddles on horse backs, and the metallic clicking of cinch rings and spurs. I never hear those sounds before daylight any more, but the memory of both the actuality and the half-dream is a part of me.

The cattle pens were on down the hill from the ranch house, about two hundred yards away. The well there was one of the oldest in the country, hand-dug and rock-curbed, about fifty feet deep, amid magnificent oaks. When the wind did not blow during the dog days of August and the big cypress cistern ran empty, water for stock had to be hauled up by pulley. One end of the rope was tied to a large wooden bucket, the other end to the horn of a saddle. Then I used to ride Old Baldy back and forth, back and forth, hour after hour, over a fifty-foot stretch, drawing water. I can see my father standing on a wide plank over the well curb and hear his hearty "Whoa!" as the bucket came up and he reached to pour the water into a long cypress trough. In time the well was sunk deeper by a driller and cased with iron up even with the old rock curb.

Water from the well was cool and delicious, but the cattle could not get half enough. At night they would stand outside the pens where the troughs were, bawling the most distressful bawls that a cow brute can make. If the pen gates were left open, the cattle would fight each other over the smell of the damp cypress troughs. I have heard them bawling all night long and all day long for water. No ranch person, no cowboy can accept "Home on the Range" as a range composition, as "When Work's All Done This Fall" surely is. That line idealizing the range as a land where "the skies are not cloudy all day" stamps the song as not belonging.

No cattle ever died on our ranch for want of water, but they died on Tol McNeill's ranch west of us, and on the Chapa ranch up about the head of Ramirenia Creek, where my father frequently bought steers. They died on other ranches. Men driving herds through the country frequently held them overnight in our pens. If a thirsty herd came when there was no water, it made too much noise for peaceful sleep. After she moved to Beeville, I heard my mother express thankfulness that she would never again have to listen to the bawl of thirsty cattle.

It was thirst in summer and hunger in winter for drouth-starved cattle. The only reserve of the land is prickly pear cactus. It is composed of about ten per cent fiber and ninety per cent water and defends itself by an armor of thorns. Before the portable pearburner — a flame-thrower fed by gasoline or kerosene and airpump — enabled one man to singe the thorns off enough pear to feed a hundred cows, ranch people fed a few of the poorest by chopping the pear down, dragging it to a fire in the open, holding it on the end of a green pole over the flames and then pitching it to the slobbering animals. In January of 1899 Mexicans feeding our poor cows reported that the frozen prickly pear pads were shattering like glass. The winter of 1898-1899 was as disastrous over southern Texas as the famous die-up winter of 87 in the Northwest.

My father and Uncle Jim Dobie, the big speculator and operator of the family, had gone into partnership in the summer of 1898 and bought several thousand cows. They leased the Dewees ranch on the San Antonio River and stocked it. During the winter that followed the cows died like sheep. The next summer I rode with a chuck wagon and a "crowd" — as an outfit was called — of Mexican vaqueros, led by my father, to gather up the remnant of cows. My chief memory of the excursion is the deliciousness of washing myself and my saddle blanket in the San Antonio River, at which, under the shade of pecan trees, we camped a whole day.

This cow venture so nearly broke my father that he decided to farm. About six lumber cabins were built for Mexican families along Ramirenia Creek, and the men plowed up several hundred acres of open sand hills that never should have been disturbed and that within a few years were turned back to the field mice and the ground squirrels and the hunting hawks. The Mexicans grew enough corn and beans to live on, shooting rabbits and trapping quail to supplement the fare, but the landlord made no money out of four-cent cotton. Incidentally, four cents a pound for beef cattle was regarded as fine. "If we can just hit a four-cent market!" I have heard my father say in talking about steers fattening on grass. When we were running cattle, the sharecroppers quit the fields to work for four bits a day and found. On rainy days they braided horsehair ropes and shelled corn. They were better vaqueros than they were farmers. It was a torture to me that I was not allowed to quit school and ride with them for nothing a day.

One of them, Genardo del Bosque, entered my life. He is still living, old and blind, on a little piece of land in San Patricio County that my father had taken in on a note and that my mother deeded to Genardo for a small sum. As long as she lived, he brought her a turkey every Christmas and received his "Christmas." From the time the family moved to town he looked after the ranch. He is little, wiry, quick, with a reddish complexion betokening more Spanish blood than most Mexicans have. He has a Spanish irony. His people once had land in Texas. His wife Emelia learned to read English in the school in which my mother taught at Lagarto before either was married. He was the best trailer I have ever known. His intelligence, energy, cow sense and responsibility would have made him a first-class manager of a big outfit.

I and my brother Elrich felt freer with him than we felt with our father and, after the family moved to town, delighted in staying on the ranch with him during summer vacations. He ruined an eye running in brush after a Rio Grande steer of enormous horns and lankiness that had jumped out of our corral while Stonewall Jackson Wright was receiving a herd there. After his men tried on two or three works to catch the steer and couldn't, I bought him range delivery. Genardo roped him but we never did drive him away. He would jump fences and leave the country when he heard brush popping, and I finally sold him range delivery to a ranchman who reported him in his pasture fifteen miles away.

Genardo del Bosque "had a *mano*" (a hand). When a horse threw me on my back across a ridge, injuring a vertebra that still gets sore sometimes, he rubbed the pain down sufficiently for me to ride to town in a buggy. After the ranch was leased he did not remain on it long under the new employer, but he did not want to leave. "*Yo tengo raices aquí*" (I have roots here), he said. Following the fancies of tradition, I have often fancied that if I were doomed to the everlasting fires of a traditional hell, could be redeemed by a substitute, and were such a churl as to call on another man to take my place, Genardo, of all men I know, would without a quiver of hesitation plunge into the furnace. My book *The Mustangs* is dedicated to him. In him and in what he represents, as well as in the land to which we both belong, *yo tengo raices*.

One year after my sister Fannie and I were old enough to be in school we had a governess. The next year, 1896, my father, Mr. Tol McNeill, "a sinner," and my cousin Dick Dobie, who improved his mind by reading law and begot a child annually, built a schoolhouse about a mile from us on our land. The teacher always boarded with us.

Our schoolhouse, on a patch of open land against blackbrush and guajillo hills to the west, overlooked liveoak slopes to the south and east. One day a flock of wild turkeys that came feeding near the schoolhouse while we were inside disrupted study. Another day just as we children burst out of the building to go home a big buck jumped a pasture fence in front of us. One evening while John Dobie and I were walking to his home from school, a coyote followed us. Ours was still wild country, we children thought.

Of several Mexican families living in the area only one sent children to school and, as I recall, they went only one year. They belonged to Feliciano Garcia, who worked for us and lived on our ranch. Neither Pancho nor his sister could speak English, and the teacher had no time for special instruction. They were ostracized by the English-speaking children both in the schoolroom and on the playground. The progress of Mexicans in the Southwest and the progress of English-speaking whites in civilized attitudes toward them is one of the improvements in life I have seen.

In time the schoolhouse was moved to another site on the ranch, a little farther away for us but located so that four more families to the northwest could attend it. We and Cousin Dick's children walked, as we had only a mile or so to go. The other pupils came horseback or in hacks. One winter my sister Fannie and I rode horseback for a few months to a one-teacher school five or six miles east of our ranch. It was taught by a man. One of the subjects was general history. The teacher dramatized Caesar's crossing of the Rubicon. After that day ancient history was something else to me than it had been.

My father organized a Sunday school that met in the second schoolhouse. What I remember about the Sunday school with most pleasure was *The Children's Visitor*, which sometimes contained stories of adventure and of pet animals. About a mile up Long Hollow, on our ranch also, were the camp-meeting grounds, where, at the time watermelons ripened, two preachers and a dozen or more families camped for ten days annually and were "revived." So far as religion is concerned, I drew more from my father's nightly reading of the Bible and praying aloud than from the sermons at camp-meetings and, every third Sunday in the month, at the Ramirenia churchhouse, eight miles away. The rhythms of the great King James Version seeped into my essence and echo in some of my prose.

Most of the preachers were of the people in ideas, conduct and language. One of them was a horse trader. At the Lagarto store, which was about six miles from our ranch, I bought a Spanish pony, still saddled, from him for twenty-five dollars. I was not more than fourteen, but I had the money. When he took the saddle off, a raw "setfast" showed on the horse's back. I said I did not want the horse. The preacher said, "You've already bought him." That was a fact. However, he let me withdraw from the trade, probably because my father was a member of his church. In teaching me never to buy a horse covered up, he gave me more than any sermon of his ever gave.

My memory of the Lagarto store goes away back. When I was very young, I went there occasionally with my father. I saw young men ride up to the store, dismount, uncoil the ropes tied to the necks of their horses, bring the ropes inside the store and hitch them around kegs holding fence staples. The store had an assortment of goods, but nothing else interested me so much as wooden buckets filled with mixed candy. I thought that if I ever got big enough and free enough to hitch my horse to a keg of fence staples and ever got rich enough to buy all the mixed candy I could eat, I'd be absolutely satisfied. That ambition has been a kind of symbol of life — something wanted and then, after it is realized or possessed, retreating as a thing of no consequence. I have eaten hardly more than a pound of candy in all my adult life.

For a while we got our mail at Dinero. I rode horseback once or twice a week to get it. I knew certain places where I had seen deer cross the road. I always remembered them, and when — very seldom — I travel that road now in a car I remember them. I knew two glades where bobwhite quail were especially plentiful. I knew an opening in the brush where I nooned once in a wagon and let the horses graze. I knew where I was almost sure to see a roadrunner running down the road. If it had rained I looked forward to seeing a certain caliche hill with more lavender and purple ceniza bloom than any other hill I have ever seen. I knew where sandy loam gave way to gravelly soil and guajillo thrived. I always enjoyed seeing cattle eat guajillo leaves. I knew where the redbirds, down from the north, were thickest in wintertime. That was when a mile was a mile and one traveled instead of being transported. Yet I don't think everybody who traveled saw particulars.

Public roads in the country were not much better than the private roads. They were all beat out by wagons. For years my father was both county commissioner and road overseer for our district. Once or twice a year he would send out a summons to men over a big neighborhood to gather at a certain place for road work. Every male citizen over twenty-one years of age owed a certain number of days to his county for road work. If he didn't want to work himself and could afford the expense, he might hire a substitute. This road work was more of a picnic than anything else. All the men, as I remember, went horseback, each carrying an ax or a spade or some other implement. All carried lunches. The work consisted of cutting out bushes here and there and filling eroded gullies so that the next rain would wash them out again. If the crossing of a good-sized creek needed repair, maybe somebody would have a team of mules and a plow and scraper for moving dirt, but generally the work consisted of riding along and getting off every once in a while for a lick and a promise.

We began to get our mail at Lagarto. I usually went after it on Saturdays. The coming of the *Youth's Companion* was a red-letter day. I might gallop all the way home in order to read at once "Land's End" or some other continued story. During the Spanish-American War I read the semi-weekly newspaper from the saddle while riding slowly. The newspaper account of Queen Victoria's death could not have been so beautifully written as Lytton Strachey's, but without historical background other than Dickens's *A Child's History of England*, I sensed the end of a great drama. Also, we had a kind of family connection with the Queen. My youngest brother, still in curls at the time of her death, was named Gladstone — Henry Gladstone, not because Gladstone was a great prime minister but because he was a "militant" Christian of great goodness. The name of Disraeli, his worldly opponent, was unknown to me.

So far as book education is concerned, the only specific pieces of learning I can recall from ranch schooling are how to spell the word *irksome*, on which I was turned down in a spelling match, and knowledge that a branch of science called physical geography existed. I remember the green binding of a textbook on the subject but don't remember a single detail of the contents. I remember in a reader the ballad of "Markos Bozzaris," which I memorized, and also the thrilling recitation of "Lasca" by a young lady older than our teacher who had studied elocution somewhere.

Then there was "Bingen on the Rhine." Only a few weeks ago I was delighted at finding a copy of this once very popular narrative, printed separately and illustrated.

A soldier of the Legion lay dying in Algiers;
There was lack of woman's nursing, there was dearth of woman's tears;
But a comrade stood beside him while his life blood ebbed away,
And bent an ear to listen to whatever he might say.

I shall not repeat what the dying soldier of the Legion said, but with all that years and sophistication have brought me, the words flood pristine feelings of pity now as they did so long ago.

Another favorite I have never outgrown is "The Burial of Sir John Moore" by Charles Wolfe. I found it again while I was lecturing at Cambridge University during World War II in an anthology entitled *A Poetry Book for Boys and Girls.* I bought the book, but did not need print to follow the words to the stirring end:

> *We carved not a line, and we raised not a stone,*
> *But we left him alone with his glory.*

Sir John Moore died, victorious against the French, at Corunna on January 16, 1809. As time has ticked off the decades, the verses have proved stronger than the battle victory in keeping green his name. They alone have kept green the name of the author, an Irish curate.

The readers — not state-adopted — we had in our one-teacher school were made up of English and American literature. They were stronger on English literature than on American.

Literary associations, aside from textbooks, with the second schoolhouse are limited to a paperback novel entitled *With Leavenworth Down on the Rio Grande.* A boy named Irving Watson brought it to school, and I read it clandestinely behind my desk. It was one of those "blood and thunder" novels that my mother positively forbade. We had a big book about Stanley in Africa, but no book pertaining to the Wild West ever entered our home, not even *The Log of a Cowboy,* although it had a sort of connection with our family in that the author, Andy Adams, was my Uncle Frank Byler's friend.

The jackdaws — grackles, as called now — that nested in the oaks about our house and lost young ones that we children rescued and made nests for in fence-staple kegs; the calves sucking their mothers and playing about them out in the pasture; the cows chewing their cuds in the milking pen; the bobwhites' cheerio to morning, the bullbats' zoom at twilight; the sandhill cranes fluting their long, long cries on a winter evening and in daytime feeding on wild onions in the prairie openings; the coyotes serenading from every side after dark; my horse Buck pointing his ears when I walked into the pen to rope out a mount and seeming to ask if I were going to ride him or Brownie; the green on the mesquites in early spring so tender that it emanated into the sky; the mustang grapevines draping trees along Ramirenia Creek; the stillness of day and night broken by windmills lifting rods that lifted water; the south wind galloping in the treetops; the locusts in the mulberry tree, the panting of over-ridden and over-driven horses accentuating the heat of summer; the rhythm of wood-cutting in cold weather; the rhythm of a saddle's squeak in the night: these the land gave me. Its natural rhythms and the eternal silence entered into me.

I never recollect the ranch as being what is called romantic. I was not a good roper or a good rider, and never shot a six-shooter until I got into the army during World War I, but from the vaqueros and my father I learned to soothe wild or restless cattle with my voice. Sometimes in a way I seemed to become one of them. I became more at one with the sailing buzzard than I have ever become with a human murderer of silence who puts a nickel into a slot to bring forth raucous sounds.

The one romantic feature of our ranch was what we called Fort Ramirez. It never was a fort, but it was a fortified ranch house built by a Mexican named Ramirez before Texas became a republic. Not within the memory of the oldest resident of the country had the fort been inhabited. Some of the rock walls were still standing when I was a boy, and a person on top of them had a grand view of the S-winding Ramirenia Creek. Granjeno bushes grown from seeds planted by birds that lit on the old picket corrals still outlined them. A patriarch named Gorgonio who lived about half a mile away and with several *parientes* (kinsmen) farmed a considerable field on shares used to tell of lights flickering about the ruins at night, also of chains making a terrifying noise. People said that a fortune in Mexican gold or silver was buried there. Almost every year strangers asked permission to dig on the premises. Many holes were dug without permission, some in the night. Digging under the walls contributed to their downfall. Some of the holes in and out from the structure were big enough to bury a wagon and team in.

Uncle Ed Dubose, my mother's half brother, had a hope for digging up treasure and a faith in divining rods and fortune-tellers not shared in the least by either of my parents. But one time he came with such a plausible legend, together with a map derived from some Mexican down on the Rio Grande — he could talk Spanish better than most Mexicans — and such specific directions from a Negro fortune-teller in Victoria, Texas, about where to dig, that my father agreed to help. He and Uncle Ed and several Mexicans spent three days sinking a big hole. They found a fill of earth not like the ground around it but that was all. Fort Ramirez contributed to my book *Coronado's Children*, which is made up of hidden treasures and lost mines.

The first thing the recent purchasers of the ranch did after taking possession was to tear down the corrals and burn up the pickets. They were the oldest old-timey corrals in that part of the country. Now they are where Fort Ramirez has gone. In my boyhood there were fifteen or so ranch families around us owning maybe seventy thousand acres, all deriving their living from the land. At the same time, there were probably more than thirty Mexican families living on these ranches. Only three ranch owners now live where fifteen once lived, and the decrease in the number of Mexican families has been at about the same ratio. Most of the land is owned by absentees; some of it is looked after by men who drive to it from town by automobile.

No matter what is discontinued, the land remains. A thousand years, ten thousand years hence, the Dobie ranch will be where it was before the Ramirez grant took in a portion of its pristine acreage. It will have other names, be divided, and then be absorbed. The land will always be grazing land, for neither soil nor climate will permit it to be anything else. It is possible that an oilfield will temporarily mutilate it. Off and on for nearly half a century oil companies and oil promoters have paid out more lease money on it than the grazing rights have brought. The time may come when people passing over it will speak a tongue that no one now living down in the Brush Country could understand.

The thought of times in which I shall not participate disturbs me no more than thought of times in which I did not participate. Nevertheless, when I consider the break now made with that plot of land on Long Hollow and Ramirenia Creek — a measure of ground to which I am more closely akin than to any other on earth, not excluding the lovely creekside that has been home to me for a quarter-century — I feel that the end of something has come.

CHAPTER THREE

Echoes of the All Gone

Christmas

THE day before Christmas all the Mexican men on the ranch would come to our house for gifts. My father would have made a trip to Beeville not long before and would have brought back a wagonload of supplies and "Christmas." Regular goods were sugar and flour by the barrel, if not in a tier of forty-eight-pound sacks, molasses by the keg, lard in fifty-pound cans, canned tomatoes, salmon, and peaches by the case, bushel sacks of Arbuckle's coffee to be roasted and ground, potatoes, onions, and dried beans. As I look back, those days seem days of great plenitude, not because of affluence — quite the opposite — but because stockpiling was necessary. "Christmas" consisted of apples, oranges, nuts, raisins on the stem, stick and mixed candy, and the presents. Each Mexican family living on the ranch received a new blanket and a sack of apples and candy for the children. To this day, common as they are now, I associate oranges with Christmas and its inevitable — and inevitably delicious — ambrosia. We had homemade candy occasionally, but Christmas was the only time of year when it snowed candy. There were no chocolates, just a mixture of lemon drops and a gummy kind of sugar in a delightful variety of colors. These candies came in large wooden buckets.

Papa went out alone to cut the Christmas tree — a comely little liveoak — and brought it in secretly. It was lighted with small colored candles, one of which usually started a blaze. Papa had played Santa Claus for several years before I caught on. He was jolly, just jolly enough, and he did not scare anybody as some Santa Clauses do. The way he called out names in a disguised voice and presented the gifts delighted his own children and our visiting cousins. When at the very last we got our firecrackers and Roman candles, we were in a hurry to run out and start firecrackering. I never heard of Fourth of July fireworks until I was grown. Firecrackers and Roman candles were as much a part of Christmas as was ambrosia. The firecrackers could be exploded by day, but the Roman candles were for darkness, when everybody gathered to watch. Probably being so eager to set off the firecrackers, to try out a new pocketknife or a new bugle and to look into a new book kept us from being curious about where Santa Claus went. When I did learn the identity of Santa Claus, the illusion was not impaired any more than knowing that a woman could not possibly live in a shoe hurt the Mother Goose fact that "there was an old woman who lived in a shoe."

My most memorable gift from a Christmas tree was not off it but from under it. It was my first saddle — a brand-new saddle made by P. Bauer of Oakville, Texas. I was not more than five or six years old. I'd ridden bareback and I had ridden old saddles, but here was one that had been made for me. In years that followed I would see *Gallup* and *Sonley* and *Victoria* and other names stamped on saddles, but P. Bauer's name led all the rest. I'd give a good deal at this date to see a saddle stamped with the words *P. Bauer*, *Oakville*, *Texas*.

Oakville, though the county seat of Live Oak County, never had more than two or three hundred inhabitants. It had Ira

Hinton's saloon, and it had Weimer's Screwworm Medicine. It had the courthouse and the jail. It had Sulphur Creek close by, beside which a saving rancher coming to court could camp and stake out his horses and boil his own coffee in a tomato can. Oakville had a tree from which either three or seven men had been hanged. But with all these it had nothing to compare with the saddle shop in which P. Bauer stamped his name on leather smelling as delicious as the spices of Arabia and, until it was broken in, squeaking as loud as an ungreased wagon axle.

Christmas was always the time for new books. We children knew of certain books we would like to have and speculated on what Santa Claus might bring. The earliest one I can recall was a paperbound, profusely illustrated book about an owl. That was before I could read. On demand, my father read it over and over to me and the next two children, Fannie and Elrich. Hoot owls talked at night in the liveoak trees around our ranch house, and my father could talk their language. Many times we made him tell us what the old owl says. It says, "I-cook-for-myself. Who-cooks-for-you-a-l-l?" You have to say it right or it won't sound like an owl. My father could say it right.

While the owl book was new and for a time thereafter, it gave me a great deal of misery as well as pleasure, but even then I would not have foregone the misery. Every night after I went to bed and the lamp had been blown out, the owl would come and sit on a tree limb — a limb that did not exist — just above my head. I wanted to cry out but he froze me into voicelessness. I would pull the bedclothes over my head and burrow under the pillow. After a while, torn between curiosity and terror, I would look up again, and there that owl would be, turning his head slightly every once in a while and regarding me with the gravity of doom. I don't know how long he would terrify and fascinate me before sleep came to blot him out. In the morning he would be gone. I never told anybody about him, but dark night after dark night he came and sat on a limb above my bed.

An early Christmas book was called *The Adventures of a Brownie*. Night after night Fannie and I poured milk into a bowl and left it out on the kitchen steps for our brownie. The milk was always gone in the morning. I won't say that the cats and dogs around the place didn't give the brownie some competition.

Beautiful Joe, about a dog, and *Black Beauty*, about a horse, came later, and I read them to myself. We named our black mongrel dog Joe after Beautiful Joe. He was as beautiful to us as any dog could be, even when he smelled of skunks, as he frequently did. We wept when he died and buried his corpse under the mulberry tree at the southwest corner of the yard.

One Christmas we got Porter's *The Scottish Chiefs*. I read it to myself, and at night as we sat by the fireplace my father read it aloud by the flickering light of a kerosene lamp. What heroes to emulate Bruce and Wallace were! My blood still stirs at mention of the mere title.

I don't recall being made happy on any night by Papa's saying that he would stop and we would have family prayers, which meant his reading aloud out of the Bible and then all of us kneeling by our chairs while he prayed. Just the same, the eloquence, drama, and picturization of the Old Testament had more influence on my life than any other reading before I went to college. They developed in me a taste for "high astounding terms."

Another Christmas book that the whole family enjoyed was *The Swiss Family Robinson*. After I grew up, I learned from Robert Louis Stevenson that it has "a plethora of good things" and is too much an imitation of *Robinson Crusoe* to be worth reading. Maybe so. It gave us barrels of joy, and I am not going to high-hat it now. I am not alone. In *This Book-Collecting Game*, A. Edward Newton says: "I believe most boys prefer *The Swiss Family Robinson* to *Robinson Crusoe;* its incidents are more varied and interesting."

My Experiences in Farming

WE raised corn, together with some watermelons, muskmelons, and "kershaws" in the valley of Long Hollow. The soil was sandy loam. My earliest recollection of this field has my father guiding a horse-drawn turning-plow while I walked alongside holding the lines. I was so young that I thought it a great privilege to "help." The horses needed no guidance. Hundreds, perhaps thousands, of blackbirds swarmed down on the freshly turned earth to pick up worms. My father was whistling, and his whistle comes to me now across the years as cheerful as the call of a field lark on the grass.

One day quite a few years after I saw the blackbirds following Papa's plow, I was myself holding the handles of a plow at almost the same spot. I hadn't had much experience plowing. Papa was away from home. I think he was receiving a big string of steers for Uncle Jim Dobie, who had bought out Dr. Simmons's cattle in the northern part of the county. Dr. Simmons was not a cowman. He had made his money by selling Simmons's Liver Regulator and his cattle brand was a liver. Anyhow, on this day I was plowing behind a gray horse named Tordillo (which is Spanish for "gray") and a bay that was quite skittish. They were cow horses broke to the harness. At that time all work horses wore blind bridles so they couldn't see behind them.

Our field made a kind of parallelogram cut into the horse pasture. Customarily only the saddle horses and milch cows were kept in the horse pasture, but at this time, for some reason, three or four wild mares and their colts had been put out of what we called the big pasture into the horse pasture. Soon after I turned a row on the back side of the field I saw or heard a movement in brush outside the fence, and, looking, caught a glimpse of the wild mares. They had some of the saddle horses with them. I stopped my team, wrapped the lines around a plow handle and went back to look at the mares. I felt more congenial toward these wild and free creatures than I felt towards plow horses. As I approached the barbed wire fence, one of them snorted and all broke away in a run that made the ground tremble.

I didn't hear any snort from the plow horses, but in an instant I knew they also were running. They were running in the opposite direction, toward the windmill, cowpens and house across Long Hollow from the field. Wild with fright, they were running as fast as they could run. Every few yards the point of the plow would dip into the ground and then it would go up as high as the traces would let it go. It looked to me as if it were going as high as a kite. The farther those horses ran, the faster they got. Within a few hundred yards they hit the barbed wire fence and took it and the plow both with them. They didn't check their speed until they raced into the milch-cow pen up at the house. I thought for sure their hind legs and ankles would have been butchered to pieces by the point of the plow, but they weren't hurt there. They were bleeding terribly from barbed wire cuts on their breasts.

As soon as I caught up with them I ran into the house and called Mama. She came out and saw the trembling horses and the bleeding wounds. The gray horse was worse off than the bay. I don't know where Feliciano was, but he was gone somewhere. Mama told me to get on a horse and ride for Cousin Dick Dobie, who lived only about a mile away. There was a horse in the pen. I got on him and loped over to Cousin Dick's, finding him at home. He came back with me at once and sewed up those wounds with an ordinary needle and thread. The wounds healed but the gray kept a deep scar as long as he lived.

I have no recollection of ever plowing again after that. I've watched a few good horse races, but no other horses I've watched seemed to move as rapidly as those two stampeded plow horses.

One year Papa told my brother Elrich and me that we might have the produce off a patch of ground if we would farm it. I don't recall that we plowed it or planted it or hoed it, but we claimed four or five acres of cotton. It put on squares, then flowers, then bolls, and finally the bolls opened and somebody had to pick the cotton. Elrich was even less given to farming than I was. I can't remember his picking any cotton at all, but maybe he did.

Good pickers can gather in a day two hundred or three hundred pounds from even half-good cotton. Ours was just ordinary. One day I picked from daylight till dark, except for time out at noon. My back at this time was plenty limber, but that night it was made up of ramrods and cricks. I had picked my best and still the scales said I'd picked less than ninety pounds. With help from Mexicans we finally got a bale picked and ginned. I don't think we got more than $20 or $25 for it.

At that time I'd never heard of Ab Blocker, one of the best cowmen who ever lived. He wasn't a boaster but he claimed he had looked down the backs of more cow brutes and drunk water out of more cow tracks than any other man who ever pointed a herd toward the North Star. As trail boss he was noted from the Rio Grande to the plains of Alberta.

Mr. Ab used to talk as if he were crying. I've heard him tell how after his first trip up the trail when he was just a boy, his parents living in Austin, he decided that he'd lost so much sleep and had such a hard time in general that he would try farming. He cultivated a field out between Austin and Round Rock and planted it in cotton. While he was chopping cotton he saw Kansas-bound herds of longhorns stringing by on the unfenced prairies. He stayed with his cotton, raised a crop, helped pick it, and sold it. Then, he used to tell in his crying voice: "I got down on my knees and promised God Almighty if I ever planted another seed of cotton I'd boil it three days first so it would be sure not to sprout." I was like Mr. Ab. All ranch work was congenial to me as I grew up, even doctoring wormy calves by day and skinning dead ones by lantern light, but the year we boys tried raising a bale of cotton remains a dark blot.

A man I'll just call Punkins because he wasn't much punkins lived on a rented place adjoining us. He didn't have more than a quarter section, which my father later bought. If he could make $2.50 on a horse trade with a Mexican he'd ride as if he were worth a million dollars. He had a patch of cotton. I didn't have any money. One time when he and his wife were going away for a few days, he stopped at our house and told me if I'd go over there and thin his cotton he'd give me two bits a day. I hoed up and down the rows for three days. When he got back he said it looked as if I hadn't spent much time thinning the cotton. As a matter of fact, I'd spent full time. He paid me six bits — seventy-five cents. I guess this was before Elrich and I raised our solitary bale of cotton. Anyhow, the experience helped enforce Ab Blocker's sentiments. I used to wish that coyotes liked cotton as well as they liked watermelons.

The only crops I remember with pleasure were the watermelon, pumpkin, and kershaw crops. When the pumpkins and kershaws ripened they were hauled in and stored in the smokehouse along with the hams and bacon. They kept well there for months.

We always had a big watermelon patch. It had to be big if we were going to have any melons ourselves after the coyotes took their percentage. The patch was in a valley field only a few hundred yards away from the house. At night we could hear the coyotes laughing over how juicy the watermelons were.

If there had been any late spring rains at all, some careless weeds and a tall wide-bladed grass that we called buffalo grass but was something else had grown up pretty well in the patch. Some mornings when we rode out in watermelon season, we boys would stop at the patch and with pulled-up careless weeds and tall grass cover a melon that plunked ripe so it would keep cool in the shade. By the time we got back around noon, we would be ravenous. We'd stop, split that shaded watermelon with a pocketknife and eat the heart out of it before going on for dinner. We are all spoiled now by ice and ice boxes, but no ice-cold watermelon was ever better to human taste, gullet, and stomach than one of those "Rattlesnake" or "Tom Watson" watermelons shaded by careless weeds and buffalo grass. Sometimes we pulled watermelons and put them in a horse trough full of water to get cold. Sometimes we wet a tow sack and put it on a watermelon to evaporate. That method will cool a watermelon well enough if the sack is kept damp.

After the disastrous winter of 1898-1899, besides putting in some fields on ground that never should have been plowed under, Papa set out a patch of cabbages in the Long Hollow field. I suppose he had read that cabbages brought a good price.

I don't remember when the cabbages matured, but it must have been in late spring after school was out. A cousin, Forrest Dubose, was visiting at the ranch when a wagon was loaded with cabbages. He and I set out to drive to Beeville to sell them. It took all day to get there, the horses having to stop now and then to pant under a shade tree, especially where sand was heavy. There was no buying of something to eat on the road. We brought with us hard-boiled eggs and sandwiches made of bacon and biscuits. They tasted mighty good. I don't remember where we spent the night in Beeville. I know we sold the cabbages to a man who ran a milkshake stand. They didn't bring much more than enough to pay for the axle grease we had used on the wagon wheels. We were drinking a milkshake when a wealthy rancher from Goliad County came in. The obsequious knee-bending and belly-crawling of that cabbage-buyer toward the rich rancher has remained in my mind all these years. I think this was the first instance of such behavior that I had had a chance to observe. You don't often find belly-crawlers among farmers and ranchers. I never had any love for belly-crawlers. After we got through with the cabbages I didn't think any more of them than I thought of cotton.

When the population of most states of the Union was chiefly rural, agricultural and pastoral, produce went begging for buyers. I grew up understanding that a farm was a liability rather than an asset.

On Milking Range Cows

EVERY time I read about wild ways on the range, I realize what a tame life we led on our ranch. A recent county historian whom I read says that it used to take two men to milk a wild cow. One would rope her, presumably outside the pen, by the neck. The other would rope her hind legs. Between them they'd stretch her out on the ground, and then while she was stretched out, somebody would milk her. Sometimes, he said, he didn't have help, and alone he would down a cow, tie all four of her legs together, and then milk her. If anybody wants to try extracting milk from a cow madder than six nests of hornets, tied flat on the ground, he needn't take a receptacle larger than a teacup.

We had only range cows to milk. Every one had to be gentled to start with. The usual procedure was to rope her by the horns, tie her to the fence so that she couldn't swish around a whole circle, hobble her hind legs, and then pull her teats, often at the same time holding her tail to prevent its muddying the milk bucket. After a few such tyings and milkings she would gentle down so that when the calf was pulled off her she would stand still and allow the milker to milk. If she proved too stubborn to learn and was something of a fighter, we turned her out with her calf and tried another cow.

Papa always chose the cows to milk. He judged them partly by their gentleness and partly by the size of their bags. Sometimes in the summer we'd milk as many as a dozen cows. Maybe we wouldn't get more than three or four gallons of milk twice a day. If we needed more, we could always bring in another cow from the big pasture. Milkers had to leave enough to support the calves. No rancher wanted his calf "knocked in the head with a churn dasher."

The earliest feed for cows that I recollect was cottonseed. It was very cheap. This was before the seeds began to be processed into cottonseed cake, cottonseed meal, etc. Two or three cows fed plenty of cottonseed in the winter would give more milk than ten cows on grass during the summer.

As a boy I had the task of going out horseback of an evening and driving up the milch cows. Out in the big pasture I would occasionally find one of the gentled cows that had just calved and would want to bring her in. If I could not see her calf, I would hang around her for an hour or two, hoping against experience that she would go to it. I would imitate the bleat of a calf; she would remain utterly indifferent. Finally, my animosity aroused by her stubborn calm, I would start her toward the pens, and then when she refused to go farther would run her, knowing that she wouldn't but hoping that she would go to the calf. Sometimes I would "chouse the daylight out of her." Her patience was always longer than mine. But if I found her with her calf and it could walk, I could worry her to the pens she knew so well.

One of the pleasing country sounds is that of a stream of milk hitting the bottom of an empty bucket, and then becoming softer and softer as the bucket fills. In the lovely romance *Lorna Doone*, John Ridd comments that one of the three fine things in the world is to come close to a cowpen in the evening and listen to the cows breathe and to the milk squirting into pails. I can see our cows now chewing their cuds and licking their calves; I can see the blackbirds picking ticks off them. I can smell their strong, good, wholesome breaths. I can hear the placid but affectionate moos with which each calf was greeted as it came through the gate from the calf pen to suck until the teats were moistened and the flow of milk started.

I never could milk with two hands, but I've seen and heard a man who could milk with both hands. The two streams playing into a bucket made a kind of tune. I've drunk lots of milk straight out of a cow's teat. I never sucked a teat but would milk the milk into my own open mouth or I might get a Mexican milker to squirt a stream into my mouth. This was part of the fun. When the bucket was full it had an inch or two of foam on top of it. A boy could drink the foam without touching the milk and could achieve a milky complexion all around his mouth and over his nose.

The milker I remember best was Feliciano Garcia. He and his family lived in a jacal several hundred yards from our house. He had the use of whatever ground he wanted for raising watermelons, cantaloupes, frijoles, calabazas, etc. He could get roasting ears out of the big cornfield.

One year he raised an especially fine crop of calabazas

(large squashes, or "kershaws"). I remember the evening that his wife sent a baked calabaza to the cowpen while Feliciano was milking. It was in halves, and the seed had already been scooped out. One of us boys ran to the house and got two or three tablespoons. Then Feliciano milked each half partly full of milk. The calabaza meat was nearly as sweet as a pumpkin pie. It was still warm, and the milk was warm. I always have liked milk with pie, but I never ate any pumpkin pie better than that calabaza with the fresh, warm milk.

I remember a pen full of our milch cows with affection. There was Old Paint, with a crumpled horn and undying fire in her spirit; a strain of Holstein blood made her give more milk than any other two cows we had. There was Hookey, a red with brindle marks so faint that they barely showed except when she was wet from rain. She would never allow our dog Joe in the pen. One evening while Papa was milking and I was watching him, my sister Fannie, maybe four years old at the time, came into the pen. Hookey hadn't seemed to mind me, but she looked upon Fannie in a dress as something alien. She lowered her head and took after the child, got a horn in one leg of her drawers and raised her from the ground. She did not hurt Fannie. Old Sabina, speckled red and white, had an excess of ticks. Her horns had been sawed off in order to cure her of the "hollow horn." Clabber, a white cow, was as patient as an ox and never kicked, but her tail was so long and active that it was tied to a leg during milking operations.

Every year we raised several dogies — calves whose mothers had died. The way we raised one was to tie a cow by the head to the fence and then let the orphan suck from one side of her while her own calf sucked from the other side. The calves were always of about the same age. Sometimes it took a good while for the cow to claim the orphan. The process could be helped along by squirting milk on the orphan so that it would have the cow's own smell on it. We had one cow, a red

With Genardo del Bosque, ranch foreman

A Mexican vaquero rides out of the brush

My father
Richard J. Dobie

My mother
Ella Byler Dobie

roan, that could be imposed upon to raise any dogie calf we put with her. Her name was Muley; she had never had any horns. She was a meek, mild critter — never fat and never poor, rather smaller than the average cow. As the eldest of the family of six children, I usually had a claim on dogies. Papa didn't give all of them to me, but he gave more to me than to the other children. Of course, I was there first to get anything.

One of my first dogies was a mottled black. We named her Pet. She was a pet from the beginning. After she grew up and had calves, she was one of the most dependable milch cows. Her first calf was a red roan bull. Papa at the time was using Durham bulls. Sabino (Red Roan), as he was named, was the best riding calf I ever had. I could put a *bosal* (half-hitch) on his nose and guide him all over the calf pasture bringing in the other calves in the evening, although they would come without being brought in. I even saddled Sabino but a saddle designed for a horse cannot fit a cow brute. My brother Elrich and I rode a good many calves. I could get more milk from the cows, but Elrich was a champion at riding the calves.

The buckets of milk were taken to the kitchen, where they were strained into pans. After a night and day, the cream was skimmed and churned into butter. I never did care to churn. We had so much milk that plenty of it clabbered, and clabber is the best form of milk there is for making bread, also for feeding chickens. After clabber formed, the whey was poured off, and the thick white residue was poured into a cotton sack and hung up to drip. The result was curd, now sold under the name of cottage cheese. I like all kinds of cheese, including the most exotic with the most fungi in it. Cottage cheese (from a factory) made out of homogenized, expurgated, bowdlerized milk can't touch natural curd with a ten-foot pole.

I have no inclination to resume the chores of milking but am glad that I did milk once upon a time. Taking care of a cow and milking her has never hurt any boy, though many a boy has had his disposition ruffled. Cows are not inspiring, but despite their stupidity, awkwardness, stubbornness, and other disposition-ruffling qualities, they exercise a wholesome effect on the mind. They are a calming influence and they tend to bring orderliness into the person who works with them.

A gentle cow is one of the most orderly creatures on earth. She is the slave of habit. She will come to a watering trough very thirsty, but if a strange animal is drinking at the spot where she is accustomed to drink, she will bear her thirst and wait patiently until that spot is vacated. A milch cow sleeps in her corner of the pen every night, and is as partial to her accustomed bedding place as some finicky old bachelor is to his bed.

Gathering Wild Fruits

As I have said, we had oranges and apples at Christmas and at no other time. The only fruits we grew were pomegranate and mulberry, both of which we thought a great treat. The chief native fruits were mustang grapes — also called cutthroat grapes — agarita berries, and sandhill plums.

As soon as the mustang grapes were a little bigger than buckshot we boys would start gathering them for Mama to make green grape cobbler, and a little later on, still before the seeds had hardened, green grape catsup. Store-bought catsup made out of ripe tomatoes has always seemed to me to have a pallid, lily-livered taste compared with green grape catsup. When the grapes ripened, my mother made gallons of preserves and jam out of them. If there is any sweet better than honey with fried venison, it is mustang grape preserves.

Gathering quantities of the ripe grapes gave me an intimate knowledge of their acidity. Provided with gunny sacks, my brother Elrich and I would ride horseback to Ramirenia Creek about three miles from the house. There the vines grew abundantly over trees and bushes no matter whether the season was wet or drouthy. Along the creek banks the roots could always reach moisture.

While climbing the vines and picking off the bunches of grapes, we would get our necks and arms raw from contact with the leaves, which have a white down on their undersides. After we had gathered two big sacks of the grapes, we would tie them up and load them on our horses, behind the saddles. We wore leather leggins and took all sorts of precautions to prevent contact between the grape sacks and the rear and nether parts of our bodies. Some of the grapes were bound to get crushed. Juice was bound to ooze out of the sacking. How the horses stood the juice I do not know. It always stung and just about blistered my legs.

This sharpness distinguishes all products of the mustang grape, however modified by sugar and cooking, from the products of all other grapes. My father's mother, Grandma White, made wine and had a jug or two around for medicinal purposes. We made no wine.

As John C. Duval tells in *Early Times in Texas*, a mustang grapevine saved his life while he was fleeing from the Mexican massacre at Goliad. He had jumped into the San Antonio River and swum across, and by means of an overhanging grapevine was pulling himself out on the farther bank when a Mexican ball aimed at his head cut the vine in two. Falling back into the water, he swam under the surface until he was safe. He lived to write long afterwards a delicious piece of exaggeration entitled "The Pure Juice of the Mustang Grape," the first sentence of which runs thus: "The mustang grape does not make a wine equal to Château Margaux, but it is an admirable substitute for dynamite." Duval's satire cannot lessen my gusto for mustang grapejuice, fermented or unfermented.

Almost the first, if not the very first, bush to bloom was the agarita, or chaparral berry, some people called it. Then it was covered with sweetly fragrant small yellow flowers. I have seen it bloom as early as Christmas in south Texas. We called the fruit wild currants when they ripened a rich, beautiful red and considered a bowl of them with sugar and cream a great treat, and agarita cobbler even better. For me the jelly has always been the best in the world.

The agarita bush is defended by very sharp points on the stiff leaves. These make picking the berries a slow, prickly job. We followed the practice, common in our part of the world, of spreading a sheet underneath a bush and thrashing the bush with a stout stick, preferably a broomstick. Good berries, leaves, and worm- or weevil-infested berries would all fall off. Then we would jiggle the sheet to get the leaves on top where we could push them off. To get rid of the light, worm- or weevil-eaten berries we would pour our gathering into a bucket and take it to an open place where a stiff Gulf breeze blew. We would hold the bucket high and slowly pour the berries into another bucket, the wind blowing the light stuff away. Mama still had a great deal of picking over to do.

While we were getting agarita berries, we had to watch out for rattlesnakes. We always did, but especially around agarita bushes. Maybe they sought protection of the well-defended plants; maybe they found prey in the creatures that came to eat the berries. I don't know.

My First Deer

To speak of my shooting career is to laugh. Sometimes I can hit a barn door and sometimes I can't.

This episode was a long time ago. I suppose there were laws protecting game, but not many people paid attention to them. I don't recall my father's ever scabbarding his rifle when he rode out. My mother killed a coyote with it once.

The rifle was an old .44 Winchester, copper-lined. I suppose I must have practiced with it a little but have no recollection of shooting it until one winter day when I was around twelve years old. I got permission to go deer hunting. It was a late, misty afternoon, the fine mist cutting down visibility but hardly wetting the ground. There wasn't much wind. I had a sharp pocketknife in my pocket and that ancient copper-bellied saddle gun in my hand. I walked across the calf pasture to the north and got into the big pasture. Before long I struck a little hollow lined with brush and oak trees; in places its bed was sandy. I crisscrossed it, hunting east and hunting west while bearing northward. I saw some fresh tracks.

The sun was about down, as I knew by the diminishing light, when at a bend in the hollow, while I was stepping softly along in the middle of it, I saw a doe stretching out her neck and looking toward me. I'm sure she hadn't smelled me, for what breeze there was was off her to me; in thick, foggy, misty weather smell does not carry far anyhow. The doe did not run. I had ceased to move by the time she got a good look at me, and in the fog I must have been somewhat indistinct against the background of brush. Does, it has always seemed to me, are more curious than bucks, except yearling bucks. I'll never forget the way this one had her neck out. She was at the edge of a motte of smallish liveoak trees. I aimed at her neck and broke it. She fell forward into the shallow hollow.

This was the first deer I'd ever shot at. The fact that the deer was a doe instead of a buck made no impression on me. If there was a law against shooting does, I didn't know it. When my half uncle Ed Dubose came to the ranch every December to hunt, he never killed anything but bucks. I had been seeing bucks all my life, but I was hunting for meat. Papa didn't like venison nearly so well as he liked beef, but I liked it better and always have.

I was not excited when I walked up to the doe and saw her already quiet. I stuck her, she bled well, and then I gutted her.

The smell and feel of blood made me brave. I decided I would carry the liver home to show as proof of my accomplishment. I left the carcass on the ground and struck out for the house, less than a mile and a half away. It was dark when I got there. I made quite a sensation when, all bloody and liver-carrying, I walked into the room where the fire in the fireplace was going and my sister Fannie and two or three very young brothers were assembled. Papa asked me where the deer was. I told him. He said we'd saddle up and go bring it in. We rode directly to the slaughter grounds. Papa tied the doe on back of my saddle.

I don't remember whether we ate the liver or not. Probably not. People used not to eat much of anything but the backstraps and hams of deer. I've learned only very recently that the heart and kidneys are the choicest parts and that the liver is better than high-priced beef liver. As I compose this recollection I'm looking forward to baked deer ribs and either boiled or broiled or baked kidneys and heart, along with fried liver from an acorn-fat buck.

This initiation into deer hunting did not make me an avid or proficient deerslayer, but I never went up that little hollow, whether hunting or riding after cattle, without looking for a deer to show up exactly where I had killed the doe. I was like a horse we had that one day while I was riding him shied away from a rattlesnake down the road about three hundred yards from the house. After that he always, invariably, upon passing that particular spot, shied. Neither he in looking for a rattlesnake at the place where he had seen one nor I in looking for a deer in the place where I had seen and killed one was using intellect; we were merely using instinct.

For me the finest feature of a hunt remains the sense of expectation, of hoping and waiting — and I confess that if I didn't like venison I would never hunt at all. I really take more pleasure in seeing wild things alert and alive than in seeing them fall.

A Hawk and a Coachwhip Snake

I HAVE remembered hundreds of times something I saw as a boy. I was with my father and two or three Mexican vaqueros driving a small herd of cattle to our ranch from the upper part of the county. We nooned on the old Timon ranch and after we had eaten lunch carried in *morrals* (fiber bags) on our saddles, my father took me and a Mexican to hunt for a wild cow lost in the Timon pasture on another trip.

We scattered, and I was riding over an open, sandy hill with tall grass on it when I saw a very large hawk, or it may have been a Mexican eagle, on the ground. It fluttered as I came closer to it and was very restless but could not rise. I halted my horse and saw that a long coachwhip (prairie racer) snake, silver-colored in that part of the world, was wrapped about the great hawk's legs and partly around its body.

Coachwhips climb trees. Also, hawks often alight on the ground. I don't know whether this hawk had caught the snake in a liveoak tree not far off and then, on account of the snake's twisting about its legs or wings, had had to alight, or whether it had swooped down on the snake on the ground. These hawks eat snakes. Also coachwhips eat birds, young ones.

I presume that the hawk had started the alliance. It had certainly bit off more than it could chew. During the time I watched, the hawk did not seem to make any move calculated to free itself from the snake. I can't recall that it caught the snake in its bill. Nor was the snake writhing. There seemed to be a deadlock between the two.

While I was watching, I heard a long, high yell. My father's yell had a lift to it as far-reaching as the opening notes of a hound. I looked and saw three or four cows running off to my left several hundred yards away, and understood that I was to cut them off from a brushy swag. One of those cows, a pale red-spotted white, was the one we were after. My horse's heart was thumping with eagerness.

I hated to leave the hawk and the snake there in the tall grass, but I took after the cow. We cut her off and put her in the herd. I did not have as much intellectual curiosity then as I have now, or I should have gone back and stayed with the eagle and serpent until something was settled, even if it took a week.

I would be willing to pay the price of two good cows on a high market to have the clear memory of the continuance of that strange contest and its outcome, perhaps fatal to both, in my mind.

A Night Ride

A RANCH boy was riding homeward along a dirt road in twilight and then in darkness. No automobile had ever made a track on that road. It wound through a silent land in which the human ear registered every sound, as in sparsely populated country every human form and face registers on the consciousness of every beholder. The boy was used to the plump of his horse's feet on the ground and to the soft creak of his old saddle, but in the quietness they made a friendly rhythm that he enjoyed. It was added to by the occasional chirp of a cricket in grass or bush beside the road. And now all the regular sounds were lost in the long and lonesome howling of a coyote, which was quickly answered by longer and lonesomer howls far off in three or four directions and which soon turned into gay, careless barkings.

The road passed a windmill that the south wind turned at a moderate rate and that made a comfortable sound every time the rod pulled up a cylinder full of water. The boy halted at the trough to let his horse drink. It was a joy to him to hear

Buck swallow with manifest satisfaction, and then to hear him lipping the water and letting drops of it run back from his mouth into the trough. The boy wasn't very thirsty, but the sound of freshly pumped water running from the lead pipe into the big cypress cistern was so inviting that he climbed a ladder and drank from a tin can kept handy.

The well and windmill, and picket pens against them, were among old, thick-trunked, wide-spreading liveoak trees. Screech owls often gave their quavering trills in these trees. This evening as they trilled, three big spring (leopard) frogs about a dirt tank, fed by overflow water from the cypress cistern, seemed to be trying to shout them down. The faster and higher the frogs croaked, the more energy the owls seemed to put into their rising and falling tremolos. This contrary duet made the boy so glad that he would have lingered longer listening if Old Joe had not suddenly whined at his feet.

Old Joe never barked at his own people; when he detected one of them coming home he would trot out to meet him and make him welcome with welcoming twists of his body and welcoming sounds from his mouth. The boy spoke to him low, and then dog, boy, frogs and screech owls were all silenced by a booming who-who-who from a barred owl, in a tree not far down the creek. "I cook for myself. Who cooks for you-all?" the boy called back to him, trying to imitate his father's basso. As if in derision at the imitation, a coyote that sounded to be in the valley cornfield let out a few yelps, and Old Joe yelped back good-naturedly as if to say, "I hear you and you'd better listen to me."

Then the boy rode on to the ranch house only a few hundred yards away. As he opened a gate near it, anyone listening through the open windows could have heard the gate slap the gatepost and the rattle of a piece of tracechain that fastened it. Somebody was listening.

"Is that you, son?" she called out in a voice that betrayed a little anxiety but that kept its calm, quieting qualities. The sound of that voice echoes across the years now as a benediction, somehow reminding me of the ringing of a bell that a certain generous soul centuries ago bestowed upon the village of Bury St. Edmunds, in England, to guide home any wanderer lost in darkness amid the fields and woods of the surrounding country.

As the boy unsaddled Buck against the feed lot, another horse kept there sometimes overnight to ride at dawn after the remuda whinnied a greeting and Buck nickered back. About this time Antonio, who slept in a room at the end of the barn, walked up softly and asked, "What is there of news?"

"No, *todo es pacífico*," the boy responded in the idiom of the country. He might have answered with another common idiom, "All is old," but on this night he said, "All is pacific." He had no intimation of how in long years ahead the peaceful sounds of that night, which were sounds common to any night, would come back to him.

CHAPTER FOUR

The Cowman Who Was My Father

When I get down into the Brush Country of south Texas, long memories always come to me. I write this in a camp by a dirt tank out in the mesquites and blackbrush. The weather is raw, and the coyotes talk about it by day as well as by night. They summon my memories, especially of my father.

I have wanted to write this sketch for a long time, not primarily to pay filial respect but to put down as clearly and concisely as I can a human reality. I have read all the books there are about ranch people and their occupation, but nothing in print about cowmen pictures the kind of man my father was. This is not to say that he was an individual beyond the much-stressed individualism of range men. The writings (and I include my own) seem simply not to get inside human lives so far as those lives belong to ranching.

Jonathan Richard Dobie was born in Harris County in January, 1858. He disliked his first name, was called Richard, and signed his name R. J. His grandfather had come to Texas from Virginia in 1830, followed within a few years by three sons. Two of them were ranching as partners in Harris County by the early 1840s, the other having died. My grandfather, Robert Neville Dobie, was drowned in a stream on his ranch in 1857, five months and ten days before my father was born. A year later the remaining brother, Sterling Neblett Dobie, moved west to Live Oak County and bought a ranch, on which he and his wife raised a family of ranchers. Along in the 70s my widowed grandmother, whose second husband, Abel H. White, had died in 1872, also moved to Live Oak County with her four Dobie sons and settled on a small ranch. Her brother-in-law ran her horses and cattle with his and continued to brand them in the Robert Dobie brand.

The country was still unfenced and a man could graze stock without owning a square foot of land. Ramirenia and Lagarto creeks, in the southern part of the county, the Dobie part, ran clear water the year around.

Grandma White was more concerned over the moral influence of the country on her boys than over grass and water. An old trail driver and sheriff from Cuero who stayed all night at her ranch not long after she moved to Live Oak County told me many years later how surprised he was to be asked to join in family prayers following supper and then to hear a blessing at the breakfast table. He said that Grandma did not like horseracing instead of church for Sunday and that she seemed to think horse thieves were more plentiful around her than Christians.

Three of her four sons became ranchmen who knew no other occupation; all four were upright, honest, sober-living, never given to wildness. Before my father married he was called Dancing Dick of Sore Toe. He loved to dance and play the fiddle, and I understand that he smoked cigarettes. About the time he married he became rigidly religious, quit dancing, disposed of his fiddle, never to play one again, and stopped smoking. I never heard anybody call him Dick. His first cousin, Dick Dobie, ranched adjoining us. The only Dobie of the generation who took a drink now and then was Uncle Jim, and he probably did not take a jigger a year.

He and my father and Uncle Neville began ranching by

raising and trading in horses. They drove horses to Kansas and sold them. When horses became unprofitable, they turned to cattle. The only one of the three who really loved horses and liked to "fool" with them was Uncle Neville. I don't think that my father or Uncle Jim ever rode a pitching horse if he could avoid it. My father advised against "marrying" a horse — becoming too attached to a horse to trade him off to advantage.

I used to think that when I got to be a writing man I'd write a long story about a cow horse that after getting too old to run in brush was sold to a trader to take east and dispose of for a plow horse. That was the end of many ranch horses. Maybe a majority of ranchmen kept a favorite horse and let him run out until he died, but most worn-out horses were sold to end up in harness — as old horses now go for dog food. I would protest to Papa against selling off any horse. I had no idea that the grass eaten by a turned-out horse would in a steer or cow contribute to educating six children. The tragedy of ceasing to be a cow horse running free and becoming a clodhopper was in my mind. Sometimes it depressed my spirits.

I never heard of any Dobie carrying a six-shooter. Over big parts of the ranching West many men wore six-shooters, but in the region I grew up in a lot of range men who belonged to the Six-shooter Age — the generation preceding mine — did not have six-shooters. My father bought a light revolver for my mother to have for protection when he was away from home. He had an old copper-bellied .44 Winchester with which he occasionally killed a varmint or hawk after the chickens, but he almost never hunted, though there were plenty of deer on the ranch. Many other ranchmen were like that; some still are.

Papa always wanted to handle cattle easy, which was not my idea, and had fairly gentle cattle. He raised some and regularly bought steer yearlings and sold them when they were two or three years old. Being pretentious and ambitious, I wanted to give a name to our ranch. Uncle Jim's ranch had a name; it was Kintuck. I thought a Mexican name would be good for ours. Papa said it was not big enough to have a name or to be a real ranch. He called it a "place." He usually had additional land leased for pasture. He was a great trader, turning his stock frequently.

He would not work on Sunday and did not want us boys riding calves and disporting ourselves in similar ways on Sunday. He helped build two Methodist churches, one at Dinero, seven miles east of us, and one at Ramirenia, somewhat farther to the west of us. Each of these places consisted of a single little store with a post office in a corner of it. We attended church regularly only at Ramirenia, once a month, when the preacher would come down from Oakville, the county seat, in the northern part of the county. Our house, like the homes of both my grandmothers, was headquarters for the preacher when it was our Sunday on the circuit he served.

Going to church was an all-day business, with a sermon in the morning, then dinner, picnic-style, at which no other woman's lemon pies and potato salad were so delicious as my mother's, and services again in the afternoon. My father sang the hymns more musically than any other man and the preacher always called on him to lead in prayer. It was usually dark when we got back to the ranch.

People came to the annual camp-meeting from long distances. A dozen or so families camped in tents. Nearly every one of them had a Mexican along to cook or help cook, haul water in barrels, bring up wood, stake the horses, and do other chores. Just before the camp-meeting was to begin the men of the community would gather at the site, a grove of liveoak trees, to repair a big brush arbor and strew hay on the ground — the floor. One day while the neighbors were working on the brush arbor my father would not eat dinner. He said it was his fast day. He observed, I believe, all the fast days officially recognized by the Methodist Church South. At camp-meeting he never shouted, as some of the participants did, but his happiness was luminous.

Once a summer a picnic or barbecue was held on the Nueces River. At it would be clean washtubs full of iced lemonade, which sold at five cents a glass. This was my introduction to ice. Also there would be what was called a Mexican band — two or three men playing "La Paloma," "La Golondrina," and other familiar tunes. I thought this music very beautiful. It would keep sounding in my ears for several days and nights.

Papa had a cheerful, though not joyous, disposition. On Sunday afternoons he liked to sing hymns in the parlor while my mother accompanied him on the piano. I do not recall this hymn-singing, which they enjoyed so much, with any lightness of heart. No man was more honest with himself as well as with other people than my father. His integrity was a substantial part of his religion. If he analyzed it, he probably ascribed it more to church and religion than I do.

As the oldest child, I got to go with him at a very early age and was often with him on trips after cattle. Perhaps I was not more than ten years old when we went into an adjoining county to look at some bulls for sale. On the way he told me that the owner was an infidel. I expected to see a monstrosity in human semblance. At that time I did not know that a man could be an infidel and also be honest and kind and have many of the other virtues commonly called Christian.

Sometimes it took only a day to drive the cattle he had bought to our ranch. Most of the ranches in the country were small and he would buy a dozen yearlings here and twenty there, receiving them at some centrally located pen. The standard price was around $10 a head, and they were good grade. Sometimes he bought yearlings so far away that it took two or three days to drive them home. Going with him and his hands to drive a herd was a signal experience for me. Often, however, I had to stay in school.

I did not go one time when a big rain fell, putting Ramirenia Creek on a boom. It was up swift, wide and deep, bringing down driftwood, when my father and his men reached it. Nobody was eager to ride into it. They had no chuck wagon; they carried some grub, a coffee pot and tin cups in morrals. My father could not wait until the creek ran down and still get to the ranch where he was to receive cattle on time. He was no hand to wait anyhow. He advised the men to take off their shoes and boots. He seldom wore boots himself and never wore spurs. Before they rode into the current he got down on his knees and prayed God for a safe crossing.

Now, this was not an orthodox procedure for a cowman. I was at one of the fool ages when I heard about this praying. (There are several fool ages for some men; in fact, for some, including myself, the fool ages are concomitant with existence on earth.) I was shamed by such humility on the part of my father. Another time — this was the year I went off to college and the family moved to Beeville — I was humiliated because he did not wear a necktie to church. He was always very neat but plain in dress. He wore a white shirt, with white starched collar, and coat, but sometimes did not wear a necktie.

I often wish that before he died my father could have known what a low opinion I came to have of myself for being embarrassed during the prolonged years of puerility at his not acting and dressing as other men acted and dressed. I had this feeling of embarrassment, something of shame, when he refused to receive a herd of cattle on Sunday.

One year Uncle Frank Byler, my mother's brother, contracted a certain number of steers to my father, to be delivered at our ranch house pens on a certain date. Neither of the men, I believe, had at the time they made the contract bothered to see what day of the week the date would fall upon. It was Sunday about five o'clock in the evening when we around the house heard the yelling and slapping of quirts on leather leggins that go with crowding brush cattle into pens. I and my brothers made a break for the big pen at the windmill about two hundred yards from the house. Papa remained sitting calmly on the front gallery. After the steers were penned, Uncle Frank rode to the house. I don't know what words passed between him and my father. After a little while, he came back to the pens and called, "Vámanos!" to the vaqueros. His keen brown eyes flashed fire as he said to me, "You can tell your pappy to count them when he wants to. They are all there." Monday morning we branded the cattle. It would have been easier to brand them while Uncle Frank's men were there to help us. After the work was done, my father rode to Lagarto to give Uncle Frank his check.

They were good friends and this episode did not mar their friendship. My father regarded Uncle Frank and Uncle Jim both as being too "worldly-minded." It must have been during the election year of 1896, when McKinley was running against Bryan and I was eight years old, that my father said to me, "Don't say anything about it, but your Uncle Frank is going to vote the Republican ticket." "Why?" I asked, not having the least idea why anybody should vote any ticket. "He thinks the low tariff advocated by the Democrats brings down the price of cattle." If he had known absolutely that voting the Democratic ticket would lower the price of his cattle, my father would have voted the Democratic ticket just the same. He was not a student of economics. His loyalty to the Democratic party was a matter of both tradition and principle. He and his ancestors had been Democrats since the time of Jefferson, but Grover Cleveland was the only Democratic president he lived under until near the end of his life, when Woodrow Wilson came in. Yet in his nightly prayer, as the family knelt beside our chairs, he asked God to bless "those in authority over us" and to direct them in justness and wisdom. By "those in authority over us" he meant particularly the President of the United States of America. The words come back to me with increasing emphasis as a commentary on both my father and the times. It would never have occurred to him or to any of his neighbors — all Democrats — to hate the President of our country. They prayed for him as all good Britishers call upon God to save the Queen. Like a faraway bell at evening time, "God bless those in authority over us" tolls tones of serenity and goodwill into the deserts of hate-for-presidents wherein I now dwell.

I grew up among men who had spent their lives on the ground, often sleeping upon it, eating upon it, riding horseback over it, gazing beyond it. They could squat upon it comfortably. They read little and many of them talked sparingly. The women were busy from the time they got up until they went to bed, but the men usually had an hour or two of free time after supper. Typically, my father enjoyed silences. In warm weather, after dark, he would sit for long whiles in a chair on the front gallery saying nothing, hearing, I suppose, the wind in the tops of the liveoak trees, or if there were no wind, hoping it would rise to make the windmills pump. I doubt that he became bored with his own company. He liked people from whom he could learn something and loved deeply his wife and children, but he did not seem to hunger after company, as my mother often hungered.

Both my father and my mother often used maxims, sayings, fables, and folk rhymes to instruct us children. To inculcate thrift my father would say,

"See a pin and pick it up
And all day you'll have good luck.

See a pin and let it lay
And bad luck you'll have all day."

He practiced this brand of thrift himself. If after he sat on his horse he noticed a shingle nail in dirt near the barn and toolroom, he would get down and pick it up. Uncle Jim Dobie was the same way. He would potter around near where a keg of fence staples was kept, expecting, not unreasonably, to find a staple dropped by some fence rider. As we boys grew older, Papa advised, "Make all you can, save all you can, give all you can."

When we were small, Papa told us about two frogs, the second of which we should somehow emulate. One was trying to get out of a well. Every time he jumped up two feet he fell back three. But against the frog of inadequate effort we learned about another. This frog was terribly energetic, and I'd say now that he had luck on his side. He had fallen into an old-fashioned wooden-dash churn containing cream. He kept paddling around in the cream until he finally churned up a ball of butter. Then he stood on the ball of butter and jumped free. He was an admirable frog. He had energy.

Papa was like this second frog. His cheerful call to us boys as we grew up was

Wake up, Jacob.
Day's a-breaking
Peas in the pot
And hoecakes a-baking.

Living as we did in *frijole* (pinto bean) country, we never had peas for breakfast or any other meal. The peas in my father's morning call had probably been brought to Texas from Virginia or South Carolina by one of his parents, and they were black-eyed peas.

Papa believed in the saying "Spare the rod and spoil the child." A teacher who boarded with us, Miss Ella Simms, received from her lover, as a boyfriend was called in those days, a leather strap with which to whip her unruly pupils. The lover was Orsineth Hatfield. When Miss Ella left us, she gave the strap to Papa. He dubbed it Orsineth's liniment. "I am going to administer some Orsineth's liniment," he would announce to a disobedient son. One time Lee giggled.

While my sister Fannie and I were still very young, a little minstrel show brought its tent to Lagarto for a one-night stand. My father drove us to see it; my mother was too much engaged with younger children, I suppose, to go. On the drive in, we saw Cousin Dick coming from Lagarto. People who are used to seeing each other ride horseback can distinguish an individual far off by his posture and way of riding just as, at nearer view, we can distinguish people by the way they walk. Cousin Dick nearly always rode in a long lope. Of course Papa stopped the buggy and Cousin Dick stopped his horse when we met. "What's the news?" he asked. Then he wanted to know where and why we were going. Papa told him. "Don't you regard the theater as sinful?" he asked. Maybe my father did not regard a minstrel show in a tent as theater. He saw more point to some of the jokes than I saw.

He had not read many books, but long and intent reading of the Bible had given him good taste in literature within certain ranges. Those ranges did not include the *Arabian Nights* tales. I heard him snort once and call them "a pack of lies." He was more tolerant toward the brownies — a species of fairy folk very dear to my childhood. He would read the brownie book to us.

So far as I know he never cursed or used coarse language. However, he was on some words and on nature's functions no orthodox Victorian. He used to laugh at the recollection of a man who came to his mother to buy "a gentleman cow." He was master of clear, simple language. I wish I could reconstruct the diction of his prayers. I imagine that sometimes while he was riding alone he composed them in his mind. The one concrete recollection I have of his letters, of which he wrote few, my mother being the main letter-writer to absent members of the family, was in reply to a complaint of mine, made in a letter home while I was in college, about an injustice that did not touch me personally. He quoted from the Psalms: "Fret not thyself because of evildoers." That quotation from Scripture has many times since given me serenity — temporarily. I can hear his calm, richly timbred voice reading this very Psalm at our nightly devotions, and I realize now as I did not then how much he enjoyed the imagery and eloquence of the Bible as literature: "Fret not thyself because of evildoers, neither be thou envious against the workers of iniquity. For they shall soon be cut down like the grass, and wither as the green herb."

He had a strong voice, well modulated. Many a time when we were working cattle I heard him "holler" a mile away. He loved to sing. He sang oldtime songs. "Kitty Wells," "She Is a Young Thing and Cannot Leave Her Mother," "The Feller That Looked Like Me," and "Old Folks at Home" were favorites. "The Feller That Looked Like Me" was the rollickiest, but I enjoyed being sad and still become doleful as I recollect Papa's singing,

You ask what makes this darkey weep
Why he like others is not gay,
What makes the tears roll down his cheeks
From early dawn till close of day.

Oh, the tune was everything. I cannot even suggest the sweet sadness by the words.

Papa sang hymns with unflagging fervor and solace to his own soul. He sang them driving alone in the buggy at night or riding horseback on the way home. Many and many a time Mama and the children at the house heard his singing long before the hoof thuds and then the creak of saddle leather announced his arrival. Often we were in the night getting home with a herd of steer yearlings he had bought up country — not a big herd, four or five hands driving it. Papa was usually at the rear of the herd, where an animal was most likely to drop out. Hymn after hymn he sang to those cattle, steadying them. The slow movement of the hymns suited the slow walk of the animals, and sometimes it seemed to me that their heads were bobbing in time with the tune. But it was at Sunday school and church that Papa sang with most fervor. His devotion to a spirit that his own spirit had created and that could respond only through his own spirit yearned beyond words, beyond melody, beyond the physical organs that sounded it. "We Shall Gather at the River," he sang. To him the marvels of *Arabian Nights* were lies, but the miracle of immortality "in the sweet by and by" was as unquestionable as that there would be coffee for tomorrow's breakfast.

We were repairing the pump at the upper mill on Long Hollow, not far from the camp-meeting grounds. I was still a small boy. Standing on the ground, my father was doing something to one of the pulled pipes that could have been more handily done from a position on the tower. About this time Andrew Polan rode up. "Richard," he asked tauntingly, "why don't you stand up there on the tower?" "I have arrived at the age of discretion," my father replied. The new word became indelible in my memory. It is still more interesting to me than the idea it represents.

At this same windmill another time, when I was somewhat older, I was struggling with a pair of worn-out pipe tongs. In a pet I asked my father why he did not buy new ones. He merely said, "Rich people have mean ways and poor people have poor ways." We were always in debt, and never had any money to speak of.

Regarding him now from the point of view of the volatile temperament inherited from my mother, I consider him about the justest man I have ever known. I recollect his being angry only twice. Once was when he heard me use to my sister a vile phrase that I had picked up from older boys and did not actually know the meaning of. Having an equitable temperament, he did not have to discipline himself to justice as fractious people do.

He had a distaste for rough men, the frontier ruffian type that Stephen F. Austin tried — unsuccessfully — to exclude from his colonies. He saw nothing picturesque about "an old stove-up cowpuncher." He saw nothing romantic about roping. He could rope fairly well, but Mexican vaqueros hired at four bits a day could rope better. He never carried a roping rope coiled on the righthand side of his saddle but carried an ordinary rope around the neck of his horse and tied by the horn string to the left side of his saddle. He was never possessed of a big red or blue bandana, but often wore a large white handkerchief around his neck or over his nose to keep out dust. He wore leather leggins against brush but never a ducking jacket. He had a kind of contempt for pretensions in dress. When a man came by one day all spruced up, riding a $40 saddle on a $20 horse, he remarked, "All it takes to make So-and-So a big cowman is two and a half profit off some Mexican on a sore-backed-horse trade."

He hoped that his sons would find something better in life than ranching in a drouth-stricken, thorn-choked country. He and my mother were set on giving each of their six children a college education — something neither of them had had. They did not look upon a college education as something to make money by. Without being much concerned about intellectual values, they felt deeply that somehow a college education would elevate us to a higher plane of living. The better things they wanted for their children were not primarily worldly possessions.

I was by my father while he lay dying in June, 1920. Decay is natural to all matter, but he did not seem natural without energy. His mind was clear to the last breath. About an hour before he died he asked, "Am I very heavy?" "No." "Then please move me next to the windows."

All his days my father carried goodness toward fellow men in his heart. His life was an almost unflawed fulfillment of the teaching "Whatsoever ye would that men should do to you, do ye even so to them."

CHAPTER FIVE

My Mother—Ella Byler Dobie

My mother was born on her grandmother Byler's plantation in Fayette County, Texas, the year the Civil War broke out. When she died, November 22, 1948, she in her long span of years had seen more changes in the ways of living in this country than had taken place between the discovery of America and her own entrance upon the scene. Her father, Rufus Byler, who had served in Hood's Texas Brigade, was presumably murdered for a fine horse and a moneybelt after the Civil War ended. He had just left his family on the Byler plantation, where they had lived during the war, and was riding to Rancho Seco on the Nueces to rehabilitate his ranch home before moving them back to it. He was traced only as far as the San Antonio River. Nobody ever knew what the murderers did with his body. Someone started the rumor that he had deserted his wife and three children and left the country for South America, but, according to all accounts, he was very fond of them. His brother, Frank Byler, eventually rode to Nebraska after two men supposed to have killed him, but either did not find them or found them innocent.

The Byler brothers ran cattle on the open range in Nueces County. One was for buying land; the other said that since the grass was free, buying land it grew on would be a waste of money — even if a man had money. After the disappearance of Rufus, his brother Frank took charge of the cattle. Grandma moved back to Rancho Seco, a small settlement of ranch people, with her "younguns." In 1869 she married Friendly Dubose, range man and a very picturesque individual, and with him reared a family of sons. He had a brother named Neighbor.

Perhaps I should say that Rancho Seco became Bluntzer, six miles from Banquete, the post office. Names of neighbors as I remember my mother's giving them sound to me like an old refrain, though I know they cannot have connotations for most people: W Six Wright (W 6 was his brand), Nick Bluntzer, George Hendrickson, Sam Fusselman (my grandmother's brother), and always the Bennetts. But neighbors were not close.

During the Rancho Seco time, before Grandma married Mr. Dubose, a fair-skinned young man came along who "looked like he might read, write, and recollect." The settlers hired him to teach school, the house of learning being a dirt-floored Mexican jacal with a board supported by stumps for a table running down the middle of it and a backless bench on either side.

"But what's the use of having school?" the Kellet children asked. "We don't have any books."

"There's the Bible," their father answered. It was the only book in his home, but there it was.

"Mr. Kellet," my mother used to tell, "was what you'd call a character. People called him 'Honest John.' Time meant little to him. If he saw somebody in a hurry, he would say, 'You must be getting rich, for only people who are hurry.' He liked to talk and when he was talking would thrash his arms about like a windmill. In those days the road from San Antonio to Corpus Christi ran through Rancho Seco, and Mr. Kellet used to go out to this road and wait there, hours sometimes, until a freighter came by and then hold him up and invite him to turn off and spend the night at his house. He wanted company and wanted to hear what was going on in the world." In that part of the country the freighters seldom camped out alone; there was too much danger.

The child Ella helped in the rearing of her brother and sister and her half brothers as they came along. Time and again I have heard her tell how she read Scott, Dickens, *Ben-Hur* and *Tom Sawyer* aloud to them and three or four other ranch boys. She could command them by threatening not to read. She attended school for a term at a Catholic convent in Victoria, but was not the kind to be confined in convents. Then she went to a "female college" at Chapel Hill, Texas. She was a good horsewoman, but said she could not hold a light as a rider to her sister Fannie. She was teaching in what was called Lagarto College, an elementary school, part free and part pay, at Lagarto in Live Oak County when, in 1887, she married Richard J. Dobie and took up life on his ranch about six miles away.

While I was still a child, my mother came upon a list of "the best ten books for young people under sixteen years of age," selected by a group of educators. It is still a good list, as the titles show: *Pilgrim's Progress; Robinson Crusoe; Ivanhoe; Tom Brown's School Days; A Child's History of England; Plutarch's Lives; David Copperfield; Black Beauty; John Halifax, Gentleman;* and *Heroes and Hero Worship.* My mother proposed to get these books for her children, and got them. The list is still posted inside the door of her walnut wardrobe.

Uncle Tom's Cabin was not on the list. My mother had been reared to regard it as evil and did not approve of my reading a copy borrowed from a neighboring ranch. She had read the *Youth's Companion* a good part of her life and kept on taking it for her children. Some of the adventure stories in that magazine remain among my most delightful memories. Her mind had more play than my father's. Yet they were well suited to each other.

My mother read to the older children and taught or tried to teach us to play the piano. She had scant time for such things — less and less as the family grew. She never milked but she made butter and curd. She raised chickens. At times she had to cook for the Mexican ranch help as well as for the family. Men might come at any hour of day or night. All had to be fed and bedded. All of her children were born on the ranch, and I realize now how much work we made. I have heard her say that for long periods of time she did not get more than four or five hours of sleep out of the twenty-four.

She never idealized ranch people, though she belonged to them from the ground up. Not long after I went to the University of Texas to teach English I was telling her how tired I got of associating with pedants and how much I'd rather associate with ranch people.

"Law me," she said, "some of 'em don't have brains enough to fry an egg in."

She saw no romance about ranching. She had seen too many drouths, too many bad times, too much drudgery and loneliness, too much lack in human relations. She was naturally gregarious and liked people with something to talk about beyond seasoning for potato salad.

When she was alone with her first children, she was always uneasy, sometimes frightened. Less than a mile to the east a family of Mexicans named Persuelo lived on half a section of land. They were reputed to be horse thieves or to harbor horse thieves. Anyhow there was always a lot of coming and going, riding and spurring around the Persuelo ranch — just a cabin under some trees, with access to a dug well a hundred yards away. When Papa was gone, Mama would have the .44 Winchester at the head of her bed. It was a great relief to her when he bought the Persuelo men out.

Papa was away a great deal, riding after cattle, buying yearlings or receiving them. In his prime he was a man of extraordinary energy and a good deal of ambition. Mama said the days were never long enough for him. Many times after he had ridden out to his own pasture it would be past dark before he came home. If he was off on business, it might be far into the night. I remember how Mama would listen for his whistle or for the sound of his horse's feet on the sandy loam.

Although she was extremely proud of her children, she viewed them with a critical objectivity, in some respects at least. She was never prouder of them than during World War I when she had four sons and one daughter in the services. After my father died in 1920, she was capable manager of her own business affairs — not big, but sufficient for her independence. She built a cottage on a high hill in the Methodist Assembly grounds near Kerrville, on the Edwards Plateau of Texas. For many years she went there to spend the summer. During the last five years of her life her younger daughter, Martha, was with her constantly.

No person in need or distress ever asked her for help without getting it. She did not wait to be asked if she knew of need or suffering. After the family moved to Beeville she would go among businessmen and others of the town raising money for a distressed family. During the terrible times of hunger and unemployment of the Great Depression, the trail to her door was well marked. Many days her kitchen fed several men. The majority of them were young, and in these she took a special interest. She thought of them as being each the son of some mother and as having an immortal soul, and with the generous plates of food went kind words out of a kind and generous heart. She kept a supply of the Gospels printed in pamphlet form, and with a free meal she gave a free Matthew, Mark, Luke, or John. She never offered to feed a hungry man on a sermon, however.

Mention of a certain woman brought this remark: "A good woman, but she has missed one big thing in life — the joy of giving. I've had my share of that. Maybe I have a softer heart for Mexicans than for any other class of the needy. They seldom save anything for the next day, but they are so responsive to kindness and help." Of course, her knowledge of Mexicans was restricted mostly to the laboring class at a time before they went to school.

Mama worried at times, but "cheerfulness was always breaking in." She never felt sorry for herself, never complained. Her spirit buoyed up others. One day when I was fuming at the wind and ice of a prolonged cold spell — other times too, but I particularly recollect this — my mother said, "Son, I will give you an old adage:

For every evil under the sun
There is a remedy or there is none.
If there is one, go and find it;
If there is none, never mind it."

When one of us boys started out for somewhere — no matter where, no matter how old the boy was — she would say, always gaily, "Remember whose boy you are."

I think of her especially at Christmas and shall as long as I live, for she was especially Christmasy. Most mothers are, but mine had so much gusto and vitality that her high spirits stood out. No child was ever more delighted with Christmas than she was. No matter how, when, or where I remember her, feelings of cheerfulness come over me. During the years of Santa Claus, with six children on the ranch, she was at her best.

Then came maturer Christmases as Time wove the swift

shuttle of life. Before long our Christmases were reunions. Mama seldom knew at what hour her "younguns" would arrive, but while busy she somehow kept watch, and as a car she expected drove up near the back door she would emerge shouting like a Comanche Indian. On Christmas morning her greeting was usually the old-time one of "Christmas Gift!" That greeting, I believe, used to be given by some servant or other dependent expecting a gift. Mama knew the gifts were coming, all right: she was elated by every Christmas card and every other form of remembrance. She outgave all other givers. "I don't always get what I want," she would say, "but I always want what I get."

After I became a kind of book man, she didn't give me books any more, for she judged, rightly, that my taste was no longer in her domain. I doubt if she ever realized how much she had done to formulate that taste. A poem entitled "The Reading Mother" by Strickland Gillilan used to be popular. The last stanza is truly of my mother:

You may have tangible wealth untold,
Caskets of jewels and coffers of gold;
Richer than I you can never be;
I had a Mother who read to me.

She had a hearty laugh and a great gusto for life, and no doubt she would have traveled more had she not taken more pleasure in giving than in receiving, for during the prolonged years of her vigor she liked to see new places and to learn. She was so eager that the night before a trip she could sleep little. "I was journey proud," she would say. Her eyes never became too dim for her to enjoy beautiful landscapes and the rising and setting of the sun.

She had many sayings out of the Bible and many folk expressions. One Bible saying was, "Whatsoever thy hand findeth to do, do it with all thy might."

Where was Moses when the light went out?
Sitting in the window with his shirttail out,

was often spoken by her and in turn by her children whenever, as often occurred, a strong breeze blew out the kerosene lamp at the ranch. I still like to say this. I don't know why. Sheer gaiety of spirit occasioned her speaking another rhyme with a biblical flavor:

Matthew, Mark, Luke and John
Saddle the cat and all jump on.

She did not play bridge or any other card game, except solitaire, but Charles Lamb's immortal Mrs. Battle never played whist with more animation or zeal than she played dominoes and "42." She kept score and she brought any delayer of the game to reality with the injunction to "shoot, Luke, or give up the gun." To determine who would have the first down in a game she would chant out rapidly an extraordinary rigmarole of syllables, one word to each person around the table, the last one she pointed to being "it." The rigmarole, perhaps older than the King James Version of the Bible, went:

One-ery, twoery, ickery Ann,
Filison, folison, Nicholas John,
Queevy, quavy, English navy,
Stinglum, stanglum — buck.

She relished what she ate and loved to see other people relish their food at her table. She walked as if she wanted to go where she was going and expected to get there. "Come on and quit piddling around," she might say to some dawdler. She was very direct. "Fiddlesticks!" was her disposal, delivered with a mild snort, of some indirection or of what she considered sophistry. "He doesn't know A from Adam's off ox" or

"He doesn't know B from bulls's foot" she might say of some muddler. She had a peculiar combination of drive, impatience and patience. Many things were out of her sphere, but she was anything but lukewarm in reaction to those things within it.

Although toward the very end her memory dimmed, she was never one to look backward. Probably she accepted the story of the Garden of Eden, but really she never believed that perfection lay behind. The "good old days" never existed for her. She did not resent change. Without analyzing the matter, she welcomed the principle of social evolution. At a time when I had almost no other interest than the pageantry of the past, about which I was writing, she said to me, "Son, why are you always looking backward? You are acting like an old man."

Having helped rear a brother and a large collection of half brothers and then having had four sons of her own, besides a husband, she seemed to take men for granted more than many women take them. She understood them. She was a man's woman and she was a matriarchal chieftain. She did not fret against nature.

Most of us remember old people as old. I remember my mother as old, too, but often I remember her without any gray hairs, eager and active, joying in little experiences. I can see her now, young and buxom, her long, thick sorrel hair coming down nearly as low — or so I remember it — as the hair of Lorna Doone in the novel of that name.

I recall her hearty description of a fiddler named Duff Hale, whom she characterized as a "Dickens character." He had a fiddle with the head broken off and at a dance he'd say, "Look, it's beheaded, just like Jesus Christ." Mama would always add, "Of course he knew that Christ was not beheaded, but he liked to talk that way to show off." Very much against drink and drinking, she used to tell with gusto about some character —

maybe she gave his name — who would say about Christmastime, "Now I've got to get on my annual Christmas drunk, and how I hate it!"

It was her way of hitting off characters that I can't equal — just an incident or a saying or a glimpse that lighted up the whole figure, the ray of light coming out with a fine heartiness and with a laugh. I was spending a few days with her in Beeville when at dinner, the meal before supper, Mama was poking fun at herself for being a little slow with eating. "Now my Grandfather Fusselman always said," she observed, "that his father — back in Pennsylvania — never would hire a man on the farm until he had seen him eat. If a man wanted a job, he'd put him off until he'd fed him. If he dilly-dallied at his food, he wouldn't have him, said that's the way he'd work. But if he went at his food like he enjoyed it and meant business, he'd hire him on the spot." She used to tell about Grandma Byler and other characters. She was a character herself.

There is the story she loved to tell of the quail pie. Our ranch neighbors on up Long Hollow from us were the Wrights. One day about noon "Bud" Wright came along. He was a large man with a large manner and a large appetite. There were other extra people for dinner that day, as happened often, and the children waited for the second table. The main dish was a very large quail pie, made of quail we boys had trapped. Mr. Bud took to it with enormous gusto. With thoughts on her children waiting for the second table, my mother watched Mr. Bud's pile of quail bones mount. He had begun by piling them on one side of his plate, but the pile grew top-heavy and finally he cleared them all off on the tablecloth. He ended by picking the flesh from another quail or two, r'ared back and said, "Ella, that pa'tridge pie was mighty good but it would have been better if you'd of fried them pa'tridges before you put them in with the dough to bake."

"I didn't say so," my mother always concluded the story, "but I was thankful I hadn't fried them."

Religion and all church services were a positive joy to my mother. Her tolerance of and respect for some dim-minded preachers and for moralistic vaporings seemed to me beyond all demands of charity and against reason. Yet, however unintellectual such an attitude was, nobody who knew her ever charged her with lacking common sense. Common sense was emphatically one of her strong points. Her religion was spiritual, only slightly ecclesiastical, not at all ritualistic. A part of her religion was to give "a tenth to the Lord," but her giving was never rationed according to what she could charge off against income taxes. She tithed her gross income, not her net. Foreign missions got part.

She devoutly believed in prayer, but she ridiculed some kinds of prayer. She used to quote as not going far enough and wide enough:

God bless me and my wife,
My son John and his wife,
Us four and no more.

She told a story of a man too lazy to get on his knees at night who wrote out on a sheet of paper his chief desires, tacked it to the wall at the head of his bed, and every night would make a weak knee movement toward the prayer and say, "Lord, them's my sentiments."

She had absolute faith in immortality and heaven. Meantime this earth was a mighty good place on which to live. Long after she began going downhill, if someone asked her how she felt, she might reply, "Slightly disfigured but still in the ring." She confidently believed that if everybody were a

Christian the world would be all right. If I argued that the people who have charge of affairs must have superior intelligence and be well informed, she would agree; at the same time she would stick to her original thesis.

If everybody were as genuinely good as she was and had as much common sense as she had, the world would not need much managing. She disciplined herself into serenity. Time and the world tamed the impetuous and wildly free spirit with which nature endowed her, but they did not break her spirit of independence, and nothing soured her wholesomeness.

In the final addition, she lived more positively than most people. She was out of the old rock. In her way, past eighty-seven, she died with her boots on.

CHAPTER SIX

Uncle Frank Byler

MAYBE I was born and brought up in the wrong part of the ranch country for appreciation of popular literature about ranch life. Looking back to boyhood and coming down to the present, I can't spot a single cowman conforming to the "tense, grim tone," shoot-'em-up, hell-bent-for-action type familiar to millions who read "westerns," hear them acted over radio, and see them on television.

I shall try to sketch a cowman whom I knew very well — Frank Byler, for whom I was named. I guess he was plenty rollicky as a boy. He was past twenty-five years old before I was born and was well settled down before my recollections of him begin. At that time he was ranching on leased land in Nueces County, where he had grown up ranching; early in this century he bought a ranch in Live Oak County, a few miles away from our ranch. He operated both ranches until the time of his death in 1933.

Letters that he wrote to his mother when he was fourteen years old, off at school at Chapel Hill in Washington County, Texas, tell which way his mind was traveling:

Dear Ma: . . . I like the school teacher and the doctor very well. Is Trinidad working for you yet and Hosay and Marcelenoso? You must tell me when one of the hands quits and send me the Corpus Christi *Free Press*. Ma, you must not let anybody ride my gray horse. Tell me when anybody gets killed. I went to church today and to Sunday School. You must have Ella's horse got up and put in the field. He is too good a horse to let die. [Barbed wire had not yet arrived and only fields were fenced.] You must not let Mr. Dubose [his stepfather] sell him, for I want to ride him myself. You must get up my black horse that Aunt Ella gave me and not sell him either.

Dear Ma: . . . Does Ed [a 7-year-old half brother] ride much? Tell him that he must ride some for me. If he don't I will forget how to ride. Tell Judge [a younger half brother] to ride some for me also. How is Browney getting along? Where is Canday [another horse] now? I am afraid that he is dead if there ain't good grass out there. Where is Ella's horse? You must take good care of my gray horse. Don't let anybody ride him.

In the 80s, Uncle Frank drove horses up the trail to Kansas. One time, as I used to hear told, while he was watering his mount at a muddy pool in the Indian Territory he saw a water moccasin and pulled his six-shooter to shoot it. He had not had the six-shooter out of its holster since leaving Nueces County and now found it too rusty to cock. He threw it at the snake and left it in the mud. He said that unless a man could shoot a gun he had no business carrying it. He never had shot much. Like many other ranchmen, he almost never hunted game.

On one trip to Kansas, while staying in Caldwell for weeks trading off horses, he became friends with Andy Adams, who had also driven horses up the trail and who years later was to write *The Log of a Cowboy* and other valid books of trail and range. *The Log of a Cowboy* was published in 1903; it is the chronicle of a trail herd driven by south Texas hands from the Rio Grande to Montana. His next novel, *A Texas Matchmaker*, is laid on the Nueces River.

Andy Adams had a way of introducing by name actual characters among the fictional. Frank Byler of Lagarto is incidentally mentioned in both books. I think it was in 1903, while he was writing the second, that he visited Uncle Frank and rode over the country with him horseback, fortifying himself on Brush Country facts and above all, on rancher language, which in that part of Texas contains many Mexicanisms. He wasn't much of a talker himself, nor was Uncle Frank, but he could draw out a man. Aunt Orrie, Uncle Frank's wife, said that while they sat on the front gallery Andy Adams every once in a while would write a phrase or a word down on a slip of paper. Andy Adams told me many years later that Uncle Frank's speech furnished seasoning for cow camp talk in his earlier novels.

I don't recollect ever seeing Uncle Frank travel in a buggy, always on horseback. Uncle Judge Dubose said that after Uncle Frank married he expected to see his saddle on the front gallery instead of out at the horse lot and that, sure enough, was where he found it when he went to see him and Aunt Orrie.

Uncle Frank could talk Mexican as fluently as any vaquero who worked for him. He liked to pike monte with the Mexicans and play poker. One year a Live Oak County grand jury investigated him and some other men for gambling on cards in a mesquite thicket close to the village of Lagarto, though I don't recall that he was indicted. He and my mother were very fond of each other, but she regretted his lack of religion. He did not belong to a church or go to preaching. She said that when he began a cow work he always timed it so that he would have to work on Sunday.

My father also considered Uncle Frank "worldly-minded." He certainly was in comparison with my father. He wore a worldly-looking moustache of reddish hairs, the color of the heavy crown on my gay-natured mother's head when I first noticed her. He habitually wore a vest and carried in one pocket of it a package of Little Joker tobacco, which he rolled into brown paper cigarettes and smoked, one after the other, except when he was working. He frequently inhaled the smoke slowly with a sound of satisfaction. He was pretty close. He never owned a watch, for he could rely upon the heavens for time, until he saved enough coupons from pound packages of Arbuckle's Roasted Coffee to send off and get an Ingersoll. He drank his coffee black and spent mighty little on sugar for his hands. I heard one of them complaining once that they had started a week's work with only a dime's worth of sugar in the chuck wagon and that it was all gone by the end of the first day. Uncle Frank had planned it that way.

Just the same, I shall always remember a special act of generosity to me. The summer when I was about sixteen years old I hired to him to run cattle. My father told me that he would pay as much as Uncle Frank paid, but I wanted to branch out. I furnished my own mounts and drew $1.50 a day — the standard price for a hand furnishing his own horses. "White" hands who rode ranch-owned horses drew six bits a day. Mexican hands drew four bits a day; they never had their own horses. There weren't any better cowhands than some of the four-bits-a-day vaqueros. Uncle Frank was gathering and delivering big steers and receiving steer yearlings that had to be branded and located.

While we were driving a herd of big steers from the upper ranch to the lower one, he put me on the point — at the head of the column. This was a proud hour of my life. I never was an expert rider or roper, but when he put me on the point Uncle Frank showed that he thought I knew how to handle cattle — and I thought so too. I was the only man in front of the steers when they stampeded down a wide land, and I brought them to a slow halt by running not too fast and not too slow ahead of them and making the soothing cries that brush hands make. That night we held them in the Barbon pasture against a fence. About midnight a fresh wind came up and they began to drift. They did not run, just walked, headstrong against the opposition of all hands called out to stop them. Some of them split off and got into brush and I was trying to hold them when Rafael Solis, Indian black in complexion and pock-marked, who worked for Uncle Frank until he died, joined me. We got the steers back to the main herd, and then Rafael told me that he and the other vaqueros could hold them all right till daylight and that Uncle Frank wanted me to go to camp. I had no idea by now where camp was, but he pointed the direction and I let my horse have his head. Camp was deserted except for the cook. I sat there by a few coals left of the campfire feeling like a piker until I heard Rafael coming in. I knew him by his whistling, for he was a great whistler; he was whistling "La Golondrina." Then I heard the hoofbeats of his horse, walking fast to be unsaddled, and then the creaking of saddle leather.

We got through delivering the steers early in the afternoon and all rode back to Lagarto, where most of the hands lived and where the wagon would be left at Uncle Frank's house. It was about sundown when he began paying us off. He pulled out from the right hand front pocket of his ducking breeches a roll of bills that looked to me big enough to choke a cow. When he went to settle up with the first man, Bud Goodwin, he said he was allowing him only four bits instead of the full six bits for that last day's work because he had not worked a full day. A full day meant from before daylight until after dark. Goodwin claimed that riding from the Barbon ranch to Lagarto was part of the day's work, but he didn't get anywhere with the claim. The other hands were paid off on the same basis until my turn came at the end. I still had an hour and a half ride home. Uncle Frank, without my saying a word, paid me a full dollar and a half for that last day as well as for each of the other days I had worked. He put an affection into his goodbye handshake that makes my heart soft now as I remember it.

CHAPTER SEVEN

Ranch Neighbors

THEY are all gone now, these people I knew as the last century was dying. I do not sketch them with any thought of rescuing them from universal oblivion. I sketch them because they keep coming before me and also because I have to try "to make a thing" in order to rest. If some readers of the sketches be interested, I should be pleased.

Our ranch house was about seven miles west of Barlow's Ferry on the Nueces River. While I was a child a suspension bridge took the place of the ferry. Near it a post office in the back end of a store to which a rider brought mail from Beeville, twenty miles on east, was called Dinero. About eight miles on west of our ranch house an Englishman named Hughes kept a store with a post office in the back end, the contents of which would not fill a fair-sized dry-goods box. This was Ramirenia. Everybody called it La Posta, for it had been a stage stand where horses were changed. About six miles south of us, on the south bank of Lagarto Creek, an older, much better known and more populous center was called Lagarto. *Lagarto* means alligator.

A railroad built ten miles away had killed Lagarto. In my boyhood several families with backyards opening into small pastures still lived on the perimeter. Perimeter, besides a store, a schoolhouse, and a church was about all left to the town. Uncle Frank Byler lived on the perimeter and operated a ranch beyond.

My father's mother, Grandma White, lived in Lagarto. Her house had the coolest hallway for a summer nap after a midday dinner that I knew. Two of her sons would let nothing interfere with their naps, but my father and Uncle Jim napped only when they had nothing pressing to do. Grandma White had the first bathroom I ever saw. It was a room built into a tower holding up a large cypress cistern into which a windmill pumped water. This bathroom was known all over the countryside. I remember Grandma White as very large, very serene, and very cheerful. She did not move about much. When she came to see us at the ranch she drove her buggy and had along a Mexican girl to open gates. I was eleven years old when she died.

The inhabitants of the Lagarto community were worldly, urbane, and cosmopolitan compared with those of the Ramirenia settlement and on up the creek. The Lagarto people had dances, for which my father had played the fiddle before he married and became adamant against dancing. The Ramirenia crowd had *bailes*, the Mexican name for dances. My parents hoped their sons would never debase themselves by living with Mexican women. My father went so far as to disapprove of our acquiring much Spanish. I didn't, but Elrich, the brother next to me, dreamed in Spanish.

When I was a small child my mother's mother and stepfather lived on a ranch to the southwest of Lagarto. We hauled groceries by the wagonload from Beeville, but we also did a good deal of trading at the Beall store in Lagarto. I never heard the matter discussed by my parents and so can't be sure why we went to church at Ramirenia. It may be because there was a more religious atmosphere up the Ramirenia; it may be because my father wanted to be free of some entangling alliances. The Methodist Church was weaker in Lagarto than the Campbellite Church, and my mother and father were both strong Methodists.

Anyhow, they helped build a church at Ramirenia. It always galled Papa that Hughes kept his store open on Sunday, though Peruna was the only form of alcohol dispensed. Peruna was a noted tonic and some people bought it by the case. A few young men would hang around Hughes's store on Sunday, not going to church hardly a six-shooter shot away. Occasionally one of the young men would take up for a while with a Mexican woman. Mexican Jim, as one of these young men was called, was a cousin of my father's. Hughes himself was a "squaw man"; that is, he had a common-law Mexican wife. I don't imagine the morals in sex behavior at Lagarto differed much from those at Ramirenia — or at London, Paris or other centers — but there weren't as many squaw men in the Lagarto district.

The preacher lived at Oakville, the county seat, in the northern part of the county, and came to Ramirenia only once a month. He usually drove a two-horse buggy. Sometimes he came to our house on Saturday and stayed all night, going on to Ramirenia the next morning. Every family who went to church took a big cooked dinner. There was always more than enough for any visitors who didn't bring their own provisions. Fried chicken, potato salad, lightbread and biscuits, lemon pies, coconut and chocolate cakes, with coffee boiled on the ground, were always plenteous.

The tallest man in the Ramirenia settlement was Mr. Perry Williams. I won't say that his legs were disproportionately long, but the bottoms of his trousers did not come down to his shoe tops. He wore cotton socks. His shoes were brogans. While most men wore long drawers that came down to the ankles, Mr. Perry Williams's drawers, if he wore any, were not visible between his shoe tops and the bottoms of his breeches. I can see him standing there now at the organ singing. He wore a moustache and had a strong voice, more whangy than musical. In order to read the hymns — I'm sure he couldn't read the notes — he wore horn-rimmed spectacles, but he wasn't used to reading anything, and he read so slowly that he was always behind a few notes and a few words on the singing. My father was a good singer and a very good leader, but nobody on earth could do anything with a song when Perry Williams was whanging out his lines away behind the others. He didn't seem to know that he wasn't in time.

He had just a little ranch and a big family. One of the offspring was a big hermaphrodite, though I didn't learn that word until long afterwards. This he-she dressed as a woman but spoke in a coarse male voice and usually sat with some of the boys. Mr. Perry Williams on occasion freighted. I think he hauled the merchandise Hughes sold from Beeville. When my brother Elrich was five or six years old, Mr. Perry Williams drove his big freight wagon to our ranch one night on the way from Beeville to Ramirenia, having turned off the public road in order to have a good lodging place for himself and his horses. He made a mighty appearance riding on the near wheelhorse and bringing the leaders around to a halt under a liveoak tree near the barn. After that for a long time my brother Elrich's ambition was to be a freighter like Mr. Perry Williams. He was upright in his dealings.

Somewhat of the peasant type were Mr. Dinn and his wife. He was a meek little gray man and she was a large-framed woman, capable of suckling each of the fourteen children they had and of taking care of the house, washing clothes and cooking unaided until some of the children got old enough to work. Most of the girls married well — indicating that they had attractions. One of them a little older than I gave me my first attack of puppy love. One married Harry Reynolds, bachelor heir to a good ranch on which oil was struck after Mr. Harry died. He built a good house in which to lodge his bride. The day before he was to be married he celebrated by taking two or three extra toddies. Then he had one of his Mexicans go down to the pen and saddle Old Sorrel and bring him up and tie him to the front gate of the yard. When he saw his favorite horse out by the gate, ears pointed in his direction, he said, "By God, Old Sorrel's coming in this house before any woman does." He poured a little whiskey on the threshold and led the horse up on the front gallery and then through the front door clear through the bedroom and into the kitchen and around and out again.

The Cleggs bought steers from Papa. It seems to me that they had the old Vantana ranch leased. Anyhow I know we were driving a small herd of steers to the Reynolds ranch and didn't have a canteen of water along. We stopped and ate lunch under the shade of a mesquite tree. Lunch consisted of sardines and crackers. We were already thirsty. Away along late in the day, maybe five o'clock, we came to a big cypress cistern and troughs at a windmill. If I live to be a hundred, I'll never forget how good that water was.

Uncle Jim Dobie ranched on west of Ramirenia. Mama didn't like it when he gave only $100 toward building the church. Early in this century he sold out and moved to La Salle County.

The brush was thicker and taller and thornier in the Ramirenia country than in the Lagarto country. Some people lived away back in the brush. The Lathams had only a small tract of land. The only one of them who ever made any impression on me was Al. The only thing I remember about Al was an illustration of how often human ambition exceeds potency. Al Latham inherited something — not over a section of land — about the time Uncle Jim was giving up leases on several big pastures. One of them was the Buena Vista of eight or ten thousand acres. Al Latham mortgaged his land to borrow enough money to lease the Buena Vista for a year. He probably didn't have to pay more than a bit an acre on the lease. His idea was to stock it with big steers. After he got control of the pasture, he had no collateral for borrowing money to buy steers; so there the poor devil was with all he had sunk in a lease that would do him no good. It was a very dry year and nobody wanted to take it off his hands.

About halfway between La Posta, or Ramirenia, and Uncle Jim's Kintuck headquarters a small, low frame house stood off a little bit from the road. By the house was a patch in which watermelons and roasting ears grew when it rained. The owner made a living, such as it was, on a few hundred acres of land, raising a few calves and a few horses. He was John Western, a Negro. Many a person stopped there to get a drink of water and sit in the shade of a *ramada*, an open shed with a dirt floor. Anybody who stopped was content to linger. There were two girls — young women when I knew them — and two sons, who were among the most noted brush hands in southwest Texas. Their names were Atlee and Nob. They worked for Uncle Jim. I heard him say that he didn't believe a more powerful man ever got on a horse and rode through the brush than Atlee or Nob Western. It took something bigger than little Mexican horses to hold up under them. Either could literally tear a hole through a thicket. Atlee drowned crossing cattle on the Nueces River while it was on a big rise. These were the only Negro cowhands in Live Oak County. In McMullen County, adjoining Live Oak, there was another noted Negro cowhand.

On out in the brush was the Lyne ranch. At church, the only place I saw him, Mr. Lyne always addressed married women as "sister" and the men as "brother"; thus for my parents it was Sister Dobie and Brother Dobie. He was probably older than anybody else on the grounds. He sat with his eyes closed but wasn't so humble as his appearance might indicate. I've often wondered about the backgrounds of Mr. Lyne and his wife. Not very long after the University of Texas was established at Austin, they sent their son Tom to study civil engineering. Tom got his Bachelor of Science degree about 1900. He worked for some time with the Southern Pacific Railroad but went back to ranching. When I came to know him, and I knew him quite well, he'd married a very enlightened woman and they had two children. He taught himself geology. He traced out a fault line halfway across Live Oak County and was always expecting leasehounds for oil companies to come to his conclusions; namely, that one or more big oil pools were under the surface of his land. Almost the last time I saw him was following Franklin D. Roosevelt's second election. With all the solemnity of a conclave of cardinals assembled to entomb the Pope he announced: "Mark my words. This is the last election that the United States of America will ever see. We've doomed ourselves to dictatorship." Tom Lyne used to laugh, but after he went to hating Roosevelt he knew no more happiness. I think he had gone to school to my mother. He always called her "Miss Ella."

He had four thousand acres of land that came to him in a rather unusual way. He grew up knowing old Don Victoriano Chapa and the son Don Prisciliano Chapa. They had a fair-sized ranch, a grant from the King of Spain, or maybe it was from the Mexican government. Don Victoriano had been a captive of the Comanches. Papa used to buy steers from them. One time I went with him. The only concession they had made to what is called progress was to have a barbed wire fence around their land. They still raised Mexican cattle; that is, of every color. Judging from how gaunt the steers and yearlings looked, half of them had been roped. They were as wild as javelinas. They had plenty of brush to hide in. The dirt water-tank had been scraped out with scrapers against the pens. I saw a cow that was going to die from screwworms standing in the water for hours, the only remedy she knew. The Chapa way was to let nature take its course. The steers Papa bought were of all ages from one to ten. After we got them to our pens a big old *josca* (brown) line-backed steer jumped over a gate and me, too. I was by the gate trying to shoo him back.

Old Victoriano lived until he was a hundred or more. His son was an old man before Don Victoriano died. He wanted Tom Lyne to be responsible for the son. He sold him four thousand acres of land at $1.00 an acre, with forty years to pay for it at four per cent interest. Then he willed the note to Tom Lyne. I have sketched Don Victoriano Chapa at some length in *The Longhorns*.

The Stonewall Jackson Wright family usually attended services at Ramirenia. Everybody called him "Bud." His ranch joined ours. His brother, born during the Civil War, had been named Braxton Bragg Wright, but Bud was a bigger bragger than Bragg was. I remember my mother's repeating once after he left an old proverb: "Brag's a good dog, but Hold Fast is a better." Bud liked to imagine himself a big cowman. He overborrowed and went bankrupt. He and his wife had good hearts. Nearly everybody had a good heart. Maybe nearly everybody still has. The Wrights had a niece living with them who committed an indiscretion, but they stood by her after her baby was born. I remember going up to the ranch not long afterward, finding nobody there but the mother and her infant. I wasn't more than ten or twelve years old and was embarrassed. I didn't know why. I don't think she was embarrassed at all.

On west of Bud Wright's ranch was the Sealey ranch. Sealey sold out when I was quite young and moved to Arizona, where one of the boys got into a difficulty that forced him to kill somebody. Uncle Frank Byler bought the Sealey ranch but lived in Lagarto and ran the Barbon ranch also, leased from Nueces County. That's where my mother's stepfather, Friendly Dubose, and his wife had gone broke. They moved to Alice, as I tell in another place.

Swinging on back east toward the Nueces to the north of us, our neighbors were Sam Watson and family, Lou Gorbett and family, Ed McWhorter and Freeman McWhorter and the Shipps. Sam Watson was a very solemn man. When I was sixteen or seventeen years old he and I rode west to buy a few steer yearlings. He didn't see anything he thought was worth the money. Not long after this I sold my horse stock out to his son Irving and helped Irving drive the stock, mares and colts, to their ranch. When we got there Mr. Watson said to him, "You ought to know better than to trade with a Dobie." So far as I know that's the only compliment I've ever had on my trading ability, and it wasn't deserved.

Mr. Gorbett was a kind of mystery man. He was small and he had a black look. People said he beat his horses. One time he came to our ranch with a heavy well rope on the neck of his horse, and after getting down he doubled it and tied the rope to a tree out in front of the yard. I was looking for the horse to explode but he didn't do a thing all the time he was tied there with a double well rope.

Ed McWhorter and Freeman were soft-spoken. Mr. Ed had gone up the trail with Papa and Uncle Jim. They were straight ranchers. I don't know how some of the other people I've mentioned made a living. One time I heard Mr. Ed tell about hard times soon after the Civil War. He was just a boy. The family had mighty little to eat. They'd sold out their stock, range delivery, everything in the brand, to a ranchman named Henderson Williams. Not long after that Cal Wright came along about dinnertime. Of course, he was made welcome, but when he sat down and saw there wasn't any meat he said, "What! How's this? Living in a cow country and no meat!" Mr. McWhorter told him that he'd sold out his brand and no longer had any range rights.

"Well, I'll give you range rights to all the meat you can eat right now," Cal Wright thundered. "I represent my own brands and the Bluntzer brands and the Henderson Williams brands. If you can't find a fat cow or calf or heifer or something handy in one of those brands, take another brand. The idea of living out here with all these wild cattle, unbranded as some of them are, and not having meat! Why, dammit, Bluntzer has advertised that anybody who's hungry can eat his beef provided it's not wasted and provided the hide's saved. That's the way we all feel."

My education was neglected by my not listening more to Mr. Ed McWhorter. I dedicated a chapter in *The Longhorns* to him.

The biggest ranch between us and the Nueces was the Shipp. The Shipps had been there in open range days. They sold out their horses in the early 80s to the Dobie brothers and the Dobie brothers drove the horses to Kansas. Then they went to raising cattle, but they didn't put down enough windmills to take advantage of the land miles back from the river. On one of the occasions when I went north with Papa to Oakville, going through the Shipp ranch he pointed off up a hollow and told me that that tree up there at one time had two men hanging from it. My chief recollection of the Shipp ranch house is of peacocks. They were the only people in the country who kept peacocks. They also kept old Ped Shelton, who was feeble-minded but no trouble. Ped made rhymes. He'd say in his very soft voice, "Gimme a little time and I'll make you a rhyme."

Joining Shipps were Mat Givens and his wife, whom a lot of people called "Aunt Mary." Mat had been in the Civil War. He must have been along in years before the War. I remember when his strength faded out Aunt Mary would get on her sidesaddle and rope calves or sheep and doctor them. She could throw down a calf, castrate and brand it. She could shoot a deer. She kept bees. She was extraordinarily vigorous.

Yet she was not at all mannish. She embroidered, and liked to laugh and chat with women. There was sanity in her mind and glee in her heart. She was religious and always supported the preacher. I believe he came to the church at Dinero only on fifth Sundays, and he usually stopped with the Givenses. One time after a new preacher had been assigned to the circuit he made his first venture on a bicycle. I'm sure he had to push it much more than he rode it over the rocky hills and through sand beds. I never saw him myself. I never saw anybody on a bicycle in that country. This is what people said. He got to the Givens ranch. Aunt Mary met him. He told his name and said, "This is Sister Givens, I suppose."

She said, "Yes. Put up your horse, and stay all night. We'll have supper after a while. We're going to church tomorrow."

He said, "No, I didn't bring any horse."

"Well, how on earth did you get here?"

"I came on a bicycle."

She said, "A bicycle is not anything for a man to ride. I don't want any bicycle person around me."

He went on somewhere else.

This reminds me of Cousin Dick Dobie, who after he moved to Mathis refused to have anything to do with a preacher who organized a baseball team among the village boys.

The Robinsons didn't belong to the up-the-creek yahoo crowd either. Mr. Alf Robinson never came to church that I saw. He was the son of the noted Sally Skull by one of her husbands. She'd had several. She traded horses out of Mexico; sometimes freighted. One time while she was going east with one of her husbands he was drowned in the San Antonio River. One of the Mexicans working for her asked if she wanted the hands to recover his body. She said she didn't care anything about his body but would like that money belt he was wearing. Almost the whole Robinson family turned out schoolteachers. Clabe Robinson had one of the best minds I met in my youth. He taught himself law and became the main land abstracter for Dougherty and Dougherty, lawyers in Beeville. He told me he was going to write a history of Live Oak County. This was after I came to the University of Texas. He wrote a chapter on mustangs and I got it published for him at a small price. Then he wrote a chapter on longhorns and I got it published for him at a small price. I don't think he ever wrote anything else on the book. He went off to El Paso in search of a lost mine and just played out. He was going to write about the Brush Country people. Nobody else could have done it so well.

Granny Hinnant was an independent soul who traveled over the country in her one-horse buggy wherever her midwifely services were needed. Sometimes she came just on a visit. She dipped snuff, said *'taint* and *sommers* for *somewhere*. Whenever she was offered coffee she said, "I'll take a sup." In language she belonged to what I came to know as the Elizabethan Age. To me her use of *sup* connected her with the Bible — the King James Version, of course: "Behold, I stand at the door and knock: if any man hear my voice, and open the door, I will come in to him, and will sup with him, and he with me."

I remember as a child standing by one of the windows in a thick-walled room of our house and looking out at drizzling rain that had kept us indoors for hours and chanting, as many a child has chanted:

Rain, rain, go to Spain
And never come back again.

My father did not want the rain to go to Spain. He had been walking up and down on the front gallery, looking out and knowing that this was the kind of rain that fell equably over all the pastures and beyond, on the just and the unjust alike.

But old Granny Hinnant, who was with us at the time, probably to assist at the birth of a new baby, though I knew nothing of such matters then, reprimanded us children. "The country needs rain," she said, "and you ort to be ashamed of yourselves. It's wicked not to be thankful for the rain, and God is listening to you. If you were Christians, you'd get down on your knees and thank Him for the rain. We did not notice her getting down on her knees, but that night at family prayers my father did thank the Lord for blessing the country with rain.

Cousin Dick Dobie's ranch joined ours. His father, Sterling Neblett Dobie, and my father's father, Robert Neville Dobie, had come to Texas from Virginia and were ranching in partnership while Texas was still a republic, as I have told with slightly more detail in the chapter on my father.

The road from our ranch to Lagarto was ungraded across pastures. One afternoon I went in for the mail on the slow, lazy horse we called Old Stray. We subscribed for the *Semiweekly Houston Post*. I got it and whatever other mail there was and put everything inside a morral, which was carried from the horn of my saddle.

On the way back, Old Stray needing no guidance and scaring at nothing, I pulled out the newspaper and began reading about the Spanish-American War in Cuba. While I was reading, I heard a voice. I looked up and there was Cousin Dick Dobie on his way to Lagarto.

"What's the news, Frank?" he asked.

"It's about Colonel Roosevelt's Rough Riders."

"I'll read that when I get my paper. How's your Mama?"

"All right, sir."

"And your sister Fannie and Elrich and Lee and Henry, they're all right, too, I guess."

"Yes, sir."

"How's your Papa?"

"He's all right, I guess."

"You mean he's not at home?"

"He left yesterday."

"Where'd he go?"

"He said he was going in the upper Ramirenia country to the Chapa ranch, and I don't know where else."

"I guess he's buying steer yearlings."

"I think so."

"What's he paying for good ones?"

"I don't know."

"Well, if he gets mine he's going to have to pay better than ten dollars a head. I'd better get on now."

Cousin Dick left in a lope. That was his regular rate of travel. He had good horses, also well-bred-up cattle. Other ranchers liked to stop for a meal and a talk. Cousin Dick was the only man I remember who would ride to a ranch for the sole purpose of "visiting."

He was a great hand to ask questions. I know he had several books of history, perhaps Shakespeare, and certainly the Bible. He read enough law to receive a license to practice, but I don't recall having heard of his practicing. He seemed always to be aiming for something beyond. One time I went with Papa to help him gather cattle out of his Ramirenia Creek pasture. After the herd was made up and we were heading it for the pens, he galloped back and forth on one side or the other of the herd, saying all the time, "Keep 'em moving, boys! keep 'em moving, boys!" All other cowmen I ever knew wanted their cattle to move slow.

While I was a mere boy, Papa bought a section and more of land called the Dickens pasture, joining Cousin Dick to the south. Cousin Dick had the idea that the division fence was off line and that some of his land was in the Dickens pasture. Papa agreed to have the land surveyed, he and Cousin Dick sharing the cost. The survey showed that an old house, rock cistern, shed, and two or three little pens owned by Cousin Dick were actually on the Dickens pasture land. Papa gave him a deed to the plot of ground for twenty-five or fifty dollars — whatever amount he had paid for that many acres.

The last time I saw Cousin Dick was in the town of Mathis, to which a good many Lagarto people moved. Years had passed, and I was teaching in the University of Texas and also publishing writings. I was standing talking to a friend in a vacant place on the main street when Cousin Dick came along. He seemed pleased to see me. He shook my hand; that is, he squeezed it as hard as he could. I was certainly pleased to see him. After asking the regular questions about members of the family, he kind of shifted gears. He was at this time, as I knew, occasionally contributing articles of opinion on religious and political subjects to a county weekly newspaper.

"Frank," he said, "they tell me that you believe in evolution."

"Well, I guess I do, Cousin Dick," I answered.

"That means," he went on, "that you believe man is descended from monkeys."

It is entirely likely that Cousin Dick had read Darwin's *The Origin of Species*. If so, he had read it not to learn but to controvert. His mind was made up. He often had a flitch in his face. Now he flitched, sniffed and snuffed and ended what he had to say with these words:

"You may have some monkey blood in you somewhere along the line, but I can tell you right now it wasn't from the Dobie side."

We both kind of laughed.

When he sold his ranch he kept the mineral rights to it. I'll bet he read all the fine print in the contract!

If Cousin Dick was a chip off the old block, my great-uncle Sterling must have been eccentric through and through. After a bank in Corpus Christi failed, he distrusted all banks. At first he hid his money secretly but an experience cured him of that practice. One spring when Cornelius Cox said that he was going to Kentucky on a visit, Sterling Dobie commissioned him to buy a Thoroughbred stallion.

"I'll give you five hundred dollars to take along," he said.

"Wait until I'm ready to start," Cox suggested.

"All right. The money will be ready when you are."

Some days later Cox came over and said that he was about to set out for Kentucky. Sterling Dobie hobbled down off the front gallery on his two canes and, with considerable difficulty, reached under the house to a sill and fell back on the ground. Two of his children ran out in alarm. He explained to them that twenty-five $20 gold pieces he had put on a sill to send to Kentucky for the Thoroughbred stallion were gone. One of the young people crawled under the house and found the $20 pieces, not one missing, on the sill at the corner.

After this Sterling Dobie buried money in small sums at different places, accompanied by a single witness — one of his own children or his nephew Neville, my father's older brother. Out in the backyard was a cabin with a dirt floor, separated from the main house, that had been used as a kitchen during slave times. This was customary architecture. After it was abandoned and left open, a daughter, Minnie, whom I knew well — Cousin Minnie — happening into it one day saw several coins on the floor that presumably had been uprooted by hogs. The coins had been spilled out of a cracked iron teakettle. Cousin Minnie reported to her father, who was ill in bed. He had her and Neville sift the dirt thoroughly, gather up the coins, replace them in the kettle, and set it on the side of his bed. He counted the coins and was satisfied. When Cousin Minnie went in next morning the kettle was gone. One time he had her bury a quart jar of gold coins near the front steps. After he died and search was made for it, it could not be found.

He might have moved it or have got someone else to move it.

He died November 4, 1880. Following the funeral at the ranch graveyard, the children and Neville Dobie, who, perhaps I should say, had been mostly with his uncle Sterling after his father's death by drowning, gathered at the house for final settlement. According to Cousin Minnie, Sterling, Jr., first dug up a jar of gold pieces that he had buried while his father leaned on his two sticks and watched, in the front yard. The money counted out $400. Neville went into a ruined Negro cabin and dug from the hearth a powder can of silver. The can had rusted away. The other children dug up the caches they had witnessed — all but Minnie, who could find neither the can nor the jar that she had helped hide under the house. Some of the coins were black and corroded from having been underground. They were turned over to Henry Newberry, merchant in Lagarto, who had a heavy metal safe. After these pieces got into circulation, people at sight of one would say, "There goes some old Dobie money."

CHAPTER EIGHT

Horses Out of My Boyhood

I'VE been reflecting on how much clearer certain characteristics of horses I knew as a boy and youth are to me than certain characteristics of people in books that I knew at the same time and enjoyed immensely. I don't know what a psychoanalyst would make of this — and wouldn't have much interest in whatever he made of it.

The horse on which I learned to ride was not a pony but an enormous work horse — probably not so enormous as I remember him. He was shockingly tame — never got out of a walk but dislodged me a few times by going under a clothesline. This must have been while I was between two and three years old. He was a light black with a bald face and we called him Bally — corruption of Baldy. I cried at his death.

A better horse for children was a white-faced bay named Stray. If a child fell off him, he would stop and graze until the child climbed on again. I shall have to explain his origin. One of the roads east from the Rio Grande, through Hebbronville, San Diego and then Ramirenia in our part of the country — ran through the north part of our ranch. The chief travelers on it, sometimes the only travelers for weeks at a time, were cotton-pickers from Mexico going to Beeville, Cuero, Yoakum and other points in farming country along in the summer and returning in the late fall. No immigration laws restricted their movements. They traveled horseback, on burros, in wagons, in old-fashioned carts and sometimes afoot. They traveled very slowly and some days had no water beyond what they carried in jugs and canteens. One of the waterings they counted on was El Papalote Solo (The Lone Windmill). It was on Long Hollow, about two miles above our ranch house. I've seen as high as forty or fifty horses and burros staked out, hobbled, and grazing free on the hillsides out from this windmill. The windmill wasn't on the road but a quarter of a mile or so to one side of it, but the pasajeros, as the travelers were called, left the wagon road for the windmill.

Once in a while they abandoned an animal that couldn't go any farther. Its back was sure to be sore from a Mexican saddle. Our horse Stray was left by cotton-picking travelers. He wasn't old; he was merely starved to extreme weakness. Scars from sores on his back never did hair over fully, but they never peeled off again from our usage. The map of Mexico was burned on his left hip and clear down past his flank. My father could have kept this strayed animal and nobody would have questioned his ownership, but he never claimed anything that didn't belong to him. He complied with the law requiring that notice of a strayed animal be given to the public and then if no claimant arose that it be sold at public auction. On the date for the auction he had Stray in Oakville and bid him in. I don't know but I imagine nobody bid against him. Certainly no rancher would have bid against another on whose land a stray had been picked up.

Stray was fine to learn to ride on and for a little boy to work cattle on, but he wasn't fancy enough to ride for the mail or to church once a month or to the annual picnic and barbecue on the Nueces River or to a summer camp-meeting.

Another strayed animal bought in by Papa was a bay mare. Exceedingly active, she was appropriated by my brother Elrich. If her rider held his hand out so she could see it and pointed his thumb down, she would kick up all over the place and run without pitching much — just enough to excite a boy.

We had a sorrel hardly more than thirteen hands high called Maudie. She was named after the famous race mare Maud S. Mares might be all right on the ranch but riding them in public wasn't done. No ranchman or ranch boy or cowboy of lower Texas at that time wanted to ride anything but a gelding or maybe now and then a stallion. Our brood mares were never broken to ride.

A very gentle stallion was named Dandy. He was a Thoroughbred. In spring he was a bright black but his hair got rusty the rest of the year. Papa bought him from my mother's half brother Ed Dubose, who was a racehorse fancier. He was a buggy horse and was pampered with corn during the winter. One time somebody saw my youngest brother Henry, a mere toddler, in Dandy's stall. Dandy was eating and occasionally stomping off the red ants, very abundant around the stable. He seemed to know that Henry was in danger. He put a hind hoof against Henry's chest and shoved him out of the stall. One of us usually rode Dandy in the early morning to get up the saddle horses. He liked to shine in public. One time when I rode him to Lagarto for the semi-weekly mail, I touched the spurs to him and entered town, if you could call it a town, in a dead run. He wasn't a stumbler but his hoofs had been allowed to grow too long and he hit a ridge or a rock in the road. When he fell, I fell off him and skinned my chin considerably.

We had a pair of bay buggy horses named Snip and Snap. It took them a long summer's day to get to Beeville, for miles of the road were through heavy sand. About a mile and a half from our house the road forked. The east prong went to Beeville, nearly twenty-six miles away. The north prong went on about twenty-four miles to Oakville. As the oldest of the family, it was my privilege sometimes to go with Papa to open the gates. I remember one morning it was still not daylight when we got to the fork in the road. Just a few steps beyond was a gate going into the big Shipp pasture. Before they got to the gate, just at the fork of the road, Snip and Snap stopped and in unison heaved a deep, deep sigh that seemed to express what later I learned was the popular translation of the initials for the railroad H E and W T — Hell Either Way You Take It. The year the family got a new hack and new harness Snip and Snap snapped up fifty per cent in their conduct. They were just as proud of that new hack and new harness as the people riding behind them.

When Snip and Snap stopped to rest in shade — and they would stop whether the driver said "Whoa!" or not — we would get out and walk around. If it were spring we could enjoy the phlox and other wild flowers. Halfway between the Nueces River and Beeville were a gin, a store and some farmhouses. The official name of this place was Clareville. The Mexicans called it Los Llanos — The Prairies. Another name for it was Ten Miles. From there on every mile was an individual in the day-long journey. Seven miles from Beeville the road turned around to leave intact a small pasture belonging to a ranch on the hill. Five miles from Beeville was the Bonce Franklin ranch, one pasture of which was prairie. I never pass it now without remembering that we camped there one night with a herd of yearlings.

A long, long time ago I was riding with my parents in a hack in Nueces County. We had not seen a soul for hours, had not met a single traveler. Darkness came, and then, away down the hill, we saw a little fire, no bigger than the fluttering blaze of a match. It was beautiful and it was a mystery. Slowly it grew larger. When we got down to the bottom of a hill we were on Agua Dulce Creek, and there we saw a lone camper boiling his night's coffee. This memory remained dormant in me for many years and was made active again by a line of verse: "He can find nothing as lovely as a cowboy's lone campfire."

The *Semi-weekly Houston Post* had what was called the Children's Page. One of its features was a running debate in which anybody's letter seemed to get printed. A debate that interested me was on whether horses or cows are of more benefit to mankind. I wanted to write a letter on the side of horses. I don't remember having written it, but I carried on a debate with my father. He said cows had benefitted people more by giving them milk, meat, hides for shoes and harness and a great many other useful things. He'd seen horse-raising on ranches change from the profit side to the losing side.

I never did think that we had enough horses. Papa thought we had plenty for doing what ranch work was necessary. Our good neighbors, the Hinnants, had more horses than we had. When we worked cattle at least two of the Hinnant boys usually came over to help, riding their own horses at $1.50 a day.

One year, about 1904, the ranch just had to have a few more saddle horses. Papa had stretched his credit buying steer yearlings at $10 around and had quite a bit of country leased. A wet summer made screwworms bad and we were riding, doctoring and skinning until after dark every day. One of the biggest horse traders in the country was Chato Velena at Alice, forty miles to the south. He was called Chat and had been reared on the Nueces east of us, his family being so prominent and so numerous that their ranch was called Velena. To show how times were then and how they have changed, one time when Chat came to our ranch, maybe buying mares, I remember Papa's asking him if he were in the habit of eating with the help or with the family. He said down in the Alice country he ate at the first table. He came in and ate with us.

The man who broke our horses was named José, and he

was from Velena. He was thick-set, heavy, swart and pock-marked. He would lead a three- or four-year-old *potro* (young gelding) off and be gone a month maybe and ride him back, leading his own horse. The standard pay was $2.50 an animal. A beautiful young bay of mine that José took to break got killed in the procedure. A spirited horse loses his head in struggles for liberty and easily cripples or even kills himself.

The instinct for self-preservation seems stronger in mules. We had a pair branded TOL on the left hip and thigh, bought at $50 apiece from Mr. Tol McNeill, whose ranch joined ours on the west. One of the mules was named Maggie and the other Tol. I've ridden many airplanes, but the fastest ride I ever made was in an otherwise empty wagon with which Maggie and Tol ran away. They didn't run into a wire fence; they didn't run into a tree; they didn't seem excited when the run was over. But an empty wagon bouncing at full mule-speed over trails, bushes, gullies, and prickly pear clumps can give an exciting sense of motion.

A year or two after the time Chato Velena ate at table with us, Papa wrote Chat to send six or eight good cow horses. The best was one we called Hippy. He was a black. His left hip had been knocked down, but there never was a better stayer than Hippy. He was about fifteen hands high and absolutely tireless. His only drawback was that once in a while he didn't want to start off. He'd sull (provincial for sulk). I don't think he ever sulled after Papa with help tied him down and gave him a terrible beating with a cow whip. My flesh crawls now at memory of that beating. My father was not a cruel man — quite the contrary. I have wondered many times what made Hippy sull just after being saddled. The girth must have pinched him the wrong way or something like that — something going back to his breaking. He was too energetic to throw off. Every movement of his had the springiness of vitality; he could not be draggy. I had no such connection then, but

My sister Fannie as a high school senior

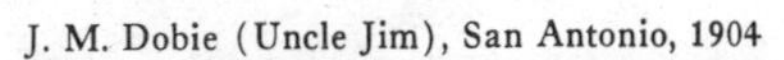

J. M. Dobie (Uncle Jim), San Antonio, 1904

A senior at Southwestern University,
Georgetown, Texas

I connect him now with a saying of Emerson's, "It is as easy for the strong man to be strong as it is for the weak man to be weak." Hippy was a good cutting horse. I never could understand why Papa let anybody ride him but himself. He wouldn't let me ride him. On a long trip we made after cattle a hired hand started a setfast on his back. A setfast is a sore that is very hard to heal. It did heal in time but never so that hard riding in hot weather would not take the thin skin off.

Not nearly so many ranch horses nowadays have setfasts as in the Horse Age. For one thing, modern horses are generally not used so hard. We had two wind-broken horses. They had been over-ridden in hot weather. A wind-broken horse would take "the thumps." His heart was racing terribly. You could hear him struggling for breath a long way off. Like a heart case among human beings, a wind-broken horse had to go easy. Setfasts, galled sides, the heaves, and other disabilities are not in the Hollywood calendar of range romance.

Papa made short shrift with horses that didn't want to go. One time we had an iron-gray stallion named Tordillo. I was just a kid. I put my saddle on him and got up. Instead of going forward he went backward. He got his hindquarters mixed up with the tongue and single-trees of an empty wagon that had been left in the shade of a mulberry tree. Papa grabbed a buggy whip and before long Tordillo was going forward in a repentant way.

I don't remember anything about a little deep bay horse that Chato Velena sent up except that my brother Elrich fancied him. He was kind of fancy himself. Elrich named him Cardinal (Spanish pronunciation, Redbird). The horse that I valued out of that bunch was a red roan we called Canelo (Cinnamon). His name brings to mind an esteem for the color that went into sayings such as this: "To hear him talk you'd think they were all red roans and natural-born pacers." Canelo wasn't a pacer of any kind; he was expert at putting his head down so that, as he hoped, he couldn't be seen or roped out of the remuda.

Range people, particularly in a brushy or rocky country, where uneven footage is to be contended with, never have had much use for pacing horses. They stumble too easily. We had a lanky sorrel that paced — and stumbled. Like other ranch people, I have always preferred a hard up-and-down jog trotter that was clearfooted to any pacer. Traditionally ranch people may like a fox-trotting horse, but have no more use for pacers than for thin-skinned, glass-eyed calicoes.

All the old-time range men of validity whom I have known remembered certain horses with affection and respect as a part of the best of themselves. After their knees begin to stiffen, most men realize that they have been disappointed in themselves, in other men, in achievement, in love, in most of whatever they expected out of life; but a man who has had a good horse in his life — a horse beyond the play world — will remember him as a certitude, like a calm mother, a lovely lake, or a gracious tree, amid all the flickering vanishments.

My own riding experiences have been limited, but I had Buck. When, before I was born, my father turned from horses to cattle, he kept a few mares from which to raise saddle horses. Buck was out of one of these wild mares. He was a bright bay with a blaze in his face and stockings on his forefeet. He could not have weighed when fat over nine hundred pounds and was about fourteen hands high. A Mexican broke him when he was three years old, but I don't think he pitched much. From then on nobody but me rode him, even after I left for college. He had a fine barrel and chest and was very fast for short distances but did not have the endurance of some other horses, straight Spaniards, in our remuda. What he lacked in toughness, he made up in intelligence, especially cow sense, loyalty, understanding, and generosity.

As a colt he had been bitten by a rattlesnake on the right ankle just above the hoof; a hard, hairless scab marked the place as long as he lived. He traveled through the world listening for the warning rattle. A kind of weed in the Southwest bears seeds that when ripe rattle in their pods with a sound a good deal like that made by a rattlesnake. Many a time when my spur or stirrup set these seeds a-rattling Buck's sudden jump all but left me seated in the air. I don't recall his smelling rattlesnakes, but he could smell afar off the rotten flesh of a yearling or any other cow brute afflicted with screwworms. He understood that I was hunting these animals in order to drive them to a pen and doctor them. In hot weather they would take refuge in high weeds and thick brush. When he smelled one, he would point to it with his ears and turn toward it. A dog trained for hunting out wormy cases could not have been more helpful.

Once a sullen cow that had been roped raked him in the breast with the tip of a horn. After that experience, he was wariness personified around anything roped, but he never, like some horses that have been hooked, shied away from an animal he was after. He knew and loved his business too well for that. He did not love it when at the rate of less than a mile an hour he was driving the thirsty, hot, tired, slobbering drag end of a herd, animals stopping behind every bush or without any bush, turning aside the moment they were free of a driver. When sufficiently exasperated, Buck would go for a halting cow with mouth open and grab her just forward of the tail bone if she did not move on. Work like that may be humiliating to a gallant young cowboy and an eager cow horse. It is never pictured as a part of the romance of the range, but it is very necessary. It helps a cowboy to graduate into a cowman. A too high-strung horse without cow sense, which includes cow patience, will go to pieces at it just as he will go to pieces in running or cutting cattle.

Buck had the rein to make the proverbial "turn on a two-bit piece and give back fifteen cents in change." One hot summer while we were gathering steers on leased grass about twelve miles from home, I galled his side with a tight cinch. I hated to keep on riding him with the galled side, but was obliged to on account of shortage in horses. As I saddled up in camp one day after dinner, I left the cinch so loose that a hand might have been laid between it and Buck's belly. We had to ride about a mile before going through a wire gap into the pasture where some snaky steers ran. As we rode along, a vaquero called my attention to the loose cinch.

"I will tighten it when we get to the gap," I said.

"*Cuidado* (have care) and don't forget," he said.

At the gap, which he got down to open, I saw him look at me. I decided to wait until we struck something before tightening the girth. Two minutes later my father yelled and we saw a little bunch of steers high-tailing it through scattered mesquites for a thicket along a creek beyond. I forgot all about the cinch. Buck was easily the fastest horse ridden by the four or five men in our "cow crowd." He left like a cry of joy to get around the steers.

As we headed them, they turned to the left at an acute angle, and Buck turned at an angle considerably more acute. Sometimes he changed direction so quickly that the *tapadero* (toe-fender) of my stirrup raked the ground on the inside of the turn. This time when he doubled back, running full speed, the loose saddle naturally turned on him. As my left hip hit the ground I saw stars. My feet were still in the stirrups and the saddle was under Buck's belly. I suppose that I instinctively pulled on the reins, but I believe that Buck would have stopped had he not been bridled. His stop was instantaneous; he did not drag me on the ground at all. He had provocation to go on, too, for in coming over his side and back the spur on my right foot had raked him. He never needed spurs. I wore them just to be in fashion.

Sometimes in running through brush, Buck seemed to read my mind — or maybe I was reading his. He was better in the brush than I was. In brush work, man and horse must dodge, turn, go over bushes and pear and under limbs, absolutely in accord, rider yielding to the instinct and judgment of the horse as much as horse yields to his.

Buck did not have to be staked. If I left a drag rope on him, he would stay close to camp, at noon or through the night. He was no paragon. Many men have ridden and remembered hardier horses. He did the best he could, willingly and generously, and he had a good heart. His chemistry mixed with mine. He was good company. I loved to hear him drink water, he was so hearty in swallowing, and then after he was full, to watch him lip the water's surface and drip big drops back into it. Sometimes after we had watered and, passing on, came to good grass near shade, I'd unsaddle and turn him loose to graze. Then I'd lie down with my head on the saddle and, while the blanket dried, listen to his energetic cropping and watch the buzzards sail and the Gulf clouds float. Buck would blow out his breath once in a while, presumably to clear his nostrils but also, it seemed to me, to express contentment.

He never asked me to stop, unless it was to urinate, and never, like some gentle saddle horses, interrupted his step to grab a mouthful of grass; but if I stopped with slackened rein to watch cattle, or maybe just to gaze over the flow of hills to the horizon, he'd reach down and begin cutting grass. He knew that was all right with me, though a person's seat on a grazing horse is not nearly so comfortable as on one with head up. Occasionally I washed the sweat off his back and favored him in other ways, but nobody in our part of the country pampered cow horses with sugar or other delicacy.

One September day I was preparing to leave our ranch for college. Although the family had moved to town, my summers were spent on the ranch. The morning before I was to leave — I always lingered as long as I could — I rode Buck out into a pasture of about four thousand acres to look through a band of stock horses. None of them had ever been broken, and they were sometimes as difficult to pen as a bunch of mustangs. There were about twenty of them. I found them on the back side of the pasture. In riding around them, I saw that a colt had a bad case of screwworms. The horses must be taken to the pen so that the colt could be doctored and kept up until the wound healed.

As I started the mares, they began to run. I kept them coursed pretty straight until we were within a half mile of the pen. Then at a snaggle of brushy hollows they circled and turned back. Buck was long-winded as well as fast-running, and it was not long before he got around a powerful bay mare leading the bunch.

Horses will run into brush to get away but, unlike cattle, they will take to the open to make distance. Those mares were determined not to go to the pens. For hours we circled, criss-crossed, dodged, and maneuvered, in the brush and across the openings. The ground had been dry for months, but we made some pretty clear trails. Finally, along in the afternoon, I penned the brutes.

After I closed the gate, I rode Buck into the shade of a big liveoak, loosened the girth, pulled some thorns out of his knees, and stood there waiting for him to cool off a bit before watering him. While waiting, I reached down for my watch to look at the time. The watch was gone. As a rule, I did not carry it with me while riding. Ranch people mostly go by the sun, their stomachs, and whatever they have to do. But I had taken the watch that morning. It had a fob that dangled loose from the watch pocket and that was, if worn when I was riding, always kept under the leggins belt. But everything I had on had undergone adjustments during the run. Now I could not be surprised that a limb had raked the fob hard enough to jerk the watch out of my pocket.

About the time I discovered my loss, Genardo del Bosque came into the pen. I told him about the watch.

"Where have you been?" he asked.

"Genardo," I replied, "I have been everywhere in that pasture, and I have been some places several times. Out there about those dry lakes there is not any ground left that we did not plow up."

"I will take the trail and find the watch," he replied.

"Can you tell Buck's tracks from the tracks of all the other horses?"

"*Sí, señor.*"

Within an hour I was gone. When I came back at Christmas time, Genardo handed me my watch.

This incident, I realize, centers on Genardo rather than Buck. Thinking about my horse called it to mind. Nobody knows what he remembers or, rather, what lies dormant in his mind waiting to be remembered.

While riding Buck in boyhood and early youth, I fell in love with four or five girls, but told only one. She was right in considering the matter a joke and thereby did me one of the biggest favors of my life. All those rose-lipt maidens and all the lightfoot lads with whom I ran in those days have receded until they have little meaning. They never had much in comparison with numerous people I have known since. Buck, however, always in association with the plot of earth over which I rode him, increases in meaning. It is a joy and a tonic to remember him.

CHAPTER NINE

"His Looks and My Ways Would Hang Any Man"

LONG before I was sixteen years old, my parents had determined that I should have a college education. I was indifferent to the idea; at that time, in our environment, college was as remote as the pyramids of Egypt. I had not raised a thirst for knowledge commensurate with the ambitions of my parents for me and their other five children, or with their willingness for self-denial in order to fulfill those ambitions. To enter college I had to know more than I knew, or, at least, to have graduated from a high school. That meant leaving the ranch and Live Oak County. Grandma Dubose, with Grandpa, lived at Alice. In September, 1904, I went to live with them and enroll in the high school.

Forty miles away, Alice was more distant in travel time from our ranch than New York now is from San Antonio. I had been there on several visits with Mama and the children. Papa went once or twice maybe; ranch affairs held him, perhaps he didn't want to go. It was an all-day drive in the hack. Meeting any other travelers was a rarity; on some trips we saw nobody at all. There were no mileposts — those indicators of distance erected by a man driving a wagon with a rawhide thong tied around the tire of the front wheel next to his seat. He kept his eye on that wheel, counting the revolutions, and when the number measuring off a mile had been made, he called "Whoa!" got out, dug a posthole beside the road, took from the wagon bed a short post into which had been chiseled a mile number, and drove it in. Speedless travel needed no speedometers.

When we reached the Avarán Pérez ranch, across which we traveled for hours, almost to the San Fernando Creek near Alice, we were in a foreign land. The title to this ranch derived from a king of Spain, and descendants of the original Pérez grantee had succeeded fairly well in remaining his contemporaries. I never knew Don Avarán, but he was a kind of legendary character. He would not take a check for any stock he sold. Upon delivering a string of cattle, he would ride to the bank in Alice with a cortege of parientes, most of them hangers-on, and his own vaqueros, receive his pay in plata and some bills, stuff all into a morral, and go back to his ranch.

The land was fenced, of course, for its boundaries were the boundaries of other owners, but the only windmill on it was at ranch headquarters. The far-scattered little dirt tanks scraped out to catch rainwater were usually dry when the cattle needed water worst. The road passed by a tank where on one trip, as I remember, sunken-eyed cattle dying of thirst stood around, too far gone to bawl. A cow and a yearling were bogged in the mud remaining in the tank. About were carcasses of dead cattle, on which coyotes suspended gnawing to trot off under wheeling buzzards.

Once we broke the drive by going to the Harry Reynolds ranch, on invitation, to stay all night. The Reynolds forebears had come from England with little or nothing and by raising sheep had paid for fifty or sixty thousand acres of land. Not a sheep was left in all that country in my time. The morning we left his ranch, Mr. Harry sent a mounted vaquero to escort us and open gates until we reached the public road — just a pair of ruts.

Sometimes in making the trip we would drive seventeen miles to Casa Blanca, called also Wade's Switch, which consisted mainly of a little store, big shipping pens, and a big ranch house. We would leave our team in the horse pasture there and catch the "Sap" (San Antonio and Aransas Pass) train to Alice, terminus of the railroad. Pate McNeill and his wife owned the ranch, she having inherited it. Nearly everybody called her Miss Maggie (Maggie Wade); she and Mama were old friends. Mama would tell her the day we were to return, and when we got off the train a McNeill Mexican would have our team harnessed, ready for us to drive. One time we found Mr. Pate McNeill in bed with a broken leg. He had roped a wild horse from the saddle, and it had jerked his horse down on the leg. No Italian countess or English gallant ever considered Byron's limp more romantic than I considered Mr. Pate McNeill's broken leg.

Casa Blanca was a romantic place anyhow. Lots had happened there and lots, in the way of riding and cow-working, was still happening. The original Casa Blanca, a Spanish ranch on the Nueces a few miles away, had a buried treasure that I was to put long afterward into *Coronado's Children* and that treasure-hunters keep on digging for. When I was nine years old I set out with my father in a buggy before daylight one morning for Beeville to the east. We found the Nueces River on a big rise that prevented the ferryboat from crossing. Here Papa learned that Mr. Wade had died and was to be buried that afternoon. We went back to the ranch and he rode on immediately to Wade's Switch, to the southwest, to attend the funeral. Death and funerals were romantic to me — remote and unexperienceable like dancing with the brownies in front of the fireplace on a winter night after everybody else was asleep. But I knew those fairy folk intimately. I never saw Mr. Wade, so far as I recollect, but he figured in my imagination. One night, four years before he died, a stranger called to him from the front gallery of his house, and when he opened the door he received a Winchester bullet in his chest. Being shot in the night seemed to me more romantic than having a leg broken while roping a wild horse. I associated Wade's Switch with men out of the past who would never sit at night in a lighted room where they could be seen through a window.

Grandpa Dubose was my mother's stepfather. She always called him "Mr. Dubose," as did Grandma also. Soon after Grandma married "Mr. Dubose," Mama — herself a child — had a decisive and victorious run-in with him over "the children," her brother and sister, but in time she and he became respectful — and to an extent fond — of each other. He was gone from home a great deal, and she was a second mother to her half brothers: Ed, Judge, Charlie, and Tom. I have heard her tell how in the seventies, while Mexican bandits were raiding up into Texas from below the Rio Grande, sometimes killing, Grandma alone with her little ones at night would stay awake near a rifle, though she was almost as afraid of it as of bandits. The Bylers and Duboses, along with numerous other people of the Nueces country, put in claims against the Mexican government for stock stolen by Mexican nationals, and for sixty or seventy years a law firm in Washington specializing in such claims would write now and then soliciting funds for their prosecution. Nothing ever came of them.

I and my oncoming brothers and sisters had no notion what the word stepfather meant. Grandpa Dubose was just Grandpa to us. He and Grandma were ranching on Barbon Creek, in Nueces County, below Lagarto, when I was born. (*Barbón* is Spanish for big-bearded man. Away back in early days a man who settled up the creek wore an enormous beard and the Mexicans called him *El Barbón;* from him the creek took its name.) My solitary recollection of the ranch on the Barbon is of the stir and bustle there. A combined panic and drouth about 1891 broke the family. After selling off everything, they had enough — probably not over two or three thousand dollars — to buy a house and lot in Alice. On the day wagons were loaded with household goods to haul to their new home, Grandpa, as I have heard Grandma tell, said, "Mattie, you have been used to buying what you wanted. Now we can't buy anything except what we have to have." Her worldly wants had always been meager.

At the time the Civil War closed, Grandpa and Nick Dunn were buying beeves with Confederate paper money for Confederate troops a long way off. They did not bother to be mustered out, and Grandpa was rather pleased with himself for never having taken the oath of allegiance to the United Sates. He did not believe in celebrating the Fourth of July, and he had company all over the South until the Confederate graveyards filled up.

He subscribed to the *Confederate Veteran*, read all the reminiscences and historical sketches that filled its pages, and kept a file of the magazine. I read it every month as it came in. I don't recall that Grandpa talked much about the Civil War, but he must have contributed to my youthful adoration of General Robert E. Lee and sentimentality over the Lost Cause. The first picture of any kind that I bought, the year I went to college, was a colored print of *Lee and His Generals*, and after I went to Austin to teach in the University of Texas I used to take off my hat every time I walked past the Confederate monument on the capitol grounds with its "Died for State Rights" inscription defying by half-truth the whole truth of democracy. My salutes in those days sprang from sentiment alone. Sometimes now when I see the small Confederate flags that people stick on their automobiles — more through hate than love — I remember how the blood rushed to my head and tears to my eyes when I heard "Dixie" played in a New York theater while I was attending Columbia University.

I recall but one war anecdote told by Grandpa. After an all-day battle in woods died down at nightfall, he and other exhausted soldiers near him sprawled out on the ground to sleep where they were. It was summertime. Grandpa was thirsty and in darkness he drank from a stagnant pool of water at hand. When daylight came and he stepped to the pool to wash and drink again, he discovered a dead Yankee in the water at the very spot where he had drunk in the night. He gave the impression that the water was more polluted by a dead Yankee than it would have been by a dead Confederate. I was disappointed with life because I had been born too late to help Grandpa fight the Yankees, and too late also to drive up the Trail with him and Papa and uncles on both sides of the house.

Grandpa drove horses and mares to Kansas, giving away, just before setting out, colts too young to travel. One year, at least, Uncle Frank Byler put horses in the Dubose herd. Grandpa said that the worst drawback to trail-driving was missing out on roasting ears, always traveling north ahead of the swelling corn and getting back to Texas by train too late for it. He was a loyal Mason and wore the Masonic emblem on a heavy chain to which a ponderous watch, carried in vest pocket, was attached. One time in the Indian Territory when a band of warriors threatened to drive off several of his horses, he made the Masonic sign. Immediately an Indian who seemed in authority responded and ordered the others to leave.

One summer — this must have been after some pastures were fenced out but before windmills were erected — while the men were in Kansas, the stock water dried up. My mother, her sister Fannie, two little boys and a Mexican drove the herd every day to a waterhole and back. Then in the middle of the night, as Grandma used to tell, she heard thunder. It must have been loud or she would not have waked. She saw lightning racing against black clouds. Soon it was raining. Grandma called the girls and they all began singing hymns and thanking God. The more they sang and prayed, the harder the rain came down. Grandma would go to the gallery and smell the rain and put her hands out in it. Now there would be plenty of water for the stock and grass would grow. Grandma went to walking in a kind of dance and shouting with joy — the only time in her life, she said, that she ever "shouted." She would never have been moved to shout at a camp-meeting.

At one time Grandpa was cattle buyer for Martin Culver's hide and tallow factory at The Mottes on the Nueces. When he rode out on his big "American horse" — the opposite of "Spanish cow pony" — he carried silver dollars and some greenbacks in a morral tied to his saddlehorn and paid cash, six to eight dollars around for grown cows and big steers. All the "packery" took from the carcasses was hides and tallow; the flesh was thrown away, to feed buzzards and coyotes.

Sometimes at home Grandpa would break into song, his voice quavering. He sang one trail song in the slow, slow tempo just right for calming wild or restless cattle — and for stirring human imagination. Mere words cannot possibly convey the song's coyote lonesomeness and its translation of the hearer to away-out-aloneness in a vast land empty of everything but solitary men driving lowing, dragging cattle at a snail's pace along a trail with nothing but grass all the way to the horizon on both sides.

It's whoop and a yea and a-driving the dogies,
For camps is far away,
And it's a whoop and a yea, get along my little dogies,
For Wyoming may be your new home.

Grandpa always said "camps" for camp, as did other old-time men of the campo. "How far is it to camps?" one might ask.

Grandpa was over six feet tall. He was a little stooped, but never had any surplus to belly or flesh. He wore a beard, and had an eye that pierced through all pretenders, especially the pretenders to religion with which this earth is so plentifully populated. He had a saying that took in many a one of them: "His looks and my ways would hang any man." He could hardly have known that amidst the "human wriggle for office" at Washington, where there were "too many pigs for the tits," Abraham Lincoln had justified judgments on men by their faces. One time after Lincoln heard and looked at an office-seeker promoted by politicians, he rejected him summarily. "Why?" the promoters wanted to know. "I don't like his face." "No man can be held responsible for his features," they protested. "Every man over forty is responsible for his face," Lincoln replied. On another occasion he told a demoted colonel seeking restoration of his rank: "You carry your own condemnation in your face."

Grandpa's characterization of some man whom he considered passingly capable was: "He can read, write and recollect." Of another he might say, "He hasn't got as much sense as a last year's bird nest with the bottom punched out." After hearing him allude several times to this and that "Spanish supper" he or somebody else had made out on, I asked what a Spanish supper was. "You tighten up your belt a notch," he defined, "and smoke a cigarette." "It is kin to a 'Tucson bed'; that's when you lie on your stomach and cover it with your back." He liked to tease Grandma at the table by saying, "Mighty good what there is of it, and, being what it is, there's plenty." When Grandma borrowed trouble, making some possible ill of the future an accomplished fact, Grandpa would cheer up the world around him by saying, "Now, Mattie, don't greet the devil until you meet him," or "Don't kiss the devil until you catch him." If his attention was called to a new hat or dress that she or some other lady he liked wore, his standard remark was, "Just as well be dead as out of style." His morning greeting to me was usually, "How does your cabrosity sagaciate this morning?" The same expression occurs in *Uncle Remus*. If a boy asked him a question he did not want to answer, he might say, "*Cuando sale el sol, yo te digo*."

He wore an old style broad-brimmed black frontiersman hat day and night, except when at the dining table and in bed. He never wore a coat except in cold weather, but the temperature could not go high enough to make him pull off his vest. It was as much a part of his dress as hat and breeches. Preparatory to going to bed, he pulled off first his shoes and socks, next his pants and vest, and then removed his hat. He wore long drawers, in summer as well as in winter. He slept in them and probably regarded nightshirts — pajamas being in his time unknown in our part of the world — as womanish. He also wore to bed his shirt, invariably white, stained by tobacco juice. The last thing he did at night before blowing out the coal oil lamp was to take the corncob pipe out of his mouth. When he got up in the morning, he put on his hat first and then got into his vest and pants. Next he loaded his pipe with Fashion Plug Cut tobacco, lighted it, and puffed while drawing on socks and shoes.

In memory I associate Grandpa with the Rawhide Rawlins of Charles M. Russell's *Trails Plowed Under*. One winter Rawhide Rawlins drifted into Chicago with a big roll of money he'd won in Cheyenne. The first thing he did was "shed cow garments" and get into a hard hat, boiled shirt, laced shoes — "all the gearing known to civilized man." Then he proceeded to spend some of his money and let a confidence man take the rest. He woke up the next morning in a small room with two bunks, and while he dressed, a fellow smoking a cigarette in the second bunk said, "Neighbor, you are a long way from your range."

"You call the turn," Rawhide Rawlins replied, "but how did you read my brand?"

"Humans dress up, and punchers dress down," the fellow said. "When you raised, the first thing you put on your hat. You don't shed your shirt when you bed down. So next comes your vest and coat, keeping your hindquarters covered till you slide into your pants, and now you're lacing your shoes. I notice you done all of it without quitting the blankets, like the ground's cold."

Every Saturday night with the regularity of Tristram Shandy's father, Grandpa stood on a rawhide-bottomed chair to wind an enormous Seth Thomas eight-day clock hanging on the wall. It still runs, the dial showing the days of the week and dates of month as well as hours and minutes. Grandpa seemed, as I reflect upon him now, to take an interest in Time as something substantive, something apart from the destinor and regulator of life. His memory held the exact date of any occurrence out of his past that interested him, just as a born bibliographer knows the date of a book's publication along with the name of the author. He had in mind the dates of all the drouths and die-ups for the preceding fifty years and told about one, before the country was fenced, that brought mustangs by the thousands from far away to water at the few stagnant pools remaining in Agua Dulce Creek.

He set a good deal of store by phases of the moon and did not need an almanac to look them up. He liked to compute them from *La Epacta*, the formula of which some wise old Mexican had taught him. While dry March winds were blowing, he might figure out from *La Epacta* the day in May when a new moon would bring a chance for rain. I doubt if he knew the English word *epact* as a term in astronomical computations. *La Epacta* is the number of days old the moon is on the first of

January. Knowing that and the eleven days' difference between a lunar year (354 days) and a solar year, one can figure out the date for any new moon in the months to follow and also the epact for the next year, the next, and so on.

After moving to Alice, Grandpa for a while drove the stage to Brownsville, about a hundred and fifty miles south by west. The Sands, bordering what later became known as the Magic Valley, exhausted every team pulling across them. Mesquite, ebony, and other brush hid whatever magic the Rio Grande Valley then had. On one drive Grandpa met, and in some small way accommodated, Catarino Garza about the time Garza was trying to raise forces on the Texas side of the Rio Grande to overthrow Don Porfirio Díaz, president-dictator of Mexico. The international excitement aroused by the revolutionist made no impression on me at the time he was active, though I suppose the *Semi-weekly Houston Post* chronicled the movements of rangers and cavalrymen in their futile attempts to catch this violator of American soil. His men bothered neither people nor property. Richard Harding Davis was on the scene as war correspondent, but judging from what he wrote in *The West from a Car Window* — not read until I was grown — the brush on the waterless land, a superficial mind, and an unguarded facility with words prevented him from seeing even a track made by Catarino Garza. It was tracks, remaining long after he himself was washed out, that made this man a name still lingering with me.

One fall, before I went to Alice, Papa hired a red Mexican named Pantaleón who had come to our ranch from down the country hunting work and paid him, in part, with a gray potro. Pantaleón named the horse Catarino Garza and spent so much time rubbing him and otherwise handling him that Papa said it was a wonder he didn't take a corncob along to wipe him after he hockied. One day while "Catarino Garza" was in a pen with some wild mares, Pantaleón manganed him (roped him by the forefeet) and in throwing him broke his neck.

At the time I went to Alice, Grandpa was justice of the peace. One Saturday official duties took him to Palito Blanco, about fourteen miles away, and he invited me to go along in the buggy. Palito Blanco — Little Hackberry Tree — was a settlement of a few ranch Mexicans. We drove to a house where we had dinner and where I saw a beautiful young woman dressed in black. On the way home Grandpa told me that she was the wife of Catarino Garza, who had made his headquarters at the house long enough to marry her, and that she had not left it once since his disappearance, about 1892 — to live in Cuba, some said, or, as others said, to be killed as a filibusterer in Honduras. For years I wondered every once in a while if she had yet left the house or put off the black clothes. She remains to me as unaging as the Venus de Milo.

Grandpa's meager earnings as justice of the peace came mainly from marrying Mexicans who could not afford a priest and from trials of misdemeanors. I suppose he held preliminary hearings on some criminal cases. According to old Trinidad Jaso's often repeated testimony, "Iffy some man tell Meestro Dubose one Mexican is kill, he say, 'Make no difference, plenty more.' "

Now and then Grandpa went with a train of cattle being shipped to grass in the Indian Territory (Oklahoma) or Kansas or to market. The Fort Worth stockyards had not been established; the cities of Texas were too small to consume much beef; the main cattle markets were Kansas City, St. Louis, and Chicago. More cattle, it was said, were being shipped annually from Alice than from any other point in the United States. They were driven there all the way from Brownsville and on down in Mexico. In the spring vaqueros sometimes held herds for days on the sparse grass south of town waiting their turn at the shipping pens. The Texas-Mexican Railroad, from Laredo to Corpus Christi, ran through Alice, but it was narrow-gauged and any cattle shipped in its cars had to be unloaded and transferred to standard-gauge cars. Its engines burned mesquite wood and stopped at various places out in the brush to load on fuel stacked against the track. Anybody could flag the train down nearly anywhere and board it; to ranch people living within reach of the rails it was as accommodating as a country town streetcar.

In the shipping season trains loaded with cattle pulled out of Alice day and night. Grandpa would say, "I've got my money, my tobacco and my six-shooter and am ready to ride." Then, without a six-shooter and with next to no money but with a supply of tobacco, he would take a small satchel of clothes, bread, fried hog-meat, and hard-boiled eggs, a railroad lantern, and a prodpole, walk to the shipping pens, get into a caboose, and leave to be gone a week or more. His business would be to get out every time the train stopped, day or night, look into the cars to see that the cattle were standing, and if one were down to prod it to its feet, so that it would not be trampled by other cattle. While he was away, I would feed, milk, turn out the cow to graze by day on the town commons and the calf by night, and bring in the stovewood.

Alice specialized in shipping cattle bones as well as cattle. The bones were gathered by Mexicans from far away as well as near and hauled in wagons to sell to merchants. One year Alice Mexicans came up to our ranch bone-gathering. I have looked upon the Rockies and the Alps, but no snow-capped peak towers so high in my memory as the great pile of whitened bones owned by the Newberry merchants beside a railroad switch in Alice. Horns were piled on with the bones. Lem Newberry told me that one time he measured a pair of horns on a steer skull that stretched close to six feet across from tip to tip. He had an inclination to keep them, but they would be in the way and he swung them onto the pile to be shipped for fertilizer and glue. Deer antlers, however, were stacked separately and one year the Newberrys got enough to fill a freight car; some fancier of horns bought the lot.

Grandpa knew all the ranchmen, horse traders, sheriffs, and rangers of the country. Captain Rogers's headquarters camp was just beyond our yard fence. He was noted for asking the blessing at meals in camp and for going to church; he was more noted for being an upright and exceedingly effective ranger captain. Three of the Dubose boys served under him.

Across the street in the opposite direction the noted Dillard R. Fant maintained a cottage to which he would occasionally drive from the large Santa Rosa ranch, on which he was going broke. During the drouth that ruined him he would, people said, sit and mutter or walk up and down and mutter to himself, "My, my, you reckon it ain't never going to rain? Oh, oh, ain't it dry!" Then after he had gone on this way a while he would change tone and call out to the house servant, "Maria, bring me a cafecito" (a little cup of coffee, which need not be little). One night while Dick Scott was at the Santa Rosa, Dillard R. Fant awoke him by walking up and down on the front gallery and carrying on in his way about the drouth. Dick Scott went to walking also and every once in a while as they passed each other Fant would say, "Dick, you reckon this drouth ain't ever going to break?" Finally he said, "Dick, it's just too dry. Let's take a drink."

Another old-time cowman and trail driver of the country was Jasper Miller. He had mortgaged lots of cattle, was large and bearded, and spoke with a husk in his throat. A saying of his current over the country illustrated his hearty generosity: he said he had never seen an ugly woman or tasted bad whiskey. On Saturday mornings I sometimes went with Grandpa to see the Sap passenger train off. One morning when we arrived at the depot, we found Jasper Miller there, ready to board the train.

"How are you, Jasper?" Grandpa inquired.

"Fine, fine, and how are you, Friendly?"

"If I felt any better, I'd be dangerous."

"Well, Friendly, I'm mighty sorry to find you in such good shape."

"Now, how's that, Jasper?"

"Friendly, I think so much of you I just wish to God you were in trouble so I could get you out of it."

Pegleg Tumlinson was around Alice too. He had waybills for many treasures, which he allowed boys to dig for. I was never among the diggers, but one night Amos Mosser, who was in class with me, and two other boys dug up three skeletons on the Agua Dulce. They were relics of men known to have been killed in the vicinity. Some Mexican had given Pegleg a derretero to the grave under the impression that the skeletons guarded money. Pegleg had lost his right leg at the knee. His *compañero* was a man named Lawrence, also called Pegleg, who had lost his left leg below the knee. They wore the same size boots and used to buy a pair together.

I owe much more to Grandma, having inherited some of her energy and spirit through my mother, than to Grandpa, but he appeals to my imagination. She was a Fusselman, partly of Pennsylvania Dutch stock. She was a dumpy little woman, fastidious, decisive, and firm, and, like my mother, she understood well the nature of men. Sorrow, disappointment and worry had quickened her sympathies and had not dampened her spunk. She had a sense of humor sometimes wry. She wrote to my mother of a revival meeting just closed: "It failed to stir up the sinner. Maybe we have none." Her warm, outgoing ways made her a close friend to several young women. At the time I lived with her, she was the main support of the household, and often helped the needy besides. No chambermaid slave ever worked harder. The four rooms of a cottage in the yard were rented to individuals, mostly schoolteachers, whom she boarded.

She was "as swift as greased lightning" in her work. My sister Fannie, who lived with her, going to school, the second year I was there, says that Grandma always called her in the morning on the way to the kitchen and that she could never dress in time to be at the table when Grandma called the boarders to breakfast. Grandpa, always up early, would have had the fire in the kitchen stove going and coffee boiling. My recollection is that for breakfast we had fried steak and fried eggs along with hot biscuits; meat, with vegetables, always abounded at the other meals.

Grandma cultivated and watered roses, oleanders, and other shrubs in the yard, along with such bright annuals as phlox and pinks, all mixed together in Mexican fashion — which is generally the fashion of wild flowers and grasses — without plan. She kept one stand of potted flowers, chiefly geraniums, on the back porch and another stand in the parlor. She loved pretty things and dressed tidily even while drudging. She had several shelves of books, including sets of Bulwer-Lytton, E. P. Roe, and Dickens, and odd volumes from Mark Twain, Scott, Longfellow, and other standard writers.

No novel I read out of those shelves remains to me as vivid as my mother's many references to Bulwer-Lytton's crime-haunted Eugene Aram, in the novel by that name. About ten years after I left Grandma's house, I experienced one of those instances in which the past and the present interpenetrate each other with flash lightning effect and weld themselves into bivious oneness for enduring memory. On a certain winter day in New York I introduced myself to Joseph Conrad by opening in a bookstore the volume containing *Youth*. I was reading the first pages when I paid a clerk for it, and I went to sleep that night in *Heart of Darkness*. Many times during the next fifteen or so years I reread *Youth*, publicly as well as privately, memorizing the apostrophes and the Judea, London, Do or Die passages. The cadences of Conrad's prose remain for me the most swelling and grandly eloquent since Sir Thomas Browne, and *Youth* remains, in its effect on my imagination, the most powerful short story I know. It led me to other Conrad narratives, above all to *The Nigger of the Narcissus* — with Singleton, the oldest able seaman in the ship:

> He sat apart on the deck under the lamps, stripped to the waist, . . . his bare back propped against the heel of the bowsprit, holding a book at arm's length before his big, sunburnt face. With his spectacles and a venerable white beard, he resembled a learned and savage patriarch. He was intensely absorbed, and as he turned the pages, an expression of grave surprise would pass over his rugged features. He was reading *Pelham.*

At this picture of old Singleton reading *Pelham* I saw instantaneously the dingy green bindings of a whole row of novels in Grandma Dubose's cottage set in a brush-surrounded village of braying burros, squeaking windmills, mountains of bleached cow bones, and human inhabitants as far away from the sophisticated elegancies of Edward George Earle Lytton, Bulwer-Lytton, as was any tattooed seaman who ever sailed out of the port of London. Mystery — the supreme mystery of the transporting power of human imagination!

Grandma went to church every Sunday, and Grandpa never went. Some people considered him an irredeemable sinner. He was a free thinker, I suppose; certainly he considered his own and every other person's soul the owner's private affair. He never advised me on my conduct beyond urging me to get an education. Lack of education had blocked him from the two best chances of his life, he said. He was as cold as a well-digger's rump toward some of the preachers whom Grandma had for supper or Sunday dinner. He liked to loiter with men in saloons, not drinking, however — probably on account of the expense. Once in a great while at home, when he felt "about forty years old" — his term for the ultimate in aged stiffness and general stoveupness — he might take a toddy. Mama said that he used to keep a bottle of whiskey on the sideboard; she and Grandma attributed overdrinking by one of the Dubose boys to that practice.

Grandpa's beard was stained by leakage from the corncob pipe constantly in his mouth. Mama said she had seen "Ma gag many a time when Mr. Dubose kissed her." Her name was Martha, but he called her Mattie. My younger sister was named Mattie for her but in time changed the name to Martha, which I like better too.

Even middle age is antiquity to most young people, but Grandpa was old, old, when he died at the age of sixty-eight in 1909. There can be no more satisfactory death than that of a captain going down with his ship. Grandpa survived his ship a long while. I was in Chicago when he died. Uncle Charlie, a son, who was with him, told me his dying words. He asked for the can. After he had emptied his bladder into it he said, "Thank you, Charlie. Now I am easy and can die like a man." And he died.

Perhaps memory ignores many particles of experience more influential on a person's life than other particles vividly recollected. I do not know. I went to Alice for the sole purpose of going to school; yet I can recall almost nothing that I learned in school and comparatively little from school life in general. I can recall many faces of pupils — one of a girl with whom I fell tremblingly in love but who, fortunately for us both, had no feeling for me. Her influence on my subsequent emotional life was as negative as that of the windmill in the yard.

Among the teachers was a German scholar. I did not at the time realize the nature and meaning of a true scholar. This German was ascetic in looks, shy and solitary. He organized a class in Latin, a subject not required, for volunteers. I volunteered but stupidly did not study. I was more interested in *The Last Days of Pompeii.* Any pupil who had an incentive to study had it from an inner source, not from the school.

During two years at Alice I was in the room presided over by the superintendent, "Professor" Nat Benton — a man to respect. Not long before we graduated he told the members of the class to write a theme on one of several subjects that he named. This was the only written assignment I had in school before going to college. Several of the nine members of the class did not write anything. I chose war as my subject and, to be striking, began my theme with Sherman's million-times quoted sentence. Professor Benton, after taking up the themes, began reading mine aloud to the class. At hearing the word "hell," the class giggled and made other noises. There was nothing funny to me about hell. I suffered humiliation and embarrassment beyond adult conception.

I always have to consult a dictionary to make sure of the ranking distinction between salutatorian and valedictorian. I don't remember which I was but think I was next to the top in grades. Anyway, I had to stand up at the graduating exercises — held in the, to me, vast Knights of Pythias hall — and make a speech. In preparing it I floundered about — for I could not think of anything to say — until Professor Benton virtually wrote it for me. In composing the platitudes, he gave me the first idea pertaining to rhetoric that I can recall. He advised me to use "three adjectives in ascending order to describe a noun." For instance, if I wanted to speak of an heroic man, I might say he was "strong, brave, and noble." If I were to say anything about pain, I should adjective it with "sharp, excruciating, agonizing."

I had a dim idea that Professor Benton might be wrong about adjectives. A letter that I came upon three years later from Robert Louis Stevenson to Henry James damning "the accursed adjective" gave me an enduring distrust. Many years later I felt hearty agreement with Clemenceau. "Some letters," Clemenceau told a private secretary he had just engaged, "you will have to draft yourself. Now listen: a sentence consists of a noun and a verb. If you want to use an adjective, come and ask me first."

I memorized my oration and practiced delivering it out in the cowshed. I knew I should be afraid when the time came to stand on the stage before all the people and say it aloud. My legs were shaking like cottonwood leaves in a breeze when I got to my position, and my mouth was dry. I started but after a sentence or two faltered. I could not summon the memorized words; they had no essential meaning to me anyhow. I had no idea at all to put into other words. Professor Benton was ready for me. He held the manuscript of my oration in his hand. He coached me by reading in a low voice the sentence I had stalled on. I repeated half of it and forgot the rest. It was no use to try to go on. If war was hell, this was worse than ten wars. I sat down in a misery and despondency for which there were not and are not any adjectives. The theme on war, the graduating oration, and the failure to study Latin are the sole recollections I have out of two years of schooling at Alice. I read books during the time and must have learned a little arithmetic if nothing else. I cannot recall a single study or textbook we had, but the life and the people of the town come back to me clearly etched.

The principal of the school was a kind man named Mr. Butler. I cannot recall anything that he ever said, but I recall gladly the braying of Mexican-owned burros at night. They were many and they roamed over vacant lots and nipped off the leaves of any shrub growing near a yard fence. Sometimes schoolboys would rope and ride them. I played baseball a little, but had no skill or pleasure in the play. I preferred walking the railroad track out to where the jackrabbits worked their ears.

Watching the big freight wagons from the King ranch in town for supplies was another pleasure. Each was pulled by six mules, the driver, a Mexican, riding on his near wheel mule. The manes and tails of the mules were always neatly roached, and every team was matched exactly for color — six black mules, six sorrels, six duns, and so on. A train of these wagons made as brave a show as the borax wagons of Death Valley. The management was responsible for breeding the mules, but the patterns in teams were out of Mexican instinct for symmetry and design. On the Mexican horse ranches down the country every *manada* (a band of mares herded and otherwise mastered by a stallion) was matched for color — and the rancheros liked variety in the matching. Even though horse raising had become much less profitable than cattle raising, carloads and carloads of Spanish horses were still being shipped from Alice to the farming country eastward.

The village had neither a water nor a sewage system. Householders not provided with wells and windmills depended upon a Mexican who drove a burro to a cart loaded with a horizontal barrel. He transferred water from it through spigot and hose into an upright barrel at the back door or yard gate of the purchaser. The price was a dime a barrel, as I recollect. This *barrilero* (barrel man) would wail out "*Agua, agua fresca*" (water, fresh water) while the burro pulled the cart and barrel over town at a shadow-moving gait. Grandma had a well and mill, besides a cistern to catch rainwater for drinking. When the windmill went to squeaking she would remind Grandpa to oil it. Sometimes the wind blew ceaselessly, covering the town with dust and sifting it into the houses. The rushing sound it made tended to drown out other sounds, but when the wind was moderate in the night, just strong enough to turn the mill wheels, their squeaking from all directions could drive a sleepless person mad.

There were two or three Mexican bakeries across the railroad tracks, and every afternoon a man with a face radiating good nature walked up and down the streets carrying on his head a large flat basket covered with a white cloth and containing loaves of freshly baked, still warm lightbread and buns. He balanced the basket on a coiled-up red Mexican sash around his head, and while carrying it did not touch it with his hands. Walking slowly, he would sing-song in long-drawn-out and faraway-sounding syllables the words *pan cal-i-ente, pan dul-ce* (hot lightbread, sweet bread). The cry, running far up the musical scale, was a joy to him, and it was a joy to hear. It was an added joy to take a nickel from Grandma and run out to meet him. He would uncover the fragrant basket and hand me a loaf of lightbread with the invariable *pilón* (lagniappe) — a very soft, warm bun, as light as milk foam, which I devoured at once. Then he would walk on, trailing aroma and melody.

The music in my heart I bore,
Long after it was heard no more.

CHAPTER TEN

Prose and Poetry

I ENTERED Southwestern University at Georgetown, Texas, in the fall of 1906. Riding on the train with me to Southwestern University was a neighbor named Harvey Robinson, several years older than I, who was going to prepare for the ministry. Despite a hope, not at all insistent, on my mother's part, I had no idea of being a preacher — and association with preachers and preachers-to-be at this breeding ground for preachers did not generate any such idea.

I was eighteen years old and could not have been greener. I had bought a pair of patent leather shoes as a part of my equipment; they were at that date several notches in style above celluloid collars, which I would never have worn. These shoes pinched my feet. While waiting to be registered as a freshman, I sat down by a table in one of the rooms of the Main Building. I looked out of a big window and wished that, unconscious of feet, I were riding Buck over a Live Oak County pasture. Presently a man of quick movement, quick speech, and countenance quickened by intelligence introduced himself to me as R. S. Hyer, president of the college, and sat down. He asked if I liked to read. I doubt if he said "read good books," for at that time people out in the country who read books at all read good ones — mostly. Drugstore literature was as unknown as drugstore cowboys.

I told Dr. Hyer that I very much liked to read. He then said something that made a profound and enduring impression on my mind. He said that he had long made it a practice to read one book a week. Right there I determined to read a book a week myself, and in the more than 2600 weeks that have passed since Dr. Hyer spoke, I have, without being methodical, been absorbed by that many books, not to speak of many thousands glanced through or searched into for something I could use.

Dr. Hyer added that he was a lay preacher and that on the coming Sunday his sermon — for he always preached on the first Sunday following the opening of the college year — would be based on James Parton's *Life of Thomas Jefferson*, which he had just read. His sermon was a finished essay fitted to the text "I am debtor both to the Greeks, and to the Barbarians; both to the wise, and to the unwise." That essay-sermon, which ranged over the great literature of the world and its influence on the mind and spirit of man, elated me with ambition to know.

I was very young when some of Benjamin Franklin's maxims from *Poor Richard's Almanack* sank into me. One became a kind of star to follow. "Dost thou love life? Then do not squander time, for that is the stuff life is made of." Yet I wasted far more time in college than I studied. I could fill chapters with recollections of inconsequential episodes, but I am trying here to track and particularize some of the debts I owe to both Greeks and Barbarians, to the wise and the unwise encountered during four years at Southwestern. I took some Latin under Professor Vaden, a scholar with gleaming gusto for Horace, but I could never qualify under Charles James Fox's tolerant dictum that while it is not necessary for a gentleman to know Latin he at least should have forgotten it. I took some Spanish under Professor Young, who ran a dairy, looked like a farmer, had buried two wives and married a third and was called Old Brigham, but I never mastered Spanish grammar or added much to the scanty vocabulary acquired from vaquero people. I took mathematics under Professor C. C. Cody, but when we got into logarithms I was so lost that I failed the course — and one had to be very ignorant indeed not to pass under Dr. Cody.

What entered into me to grow were things like Dr. Hyer's introduction to James Parton as a biographer. To this day I have not read his *Jefferson*, but during World War II while lecturing on American history at Cambridge University I read his *Life of Andrew Jackson*, and agreed with a delightful Cambridge scholar much more learned in the subject than I am that this work gives a clearer conception of what is called Jacksonian democracy than anything else published up to the year 1944. Nor have I read Parton's *Life of Voltaire*, but my friend Roy Bedichek considers it as liberating to the human mind as Voltaire himself and attributes its obscurity to fear of truth and deference to the papal Index of Forbidden Books kind of thing. Dr. Hyer began one thread, made golden more by conversation than by study, a-weaving through the pattern of my life.

But back to college. For the first year I lived at Giddings Hall, a two-storied wooden structure fronting several four-roomed cottages, on grounds joining those around the old stone Prep building. The principal of the Preparatory Department, Professor Burcham, presided over student conduct and meals at Giddings Hall. He was lame, but active, and the barbarians called him — to his back — Old Crip. He might have been thirty years old at this time. If I had a roommate at Giddings Hall, I do not remember him. I paid $10 a month for room and board.

The food was abundant. It was set on the tables in great platters and bowls. According to my recollection, besides the skimmed milk in pewter pitchers that stood on every table, we had fried steak and hot biscuits three times a day, except for

A group of Texas Rangers, one of whom was a Dubose, about 1900

A lieutenant in World War I

Branding

Even while teaching at the University of Texas, I got down to the Brush Country for a few weeks in summer (1919)

chicken or some other specialty at noon Sunday, and for Sunday supper cold canned salmon and cold stewed prunes. All food was cheap, but nothing was cheaper or less trouble when the cooks were gone than canned salmon and stewed prunes. Many years were to pass before I could relish either, and, so far as taste goes, I still prefer a hot corn pone sopped in a mixture of melted beef tallow and sorghum molasses — a cow camp dessert — to the finest California prunes ever boiled.

I recollect one very tall, very slender, very red collegian solely because of his gormandizing. He seemed unable to fill up. It was popularly believed that a giant hookworm devoured down below as fast as the man could devour up above. Hookworms were at this time regarded as a major affliction of the South and there was plenty about them in print, but I had skipped it all, as I continued to skip it. Just the same, Red, as the hookworm man was called, gave them a bizarre reality — and he may have been as free of them as many a man in these times called communist is free of communistic ties. Red sat at one end of my table. He was always at the dining room door when it opened; he was always in his chair and reaching as soon as Old Crip had finished a blessing that not many of the boarders felt like amening, and his arms were so long and his manners so short that he reached for whatever replenishment his plate required. I was well acquainted with Ichabod Crane, and devouring Red now gave a peculiar realism to that character. Several years later, at Columbia University, Chaucer became my favorite poet next to Shakespeare, and Chaucer's Clerk filled out Red:

As leene was his hors as is a rake,
And he nas nat right fat, I undertake,
But looked holwe, and therto sobrely.

At $10 a month we furnished our own linen and other bedding and did most of our room cleaning. On certain days water was hot in an outside bathhouse. The plumbing was not very far ahead of the plumbing on farms and ranches over the country at the time. Every room had a coal stove and coal was free to whoever would scuttle it in from a pile of Bunker Hill proportions out by the cow lot.

My English teacher was Professor Albert Shipp Pegues, M.A. I still cherish a copy of *The Principles and Progress of English Poetry*, edited by Gayley and Young, that we used in the freshman year. It is a handy-sized quarto containing the cream of English poetry down through Tennyson, much more conducive to development of a taste for poetry than the encyclopedic tomes that Ph.D.-minded instructors later loaded upon undergraduates. In introducing literature to freshmen and reserving composition for sophomores, Professor Pegues had the idea, evidently, that if pupils learned to read they would absorb enough of form, or what is called style, to enable them to compose clear sentences.

His survey course in English poetry transmuted the world for me. In recollection this course has blended with one more advanced in the Romantic poets that I took as a junior. I had read some narrative poetry — Macaulay's *Lays*, Scott's *Marmion*, Tennyson's *Idylls of the King*, but only Tennyson had held me in thrall, and he seemed always of the afternoon. The Romantic poets, Burns as well as Wordsworth, Coleridge, Byron, Shelley and Keats, were of the morning, and they were as much a part of Albert Shipp Pegues as love is a part of Juliet. Pegues himself was regarded as being very romantically in love with his comely wife. He drilled us on metrics and illuminated the language and thought of poets; above all, he made us enjoy poetry. The juices of vitality pulsed through his handsome body and features, and he read poetry with burning eyes and absorbed voice. He knew much of it by heart and required us to memorize "touchstone passages." No other teacher I came under, least of all in graduate work, so enlarged and enriched life for me, so started up growths inside me. He opened windows; he carried whoever would go with him to the Elysian fields. Many students, perhaps a majority, did not have it within themselves to dance to his piping of divine poetry.

Although in time I became hail fellow well met with most people who came along, led in baseball yelling one year, managed the business of the weekly newspaper, edited the annual, reported for the Williamson County *Sun*, and otherwise squandered the stuff of life upon activities that seldom activate the mind, I was my essential self when I walked alone up the San Gabriel River with a volume of Wordsworth, reading him there as I imagined he had walked and composed by "sylvan Wye," and making his lines an integral and abiding part of me.

These beauteous forms,
Through a long absence, have not been to me
As is a landscape to a blind man's eye:
But oft, in lonely rooms, and 'mid the din
Of towns and cities, I have owed to them
In hours of weariness, sensations sweet,
Felt in the blood, and felt along the heart;
And passing even into my purer mind. . . .

From the time I noticed anything I have loved the pale pink evening primrose that we called, and I still call, Mexican primrose. It is not at all the primrose that Wordsworth knew, but Wordsworth's lines have made it more to me than it was before I heard Professor Pegues read them:

A primrose by a river's brim
A yellow primrose was to him,
And it was nothing more.

The dining of Elizabethan dramatists at the Mermaid Tavern to which Professor Pegues introduced me has lighted up and savored dinners with friends at less romantic taverns.

Before entering college I had had no particular course in English composition, though I had studied grammar. However, words, their sound more than their meaning, fascinated me. While riding horseback alone on the ranch I used to compose phrases and say them over and over aloud with variations. From that exercise and from my reading of literature and from my father's nightly reading out of the Bible, I went to college with some sense of the architecture of sentences and with a consciousness of the harmonies in the prose of master writers. During college years and for several years afterward I used to make lists of new words learned from Robert Louis Stevenson, Charles Lamb, Hazlitt, Sir Thomas Browne and some other writers. I would write out the definitions of newly acquired words — veritable riches they seemed then — and devise occasions for using them in talk or writing. I was delighted when I learned that to Oliver Wendell Holmes the dictionary was the most romantic book in the world and that it was O. Henry's favorite reading.

As soon as our class in English composition got well organized, Professor Pegues assigned a theme to be written on any subject of our own choosing. To explain mine, I must revert to the school on our ranch.

On one side of the schoolhouse the land was open except for scattered liveoak and mesquite trees; on the other side for miles extended a thicket of black chaparral, guajilla, colima, catclaw and other thorned brush, along with thornless Mexican persimmon, whitebrush and guayacan. At noon, after bolting down the contents of our lunchboxes and buckets, the boys would take off for a game of cats and dogs. The "cats" on foot were allowed a fair start to scatter and hide in the brush;

then the "dogs" would set out on horseback after them, yelling and popping the bushes. The object of the dogs was to rope or hem up the cats. Experience as a cat in this game convinces me that hunted foxes sometimes have a fine time. We were often late getting back to school; one day, having roasted sweet potatoes dug up out of Cousin Dick's patch, we stayed out until afternoon recess time, and after school received a wholesale thrashing that left the teacher, a gentle and not sturdy lady, worn to a frazzle. We were a bunch of bullies.

My first theme, three or four pages long, for Professor Pegues was on our ranch school and this game of cats and dogs. In the course of description I said that the game was "the anticipation of morning, the delight of noon and the recollection of night." When after a few days Professor Pegues brought the themes, marked and graded, for return to his scholars, he said he would read one as an example of good composition. Our class met on the second or third floor of the Main Building, and I had a seat by a window looking over beautiful rolling country to the south. I often looked out this window while listening, especially if the master were lending to the rhyme of a poet the beauty of his voice; at the same time I would be riding in fancy over other hills, far, far away. On this day of the themes I must have been riding more than listening, for I did not comprehend that my own theme was being read until I heard "the anticipation of morning." My heart was in my throat. When I went up to get my paper at the end of the hour, Professor Pegues spoke hearty words.

I did not set out immediately giving my days and my nights to trying to learn to write, but I became increasingly conscious of the craft and found pleasure in the practice of it. I still have pleasure in a writer's craft and still have to work at it. A long time ago now I thought that by the time I had written a million words all I would have to do would be to open the gate and the words would file out in decent, exact order. I have written several million words; yet words remain as stubborn, as elusive and also as effusive as they ever were.

All the shelves in the college library were open to undergraduates. (I never have thought anything of card indexes as an invitation to reading.) Through allusions in required reading and by means of the open shelves, I discovered Leigh Hunt, John Morley and other minor writers. Many books I picked up and merely glanced into, as a speaker on a rostrum, waiting for his time to come, picks out certain faces in front of him to read.

History interested me next to literature. I liked "Sleepy" (S. H.) Moore, the history professor. He led me out on the vast plains of human experience, but never through what was in himself did he send me spurring up to a mountain top to see what might be on the other side; I found the spurrers in history.

As I look back on the first college professors I became acquainted with, they all appear as "characters." Probably nobody on the faculty had read more liberally than Reverend John R. Allen, D.D., professor of philosophy. One day while coming out of the library with four red-bound volumes of beautifully printed rag paper stacked in an arm, I met him.

"Young man," he queried, "what work have you there?"

"Victor Hugo's *Les Misérables*," I replied.

"Ah, young man," he exclaimed, sucking in his breath, "how I envy you reading that masterpiece for the first time!"

Dr. Allen taught economics as well as philosophy and had given a course on the Bible. He was the author of a volume slight in size and agreeable in style entitled *Man, Money, and the Bible; or, Biblical Economics* (published by the Methodist Episcopal Church, South, Nashville, 1891.) "Some wa-a-ag," he said, "dubbed it *Man, Monkey, and the Bible*." The innocence of the old age that believed in Garden of Eden perfection far behind is summed up in the book's subtitle: *A Treatise upon the Economical System of the Bible and Its Solution of the Social Problems that Confront the Nineteenth Century.*

All I remember from the economics course — which did not require a reading of *Man, Money and the Bible* — is "unearned increment" and Henry George's idea that it belongs to the society responsible for it and not to some accidental owner of a deed. Many years after acquiring this fragment of information I became well acquainted with a man who while peddling vegetables from a wagon in Austin took a course in economics at the University of Texas that opened his eyes to the fortunes lying in seizure of the unearned increment. He became a multimillionaire through investments in low-priced real estate that population and the industry of others would make valuable while he Miltonically only stood and waited. Neither in college nor for a long time after had I the slightest interest in the economics of society or in making a fortune.

Dr. and Mrs. Allen lived in the Annex, as the women's dormitory was called, and were guardians over the uniforms, study habits, social life, manners, morals, virginities and all else of the female students living under their eyes. A young lady could not even walk to town without a chaperon. On Sunday all the young ladies marched to church in a chaperoned phalanx as unbroken as a regiment of soldiers on review. Despite his responsibility for women students, Dr. Allen never seemed conscious of their existence in his classes or of their intellectual potentialities. He invariably addressed a class as "young gentlemen."

According to a story often told, word once reached Dr. Allen that girls on the second floor were letting down a rope at night and hoisting one or more cavaliers up. He and Mrs. Allen occupied rooms on the first floor. One dark Saturday night he went outside and, feeling along, found the rope. He sent two or three waves up it and then gave the kind of jerk that he imagined signaled "Ready!" He was low, chunky, but not flabby. Presently he felt the rope being pulled. He held on, partly helping with his feet braced against the stone wall. He could hear titters and then something about "heavy." Just as he got nearly to the dark, open window, somebody struck a match. All at once the rope was let go.

In the philosophy course Dr. Allen seemed, according to my dim recollection, to be always sounding on Immanuel Kant. I comprehended absolutely nothing from the entire course but Kant's "categorical imperative": the rule by which you do only what you would have others do and thus would have become "universal law." For Dr. Allen the categorical imperative was a sublime enlargement of the golden rule. He probably followed it. He was, I judge now, a true Kantian. At that time I did not know enough to admire Kant for his steady opposition to the closed mind of the church. It may be that my own ever-increasing admiration for dissenters from torpid conformity and for heretics and intellectual rebels has brought me to regard Dr. Allen as more independent-minded than he actually was. As a Kantian, he paid no attention to dunces, took it for granted that any genius who might appear would go ahead anyhow, and devoted himself to intermediate talent.

I did not read any systematic philosophy under him and have read very little away from him. Because of constitutional obtuseness or from lack of mental discipline, all philosophical, ethical, logical, philological, theological, economical, political and critical theories, theorems, platforms, exegeses and the like are beyond the spontaneous grasp of my mind, and what it grasps through sheer will power soon escapes. I laughed within myself a few years ago at the charge some ignoramus made in print that I had fed too much on Karl Marx. It would take commissar methods to make me wade through the turgidity of any Teutonic thesis. I take no pride in my obtuseness. It is shared by millions of lowbrows, business executives and individuals who regard information quizzes over television and radio as educational. I admire intelligences that create systems of thought, but I cannot follow them, except by an effort that I am unwilling to exert. Doctor Johnson's disposal of the theory of the nonexistence of matter by striking his foot against a rock and punning, "I refute it thus"; Lamb's hope of spending his last breath inhaling tobacco smoke and exhaling a pun; Herrick's injunction to "gather ye rosebuds while ye may"; Wordsworth's placid satisfaction with sitting on an old gray stone and letting "authentic tidings of invisible things" — also of visible things — soak into him; Stevenson's justification of idleness; Benjamin Franklin's urbane example of usefulness to mankind; Matthew Arnold's persuasiveness to tolerance; Shelley's reach for the stars, mothlike though it be; Mirabeau's advocacy of his own magnificent "art of daring"; Cyrano de Bergerac's desire to be "always admirable"; Byron's regret at not having taken advantage of more opportunities to sin; Robert E. Lee's example of integrity; Montaigne's frank validation of all the body's appetites and senses — these are the forms of philosophy congenial to my nature.

Dr. Allen's manner of sucking in his breath and grinning out both tolerance and a mild sort of you-be-damned judgment had more effect on my imagination than his iteration of *Cogito, ergo sum* from Descartes had on my thinking. On a final examination question concerning Plato I quoted a good part of Wordsworth's "Ode: Intimations of Immortality," for Platonism was too vague in me for exposition. Plato's account of the trial and death of Socrates means more to me today than all the arguments of both these great philosophers. I received a good grade in the course. According to collegiate folklore, Dr. Allen read examination pads upside down so that he would not be tempted to waste time over indecipherable handwriting.

His Bible course had been considered as much a crip as any

course in Education now is, without being so dreary. A playboy who registered for it and did not "crack a book" during the term was assured by fraternity brothers that he would easily pass if he memorized the names of the prophets and kings of Israel, their approximate dates and something that each said or did. He could do this in an evening, for the data were all in form. He applied himself for the evening. The next morning Dr. Allen chalked one, and only one, examination question on the blackboard: "Write an exhaustive criticism of Moses." The playboy pulled his hair, rubbed his nose and nibbled his pencil for a long while; then the light came to him and in his bluebook he wrote: "Far be it from me to criticize so great a man as Moses, but if you would care to have the names and dates of the prophets and kings of Israel, with a significant fact about each, here they are." He passed the course. Long after my Southwestern days I learned that this was a traveling anecdote, probably pinned on Dr. Allen through no action or inaction of his own. In A. A. Milne's *Autobiography*, published in 1939, the following passage occurs:

> There was once a young man who went in for a Divinity. Having heard that the examiners were likely to be interested in the Kings of Israel and Judah, he made a list of the Kings of Israel and Judah and committed it to memory. He now felt confident of answering one question anyhow. However, when he got into the examination room he was horrified to discover that there was absolutely no demand for the only information which he could supply. Luckily Question 8 asked, "Who were the Minor Prophets?" He replied with dignity: "Far be it from me to make invidious distinctions among the prophets. Rather let us turn to the Kings of Israel and Judah, as follows . . ."

One winter I boarded in a private house toward town from the college, sharing a cottage that had a wood stove with John E. King, several years my senior in maturity as well as in years. I remember the wood stove from reading by it one cold, rainy afternoon Jack London's *The Call of the Wild.* John King reached his zenith in amplitude of mind and nature as managing editor of the Dallas *Morning News.* His realism was good for me. I was absorbing, but my mind was not developing sinews.

Mood Hall was built while I was in college, and I remember with gladness companions there. Lowe Simons, my roommate, had a very soothing voice and temperament, and his gay charm never jarred on the "divine melancholy" I sometimes cultivated. Mid Westbrook used to start my mind gallivanting by reciting,

> *For, my friends, we were actors then,*
> *In the good old palmy days.*

But he never got beyond those two lines, and the only place I gallivanted to was up in the air. I recall one prolonged discussion over immortality, and about that time began a doubt, never troublesome to my spirit, that soon ended in comfortable indifference.

All the more active-minded men in college belonged to either the Alamo Literary Society or the San Jacinto. These were primarily debating societies for men only, and the highlight of Commencement was a debate between two elected men from each society. During four years of attendance I never stood up in a meeting of the Alamo Society to say something without trembling. I marveled at young men who could stand and think out loud in orderly, clear language.

One such was Lyndsay D. Hawkins, who became a lawyer. He said that his father, a lawyer, had trained him to rise and make a speech at any time on any subject announced — on clocks, for instance. I began consciously associating ideas, instances, words, experiences, quotations — every concept I could summon — on clocks, and then on other subjects. My memory is weak, but I have cultivated the faculty of calling up what it holds — though many a time after making a talk I have noticed that the aptest stores wait several hours to rise from latency into consciousness. The best after-dinner speeches come after midnight while the speaker perfects, alone in bed, what his dispersed listeners have forgotten in sleep.

The faculty of being reminded is universal. In some bores it is confined largely to jokes; in others, the subjects strung together have only a physical connection, without play of mind or growth of idea; to people of the Dame Quickly habit of being reminded, relevancy is without pertinence. Illustrative of my own habit of connotation, that word *relevancy* instantly brings into consciousness "no relevancy bore" in Poe's "The Raven," and but for the sound I might write *relevancy no pertinence bears* instead of *relevancy is without pertinence*. To illustrate further, the word *worm* comes into mind asking, it seems, for associations. I think of Poe's "The Conqueror Worm," of the royal "progress" by means of a worm that Hamlet sends a king on "through the guts of a beggar"; of the Diet of Worms, which has nothing to do with either physical diet or worms; of the line "For such a worm as I," in a hymn my father used to join in singing at church; of Andrew Marvell's delicious argument "To His Coy Mistress" on relenting before

worms shall try
That long preserved virginity,
And your quaint honour turn to dust,
And into ashes all my lust.
The grave's a fine and private place,
But none, I think, do there embrace.

Worms — the very word is like a bell tolling up that scourge of Southern ranches far more devastating than all cow-thieves combined, though never mentioned in cowboy romances —

screwworms. Race now into recollection gallons of E. O. Weimer's screwworm medicine, mostly chloroform, bottled at Oakville, Texas, that I as a boy poured into cattle wounds, and my horse Buck's sense of smell directing me to some worm-eaten animal hiding in brush or high weeds.

Perhaps the subject is unpleasant to some people. Turn to the skylark. Ever-soaring and ever-singing, it lifts up the spirits of all earth-dwellers, but only the accretions of English poetry have made it a primary bird of the world, transmuted into an abstraction of the human spirit's loftiest reaches. Nobody who regards this skylark, on the ground or in the air, silent or singing, can comprehend it without consciousness of poetry's enrichments. The habit, cultivated in the beginning, of connotation has given significance to and enriched for me, as it has for myriads of other people, all sorts of objects on this earth. An unabridged dictionary and Bartlett's *Familiar Quotations* and *The Oxford Dictionary of Quotations* make much wit handy and for many a modern writer increase awareness of the prolonged shadows cast by words. No shadows, no art. Although connotation works in an essayical manner, no encyclopedia of connotations could have enabled Hazlitt to write an essay on sundials or Lamb to write a chapter on ears.

Cultivating the art of connotation has helped me in an unending strife to be precise, specific, concrete, definite. It affords, sometimes, apposite illustrations; oftener, it clogs directness and simplicity, so that I am always being forced to compromise between admirations for a plain, economical style on one hand and for cumulative effects and divagations on the other. Literary allusions are enjoyed only by those who recognize them, and when I retain one in a narrative about a wild horse I realize that I am writing more for myself than for most readers of Western wildness.

It is very hard to know about one's own mind, to say nothing of another's. It is very hard to be honest with oneself, partly out of ignorance. I doubt that I ever forced myself for five minutes on this business of connotation. It comes voluntarily or not at all. "Your dull ass will not mend his pace with beating." Play of mind is another term for connotative activity. In a prologue to a talk on water and soil conservation he once made, Roy Bedichek compared his diffidence to that of the Negro in a folk rhyme who confronted a medical emergency:

Ah ain't no doctor nor no doctor's son,
But ah kin hol' de patient till de doctor come.

This is play of mind through fantastic association of ideas.

In the Alamo Literary Society, where this subject got started several paragraphs back, E. V. Cole frequently spoke in his easy, droll, sardonic and unsubtle manner. At one meeting he read the more devastating parts of Mark Twain's essay on "The Literary Offenses of Fenimore Cooper." If a Spanish Inquisition had been available, and if I had been director of it, E. V. Cole would have been boiled in salted lard right there. I had been reared on Cooper's novels, he was a veritable idol; a public attack on the honesty of my father could hardly have been more personal to me than this attack on the creator of Leatherstocking. But I was too bashful to take part in the heated debate that followed Cole's reading. Talking in public is to this day the hardest work I have ever done. When I see a schoolboy glib and ready on his feet, he seems far more extraordinary than a parrot that can swear in six languages.

It did not take me as long to forgive E. V. Cole as it took me to approach a preference for truth over prejudice, and while I still cling to some "imperfect sympathies," I hope I have evolved far enough not to repulse facts, however distasteful they may be, that demand a reversal of opinion.

I had no militant feelings against fraternities, but was an out-and-out barb. Campus elections and other politics, which seem increasingly to obstruct intellectual pursuits in American colleges and universities, were too limited to stir up much barb-frat strife. Owen Johnson's novel *Stover at Yale*, which I read a few years after leaving college, characterizes the seriousness with which frats take their fraternities as "guarding an empty tin can with sacerdotal righteousness." Other empty tins guarded by society with sacerdotal righteousness have concerned me far more than those designated by Greek letters ever did. No college fraternity rushed or invited me; I was as actively satisfied with my friends and with dormitory life as Dr. Johnson was on his "throne of human felicity." I had the barb contempt, generally shared by frats, for "frat suckers."

There were no picture shows, dances or other such diversions in Georgetown. The nearest thing to a conversation center off the campus was an "ice cream parlor," but it was parlorish. Two stores downtown sold textbooks, and one of them had a shelf or two of books written to be read, some priced low from having been there so long. This was my main idling place off the campus. It was the nearest approach to a bookstore I had seen and was the precursor of several secondhand bookstores in cities and in certain English towns in which I have spent many eager hours. Here I bought my first book not for class work. It was *Rubáiyát of Omar Khayyám*. No other place I have known came as near realizing the unworldliness and simplicity of Cranford as Georgetown.

Occasionally a worldly student hired a livery stable rig and cut a swath driving around in it. Once in a blue moon some of the students went to Austin by train to see a play in the Hancock Opera House. I had neither money nor inclination to go to Austin on weekends for larks credited to certain fraternity men. Two blind ministerial students caused a great commotion by being caught one night in an Austin house of ill fame, as such domiciles were called. I don't know who caught them. They were cheerful fellows, and I wondered at the holy outcry against them. They were expelled from college, as I recall.

Two off-campus diversions were first Mondays on the courthouse square and trials in the courthouse. On the first Monday of every month hundreds of horses stood for sale around the square, while horse traders from all over the country stirred about. The welter of men and horses was as good as a gipsy caravan. The horse smells took me back to old Dandy's stall on our ranch in Live Oak County. One Monday Booger Red came with his pitching horses and, for those who paid admission at a gate out from town, rode a ram-nosed black whose squeal of rage comes to memory yet when I see or hear Booger Red's name. Before rodeos, Booger Red — he was called by no other name — went about the country with a wagon carrying bedding and grub and with a helper or two driving or leading several horses. He stopped at towns, barbecues, wherever an exhibition of riding might pay.

Many criminal cases, especially of murder, were transferred from other counties to Williamson County for trial in the district court. In my senior year I dallied with the idea of becoming a lawyer and took to attending criminal trials with as much interest as I took in habituating theaters after I went to New York as a student at Columbia University. The relentless prosecuting attorney, James R. Hamilton, added drama. Among Georgetown lawyers on one side or the other in any big case, Captain Armistead Fisher looked as majestical as Daniel Webster, but it took Frank Taulbee to stir the blood.

Frank Taulbee knew the principles, emotional proclivities, and prejudices of many voters in the county and his cunning in selecting a jury was said to be worth any amount of evidence. His long, sparse red-roan hair had a tendency to stand up on his head and his complexion matched it. He wore high-topped, laced black shoes, black trousers, black alpaca coat, white shirt with broad starched cuffs, and high-standing collar with black string tie. He had a way of seeming to make jurymen ask questions he asked witnesses.

After all the testimony on a case was in, the judge allotted time for speeches by both prosecution and defense. Frank Taulbee always knew when the prosecution was about to conclude and his own hour was arriving. Then he would arise from the seat in which he had been ostentatiously squirming and begin stalking up and down an aisle, pulling up the sleeves of his black alpaca coat and drawing back over them his magnificently unlinked cuffs. Thus he would stalk, running a hand through his hair to make it stand up straighter. I wondered that the judge, Charles A. Wilcox, superb in both justice and civility, would allow him so to distract the attention of the jury from the earnest logic of the prosecution. He was as distractive as a mouse I once saw playing back and forth on a wall high up behind the Honorable Clarence R. Wharton while he addressed with forensic emphasis a historical society that became increasingly attentive to the mouse and decreasingly attentive to history.

I wondered, too, if this actor-lawyer on the courthouse stage had read the life of Lord Erskine, perhaps the greatest advocate the English bar has known, one of whose great defenses of free speech I had outlined and analyzed in the argumentation section of Professor Pegues's course in composition. Professor Pegues had drawn a picture of Lord Erskine's arrival in court wearing very long gauntlets and standing while he deliberately removed them from his expressive hands just before addressing the gentlemen of the jury.

One night during a crowded docket in the district court, Colonel W. K. Makemson, a highly civilized lawyer who had fought in the Civil War, ended the pleadings of the prosecution in a murder case. The district judge asked the lawyers if the court should recess or if pleadings should continue. He ruled in favor of continuing. Frank Taulbee leaped — literally leaped — to the space in front of the jury. Colonel Makemson, already at the age when weariness is constant in the human frame, had been sitting on the edge of a table while he tiredly argued the guilt of the accused. Taulbee with a swing of his whole body shoved that table out of his prancing space.

"Gentlemen of the jury," he began in harrowing tones, "you are tired; the court is tired; that toil-marked woman beside the prisoner at the bar holding a sleeping baby in her lap is no doubt tired, too — terribly tired. But the court has, I think, wisely decided that you should not go to rest without being reminded that the destiny of an immortal soul and of souls dependent on him rests with your conscience. God knows how the attorney for the prosecution will sleep after urging you to send a man to death — and his family to penury and shame. 'Vengeance is mine, saith the Lord.' Oh, gentlemen of the jury, is vengeance yours, and yours, and yours?" Here Frank Taulbee half knelt so as to bring his burning eyes level with the faces of the jurymen. "It is," he went on, "pity and not vengeance that we shall ask for when we come to the Bar of Judgment, and I must think we shall receive it accordingly as we have given it." His voice became almost magical as he quoted,

Not all the herd that roams the dale
To slaughter do I condemn.
Taught by that Power that pities me,
I've learned to pity them.

In another trial, a civil case, a man was accused of having moved a survey stake or rock over onto his neighbor's land so as to widen his own acreage. No good fence marked the dividing line between these two making them good neighbors. A lawyer from Austin defended the accused and in his argument kept quoting Plutarch — without much pertinence, it seemed to me. Frank Taulbee followed him.

"Gentlemen of the jury," he began, "we have been hearing over and over what Plutarch says about this and what Plutarch says about that. Who is this man Plutarch, anyhow? I don't know. Perhaps some of you don't know. But I can cite you an authority that we all do know — the Good Book itself. Therein you'll find written these words: 'He that removeth the ancient landmark shall have his eyes plucked out by the buzzards of the air.' "

As soon as I got to my room I consulted the Bible presented by my mother when I went off to college. There is a curse in it all right about removing a neighbor's landmark, but I haven't found Frank Taulbee's yet.

While I was a sophomore, Senator Joseph Weldon Bailey ran for delegate-at-large to the National Democratic Convention against Cone Johnson. He had been accused of accepting money from an oil company and was familiarly known as Coal Oil Joe. But this accusation had not weakened the spell of his oratory. Feeling was at white heat over Texas. When it was announced that Senator Bailey would "address the citizens" on the courthouse square at Georgetown, a "Bailey Club" was organized among the men students of Southwestern University. Looking back now, I do not know why I joined it unless because, hero-worshipper that I was, I considered Joseph Weldon Bailey a hero.

He began with a eulogy on the Lost Cause and the Confederate Veterans, of whom a good many still lived. This eulogy may have lasted half an hour. A natural-born orator must have a silver tongue, and a silver tongue is necessary to prolongation of eulogy without boring, for eulogy is one of the most boring as well as lying forms of speech. I don't remember how much the Senator touched on his record. I know that he did not allude to the charges of bribery. He was strong on motherhood as he approached his climax. That was after he had spoken maybe an hour and a half. The weather was hot, and he had taken off his black alpaca coat. Sweat running down his bleached face had wilted his white starched collar. The climax came: ". . . the God of my sainted mother up there beyond the farthermost cloud that gilds with the rising sun and blushes with its going down." The look of reverence on the senator's face as he reached this height would have stirred to envy any actor who ever impersonated a piety-professing hypocrite. Many people were deeply moved.

"Georgetown is staked off with bell ropes and pegged down with bell clappers." So Ned Springer, from a ranch on the plains, used to say. On Sunday morning the air was clamorous with the bells, but they never made for me the joyful noise unto the Lord that I heard from the bells of Cambridge, through professional bell-ringers, long afterwards. At Georgetown I memorized, the first time I met the poem,

O little town of Bethlehem!
How still we see thee lie;
Above thy deep and dreamless sleep
The silent stars go by.

Now, whenever I hear it sung at Christmastime, it connotes Georgetown. Some students seemed to get as much pleasure out of sermons as I got from murder trials. For a good while I went to church regularly every Sunday. During the annual revival meeting at the town-and-gown Methodist church, college work was all but suspended by some professors — not by "Piggy" (Pegues). I heard about one student who when reprimanded for not attending services replied, "There is no sin but ignorance" — he had read Marlowe — "and I am serving the Lord by dispelling that sin from my own brain."

Of all the sermons I heard at Georgetown I remember but

three: Dr. Hyer's on being debtor both to the Greeks and to the Barbarians; another, highly poetic, by Dr. Charles M. Bishop, who succeeded Dr. Hyer as president, on "When My October Comes"; and a revival sermon by a sensation-rouser named Hugh D. Knickerbocker on putting off repentance until too late to avoid eternal damnation. He pictured man after man as being almost persuaded to accept Everlasting Mercy but fatally procrastinating. His climactic cry rings in my ears yet. A brother sitting by a dying sinner's bed saw a look of terror contort his features and then heard him in the final struggle for breath half scream, half whisper, "Lost, lost, lost." No actor on the dying words of wicked kings and ruined lovers could have exceeded Mr. Knickerbocker in raising, prolonging, lowering those repeated words "Lost, lost, lost" and making them echo and linger up against the high ceiling and whisper like dusky death itself into the organ pipes. The blood came up into the back of my head, as it always comes when something grandly brave or beautiful or noble or dramatic fires my imagination. Had I heard this sermon at a camp-meeting of my boyhood, I should probably have joined the procession to the mourners' bench. Now its drama was in the category of Lady Macbeth's sleepwalking.

It was about this time that I read Marlowe's *Doctor Faustus* and became haunted by the scene in which at the stroke of midnight Faustus must deliver his soul to the ruler over eternal gnashing of teeth. As the knell of finality approaches, Faustus cries out, "*O lente, lente currite noctis equi*" (Slow, slow, coursers of the night). Whenever I returned from college to the home of my parents at Beeville — whence I would quickly go to the ranch — I had to change trains at San Antonio, generally staying overnight to catch the "Sap"; then at Kenedy, a railroad junction, there was another wait. I might read there, but I liked to walk up and down the wooden platform and watch an engine switch freight cars and listen to the rhythm of the wheels. They said, over and over, "*O lente, lente currite noctis equi.*"

Two railroads afforded entrances to Georgetown, which is on the main north-to-south line of the Katy (Missouri, Kansas and Texas) railroad. The I & GN (International and Great Northern, later amalgamated with the Missouri Pacific) ran a branch, no longer operating, from Round Rock to Georgetown. One time the ticket agent at Beeville routed me over the I & GN. After spending a good part of the day in San Antonio, I took the I & GN to Round Rock, got off there about midnight, found my way to the hotel, in front of which a lantern was burning, and rang a cow bell at the door. A stringy-haired, mother-hubbarded, barefooted young woman whose name I later learned was Kate, met me and escorted me to a room. She was not designed to arouse interest in a young man whose ideals were the Blessed Damozel, La Belle Dame sans Merci, Highland Mary, Queen Guinevere, Maid of Athens, and several other ladies fairer than the evening air. In fact, I doubt if she ever interested any man. I would have to wait in Round Rock until the following afternoon to catch a train to Georgetown, about eight miles away. But for a heavy bag I should have walked.

The next day was a Sunday following New Year's. The hotel proprietor was known to drummers — now called salesmen — over the country as Old Lady Smith, and they circulated a parcel of yarns about her. According to one, a drummer bawled out Kate one morning at breakfast because his eggs were too soft. Sniffling, barefooted Kate took them back to the kitchen, where Old Lady Smith was cooking. After a good while Mrs. Smith appeared with a dozen eggs in a bowl. "I think you'll find them hard enough," she said. "Thank you, I only want two," the drummer replied. "You'll eat the dozen right here and right now," Mrs. Smith said, displaying a butcher knife, "and if you ever say another cross word to Kate you'll have to get your throat sewed up before you can swallow a bite." The drummer ate the dozen hard-boiled eggs.

At dinner we had turkey hash. Three or four regular boarders made the regular jokes about left-over turkey, Mrs. Smith out-roughing them. I considered the hash and everything else good enough but didn't want a rehelping and declined when Mrs. Smith passed the dish a second time. "Young man, don't you get fresh with me," she said, "or you'll have turkey hash running out your ears." After dinner while we were sitting on the front gallery waiting for train time, a man who had been downed by life shuffled by. "I wonder what that damned old codger is doing out today," Mrs. Smith remarked. That was the first time I had heard a woman use "damn."

Association with womankind in our college was at this date about as limited as in any academy strictly for men. Both sexes attended the classes and might greet each other, but it was against rules for them to converse in the halls or even walk up the stairs side by side. Once a month the Woman's Annex gave a reception at which the more sophisticated men got in plenty of talk — in full view of company — with their girls. About all we country greenhorns did was to be escorted from girl to girl sitting receptively in chairs. I fell slightly in love with one girl but never said anything to her about the matter. In my senior year I really fell in love with the girl I later married but had no opportunity, at least no opportunity surmountable by my timidity, to bring up the subject of love until we were out of college.

Despite a more than casual interest in writing, nothing inside me cried out to be delivered. A file of the college literary magazine shows that I wrote pieces on Robert E. Lee and Napoleon; I remember the admirations, now ashes, but the compositions have utterly vanished from memory. One on a dying vaquero has not. He was imagined out of an old Mexican who had driven horses up the trail with my father and in my boyhood, too stiff to run cattle, took care of the remuda. I had him calling up the days of free grass and bountiful water. The day after the sketch was published, just as I was stepping out of Richardson's Book Store Dr. C. C. Cody stopped me and, in his always kind way, said, "Frank, your story is interesting enough to be in the *Youth's Companion*." It wasn't, but no critic's approval of a book attached to my name has lifted my spirit so high. It was very liftable. I had grown up on the *Youth's Companion*, anticipating its weekly coming as eagerly as a horse nickers for his morning corn.

I often yearned to write in "high astounding terms," but matter for those terms was lacking. I would have Hotspurred it to the bottom of the vasty deep to "pluck up drowned honour by the locks," but the deep was not in me, and for a writer that is the only place the deep can be. "Marlowe's mighty line" was the thing for me — and I never even tried to write a ditty. Inhaling with delight the loveliest lyrics of man's heritage, I had not the breath to exhale a single verse. Perhaps I felt then, in my late developing, what I have now long known: that while a certain amount of talent may approach mastery of craftsmanship, supreme literature comes only from that plus — the plus beyond craftsmanship, though through it — of energy, of passion and of power not so much possessed by as possessing genius. Wise men have simmered down the definition of genius to "a supreme capacity for taking pains." No amount of application and taking pains by a million writers of mere talent could in a million years produce the electricity in

Was this the face that launch'd a thousands ships,
And burnt the topless towers of Ilium?

or in:

Absent thee from felicity awhile,
And in this harsh world draw thy breath in pain
To tell my story.

or in:

Golden lads and girls all must,
As chimney-sweepers, come to dust.

I longed for the magic of the stars and the soul of a North Sea storm. I wanted to look into eyes that would burn holes through a saddle blanket, under a light that never was on sea or land, perhaps

Where burning Sappho loved and sung.

Still, no urge impelled me to venture forth and begin sucking the juices out of life. In fact, I would have done nearly anything to put off leaving college. I wrote a few short newspaper articles against the proposal to move Southwestern University to Dallas. The church finally decided to establish Southern Methodist University at Dallas and leave Southwestern where it was. Prolongation of the present was about all I wanted. I had not yet formulated the maxim *Never let the future interfere with the present*, but I was acting upon it.

Up until a few months before Commencement I had settled on no profession or employment, but had ruled out ranching. I was just drifting. Time was of little consequence. Finally I decided to teach English, for a while at least — in order to keep on reading poetry and to communicate it. The recourse was not forced, as it was with an academical-natured English instructor I later knew. He had, he said, "no aptitude for anything else." I seemed to be afraid that if I got away from poetry, "shades of the prison house" would close down and make me no better than one of the damned. This fragile vase in which the flowers were to be kept fresh might crack on any rough road. I had the tender shrinking from actuality expressed in a shriek I once heard a girl emit at sight of a cow trampling down bluebonnets. Had I joined the Madero revolution in Mexico, as I had an impulse to do late in the year, I should not have experienced a hothouse shock at finding, not long afterwards, a small marble bust of Edgar Allan Poe stuck away, temporarily I suppose, in a men's toilet at Fordham University — a Poe "shrine."

Teaching in a college was beyond my ambition at the hour. Nor had I the faintest intimation of the hard fact that in most universities a passion for literature and an ability to engender that passion in students has little weight with Ph.D.'d sanhedrins in advancing an English instructor.

The accidents of time and place and the complex weavings of myriad threads in the spinning of a human life make it almost impossible for a person to say that this man, this book, or any other single fact has determined his course. Charles Darwin inclined to the belief "that education and environment produce only a small effect on the mind of anyone, and that most of our qualities are innate." The qualities yes, but if Darwin had been put out as a child with and had become one of the gauchos about whom he wrote in *Voyage of the Beagle*, he would hardly have gone on the voyage that led to *The Origin of Species* and a revolution in human thinking. An English teacher named Albert Shipp Pegues did not create a quality in me, but he cultivated one and seems to have been largely responsible for my decision to teach.

CHAPTER ELEVEN

A Schoolteacher in Alpine

After four years (1906-1910) at Southwestern University, I was soon to graduate with an A.B. degree. I had not yet settled on a career, had not resolutely applied myself to anything, had merely drifted, reading what I wanted to read, neglecting courses that required application of will, wasting much time that I did not want to waste on "bull sessions." I had found the drifting so pleasant that I did not want to leave college, college town, and college friends. Had I announced that I was going to be a preacher, my mother would have been equally surprised and pleased. My father never advised me beyond the simple injunction to live an upright life and to "be a man, or a mouse or a bob-tailed rat."

When, in my senior year, I enrolled for a course in Education, I must have had some notion of teaching — teaching English. Without any consideraton of a professional career, I drifted into teaching solely because I had fallen in love with English poetry and wanted to continue and communicate that love. The course in Education spurred nothing in me and added not a whit to my fitness to teach anything or anybody. Many collegians took it as a crip. Everything I took was a crip: if I liked it, it was easy; if I didn't like it, I took it easy.

A state law — promulgated by the Education hoaxers —

required credit for nine hours of their pabulum in order to get a teacher's certificate. Any moron who slept through the classes could have got the credit. The Educators, working according to "Parkinson's Law" — the incestuous law of all bureaucracies — later demanded more and more Education courses for a certificate to teach. I learned, in nine months, to open the schoolroom windows if it was warm and to close them if it was cold. Though air conditioning has revoked that particular banality, the course I took over half a century ago remains as modern as spaceships. The majority of Educators, including high-school executives, their minds dulled by quackery and prevented by quackery from becoming cultivated in a civilized way, develop into quacks themselves. I have never encountered one possessed of a first-class mind, though I have encountered a few fairly good ones. Many are dull well-meaners, cunning climbers, exponents of the paltry, and, worst of all, quellers of eager, searching intelligence — especially of intelligence lodged in teachers not willing to knuckle. Education-molded executives are usually strong on religion. Considering their contribution of flabbiness rather than of fiber to the minds of tens of millions of Americans during the twentieth century, I accuse them of having been far more lethal enemies to society than all the Communists dreamed up by the late Senator Joe McCarthy along with all the Communists put down in his books by FBI Hoover. The history of education, be it added, is a legitimate subject.

I am better acquainted with the public school system of Texas than with that of other states, but corruption by Educators is common to all. The Texas State Teachers Association, largely financed by dues from genuine teachers, is dominated by superintendents and their lackeys. The powerful teacher lobby is operated by them. In Texas, and in Mississippi alone among other states, the legislative objective of the teacher lobby is confined to salaries — and the more teachers a superintendent has under him, the higher his salary. The conception of education held by these superintendents is mostly limited to what can be bought with money — buildings and equipment, to winning athletic teams, and patriotic palaver. They are as mouthy on patriotism as on religion.

In the Education-wheels-within-Education-wheels procedure for selecting and adopting textbooks, all bought by the state, a few bona fide teachers are given a sop, but the Educators ruthlessly rule. Crammed to the upper end of their gullets with Education courses on "methods," they cannot distinguish between intellectual vitality in writing and neon sign flashiness. They take theatricality for humanity and banal moralisms for thought. Dullness in schoolbooks is not boresome to them; dullness is their trade; it is safer than vitality. The few and scattered superintendents with a civilized sense of values and with a realization of what intellectual integrity means are powerless against the crassminded dominators — the climactic product of Education.

I have turned aside, not unconsciously, from a relation of my own schoolteacher experiences. Southwestern University, like other colleges, had a bureau supplying information on teaching jobs. I recall applying to only two schools, both in Texas. From the superintendent at Amarillo I received a questionnaire on Southern ancestry, church affiliation, and other personal matters. I could have answered in a way to influence people, but did not propose to suffocate intellectually. A job was open at Alpine for principal and English teacher. I applied and was hired — without questionnaire. I spent the summer reporting funerals and fires on the San Antonio *Express* at $15 a week and had such a good time that I rather wished I hadn't tied myself up for a teaching job. The newspaper offered me a dollar raise if I would stay. The teaching job paid a hundred dollars a month.

I traveled from San Antonio to Alpine on a Southern Pacific Railroad train, and every mile I looked out upon was a new world. I liked it. Alpine, a cowtown set among the mountains of west Texas, had a new schoolhouse, and near it a new boardinghouse designed especially for teachers. There weren't enough teachers to keep it going, and among the other boarders were a man who drove the stage — an automobile — from Alpine to Fort Stockton and back every day; a bookkeeper; the county attorney; the owner and operator of a pool hall; a consumptive from Gonzales who hoped the dry air would cure him. The pool hall operator was the largest-natured and otherwise the best man of the lot. While he was gone from town one day his hall caught fire. I led in removing the billiard tables. After that we were silent friends to each other, though I never entered his "place of business." I have never learned to play billiards for the same reason I have never learned to play poker; there have always been more interesting ways to spend time. I was the only man on the school faculty except "Professor" Page, the superintendent. Three or four of the single women teachers roomed as well as boarded in the house where I also had a room. We teachers, especially the women, were rather patronized by the worldly-wise boarders. I soon came to feel at home with various people of the town. Several had come from the lower country — my country — to Brewster County while it was open range.

One December night I had sat in my upstairs room grading papers and preparing lessons for the next day. About midnight I began reading *Treasure Island*. If I had read it earlier, I have no recollection of the fact. The first chapter released me. I read on utterly absorbed. I was reading this passage: "When we were about half through with the counting, I heard in the silent, frosty air a sound that brought my heart into my mouth — the tap-tapping of the blind man's stick upon the frozen road." At this instant in my reading a fresh norther banged open the door at the end of the hallway and scurried loose paper down the hall. For a moment I thought old blind Pew himself, with his stick, was walking there. My hair stood on end. The wind was icy cold. I got under the blankets. Sleep was impossible. I finished *Treasure Island* before a daybreak nap. It wasn't the wind that took me away. It was Robert Louis Stevenson, master taleteller.

I went to church nearly every Sunday, and had as well pause to say that this year marked the end of my regular church attendance, soon to become regular nonattendance. At no period in my life could I have joined my mother in one of her favorite verses from the Psalms: "I was glad when they said unto me, 'Let us go into the house of the Lord.' " After services in the Methodist church at Alpine, I went regularly to dinner with Mr. and Mrs. W. B. Hancock. He had driven cattle up the trail to Kansas and sometimes took me to his ranch out from town. I became almost one of the Hancock family. Some people thought I should teach a Sunday School class; I didn't.

I had plenty of teaching in the school, though "principal" was purely an honorary title. I suppose Mr. Page did some supervision, but remember his coming into my room only once. A man of common sense and imagination, he had a hearty laugh and had not suffered the intellectual stultification that most superintendents and other school executives exhibit after having tamely submitted to multiplied Education courses. I had no trouble with discipline. Perhaps I flogged a boy or two. The chairman of the trustees came to me once and told me that if I whipped his son, the son would rebel and quit school. He made no threats; he just told me the fact. I managed not to whip the son; he gave no trouble but learned nothing. He had only one thing on his mind — if consciousness is mind. That was sex. This was before Hollywood and then TV, along with *Tropic of Cancer*, *Lady Chatterley's Lover*, and the likes "corrupted our youth." It was not before Adam. The lad was not alone among the pupils in arriving at the explosive age of puberty. No discipline of mind or interest in anything else had prepared him to take sex as a part of the whole instead of as the whole thing.

My pupils varied. Shy, bold, genial, generous-natured, they were for the most part as intelligent as university professors. I asked Georgia if she had "gone over" an assigned book. "Twice," she replied. Then, too honest to deceive, she, laughing and blushing, explained that she had "gone over" the book by stepping over it. A kid would try to embarrass me by asking, "What is a cowchip?" I would refer him to the unabridged dictionary with which, thanks to Mr. Page, my room was furnished. I look back upon these kids with fondness. I was young myself. I call them *pupils*. A *student* is one of some maturity who studies. Before long, I suppose, the kindergarten infants will be called "students."

I don't remember how many courses I taught in English, maybe only two. I was assigned a course in history, a course in Spanish, though I knew almost no grammar and spoke "cowpen Spanish"; a course in geology, one in physical geography, and maybe something else. My knowledge of geology was confined to two facts: I knew the difference between flint and limestone, and I knew that the theory of evolution was inherent in geology. A very limited knowledge of the theory did not prevent my setting out to convert the heathen to it. (To scientists it is no longer a "theory.") I found a little to read on the subject. It was more interesting to me than the Pleistocene Age, the Miocene Age, and so on. My unorthodox — to fundamentalists — views were carried home by some schoolchildren, and before long, as Mr. Page told me with a laugh, a fundamentalist trustee, very pious in his profession, wanted to fire me. He did not have his way. Had Darwin's writings been available I would have prolonged the evolutionary theme, but as it was I soon ran out of soap.

The town — and county — supported two weekly newspapers, the Alpine *Avalanche*, run by Mr. Yates, and the Alpine *Guide*, run by Bill Easterling, who had roved far and often as a newspaper man. I established a school monthly called the *Alpenstock*, editing it and prevailing on some pupils to write for it. After Christmas I stirred my pupils up to produce a play. Nothing short of Shakespeare would do. Josephine Linn acted Lady Macbeth, and I took on Macbeth. I don't remember how Banquo and other characters came off.

The *Alpenstock* was printed by Bill Easterling, an intelligent talker. He told me one day that he had known Roy Bean, "Law West of the Pecos," well. He had run a newspaper in Del Rio, to which Langtry, where Roy Bean held out, was tributary. He was going to write a life of Roy Bean, he said. Along in the 20s, after I had become active in collecting and writing down — or up — the lore of the Southwest, I learned that Bill Easterling had moved to Ozona. While I was out in that country, I stopped to talk with him about Roy Bean.

"How are you getting along on that book?" I asked.

"Oh, I decided there wasn't any use for me to write it. It's already written."

"Who wrote it?"

"I don't remember the fellow's name, but I read it."

That was the end of our conversation on Roy Bean. Whiskey had not helped Bill Easterling's memory.

I went on west to Alpine and hunted up Jim Wilson, a cowman and a mighty interesting talker. I gave him Bill Easterling's word on a book about Roy Bean.

"Why," he said, "there never was any such book written, much less printed, but maybe Bill Easterling saw or heard of the fellow who was going to write one. He was a kind of tramp schoolteacher. When he got to Langtry he found Roy Bean's saloon a congenial place. After hearing Roy Bean talk and hearing some of the talk about him, he told Roy that somebody ought to write his life and he'd like to do it. Old Roy always kept any clipping about himself in a trunk. He was terribly wrapped up in himself. He offered to board the tramp schoolteacher if he would stay and write his life. He stayed three months or so. Board included beer as well as frijoles. When he was awake he was too beery to write, and when he was asleep he couldn't write. Old Roy finally fired him — sent him on west. That's the life of Roy Bean that Bill Easterling read."

The first of three books on Roy Bean — the faker — became available within a few years. Jim Wilson told me of another book that never saw the light. One of the characters of the Big Bend yet traditional was Alice Stillwell Henderson. Stillwell Crossing on the Rio Grande perpetuates the name. Her husband got into trouble and for years she kept on ranching without any man to boss her. One time she crossed alone, except for her.30-.30 rifle in a scabbard and a six-shooter, into Mexico on the trail of thieves who had driven away several of her horses. She came back with the horses. Every man and woman who knew her, though women were mighty scarce over her range, respected her. Jim Wilson said that when cow people got together to work the unfenced Big Bend country, Miss Alice might ride into camps at any hour. When she did, talk became careful without being cramped and at night some man would persuade her to take his pallet and put down a little to one side, while he doubled up with another man.

One time, Jim Wilson said, the cow crowd camped for several days near the Henderson ranch house. He took to noticing a light in it late every night. Mrs. Henderson was riding with the cow hunters — in very rough, brushy country. One morning when she joined them, as usual before daylight, he said to her, "Miss Alice, you seem to be sitting up mighty late these nights. I see your light." "Yes," she replied, "I am writing the life of Sally Skull."

Wondering if the Sally Skull book had ever got written, I went on from Jim Wilson at Alpine to Fabens, Texas, below El Paso, to interview a son of Mrs. Henderson's. Yes, he said, his mother had written about Sally Skull; he did not know how much. The manuscript, the last time he saw it, was in an old leather trunk left as worthless in a house on the Kokernot ranch north of Alpine. A man working for the Kokernots assured me the trunk was no longer there; he remembered when it was. I have often blamed myself for not having taken a look myself and pursued detective procedure in trying to locate the manuscript.

Going back to my schoolteaching, Alpine didn't have a picture show, and radio was as yet hardly dreamed of. Looking at the sunset was one of my chief entertainments. Nearly every evening I walked toward it, watching the deep shadows from the mountains come over the land, and then the fire disappear beyond. I was always alone on these sunset walks. At Christmas I went with a pupil of mine named Harris and his father in a wagon up into the mountains to hunt. We must not have been on good hunting grounds, for no one of us even got a shot at a deer.

The Madero Revolution had started. I had been in college with Vicente Ramos from the Ojinaga country across from Presidio on the Rio Grande. He somehow learned that I was in Alpine and about the first of December I received a letter from him inviting me to spend Christmas on his parents' ranch. I had a strong inclination to join Francisco I. Madero in revolution against the old dictator Don Porfirio Díaz. Had I gone across the river and gotten a good taste of realities from Vicente and his people, I might not have kept on as schoolteacher.

An elderly, gray gentleman, English and gentle, with his wife ran a tailor shop in Alpine, making clothes to order. They made me a gray suit of such durability that I thought it never would wear out. The world was as yet far from being mechanized. A Mexican bakery sold lightbread. The only heat was from wood and kerosene stoves. Wagons pulled by burros as well as mules hauled freight to Terlingua, where quicksilver was mined, down near the foot of the Big Bend.

The Alpine character most arousing to my imagination was "Doctor" Stuart, who filled prescriptions and sold everything for sale in Bob Slight's drugstore. His speech was as Scottish as *Tam o'Shanter*, and his contempt for fools was as strong as that exemplified by Carlyle when he wrote across the front page of an unsolicited manuscript, "A pack of damned nonsense, you poor unfortunate fool." He admired Hume. Some people considered him an infidel. Nobody could have shown less concern for their suffrages. On St. Patrick's Day he flaunted an orange ribbon in his buttonhole. I don't remember now whether he or someone else told me that he had attended the University of Edinburgh. Anyhow, after coming to America — and there were surmises on why he had left Scotland — he served in some capacity with the commissary department of an army expedition sent out against Indians of the West.

He ended his military career as a sutler or sutler's clerk at Fort Davis in the mountains twenty-four miles northwest of Alpine. He had acquired some knowledge of medicine and after the army abandoned the post stayed on as a pharmacist, in time coming to Alpine. He was not a licensed pharmacist but could read a doctor's hieroglyphics and mix drugs. He knew more about patent medicines than any doctor around.

The Mexican population relied on him absolutely and bought whatever remedio he prescribed. I saw him once administer physic to a pain-racked old Mexican reprobate, maledicting him all the while with the utmost of contempt — but bringing him relief, even if only temporary. "Everybody is temporary," Doc Stuart would say.

There was a hard glitter in his eye. He was reputed to have killed a man, but I can't imagine anyone's asking him for facts on the matter. He wore a fringe of gray-red hair, not long, around his bald head and hobbled about the drugstore in carpet slippers like some character in an ancient novel recovering from the gout. He was in demand for mixing punch at certain convivial gatherings of men only.

He lived by himself in a two-room shack, the yard in which it stood enclosed by barbed wire. If he had visitors, I was not among them. He was said to be a woman-hater — another subject we did not discuss. His lack of deference to schoolgirls coming in to buy was marked. A Mexican woman cleaned his shack once in a while and washed his clothes. He never asked about anybody else's business and never spoke of his own. Other people talked about it. Rumor went that he had married somewhere, sometime, high up in society but had broken away from the marriage yoke. One day, rumor continued, when the west-bound transcontinental train stopped at Alpine, Doc Stuart and various other citizens having, according to custom, stepped over to the station from the front street to meet it, a finely dressed lady of proud carriage descended from a Pullman. While the porter was watching her bags, she asked some man where she might find Mr. James B. Stuart.

"Yonder he is," the man said, pointing to Doc Stuart, who stood — in his carpet slippers — a little apart. The lady approached him. What words were passed, nobody heard, but the glowering that Doc Stuart gave her everybody saw. The fireman was ringing the bell, the conductor was calling "All aboard!" The lady rushed back to the porter and, followed by her luggage, disappeared into the car.

In the back end of the drugstore a few books, some of them standard novels, took up about three feet of shelf space. If one was sold during my time, I did not miss it. Occasionally after supper I would walk the few blocks to town and step in for talk with Doc Stuart. If he were busy, I'd go to the bookshelf and read a page or so before he came. One night I began quizzing him if he had read this title and that title. Incensed at my impertinence, he burst out, "Young man, it's not many books worth the reading known to you that I hae not read." He did tell me on another occasion that he had read every book written by Sir Walter Scott. He was a great hand to quote Burns.

In those years of callow sentimentality I inclined to moralisms more than I have in the long period of mature-mindedness that I now enjoy. While I was idling with Doc Stuart one evening, three flouncing, giggling young females came in, spent two bits, and left in loud laughter. When Doc Stuart returned to where I stood, shaking his head, I quoted this quatrain:

That loud and boisterous laugh
May attract the attention of some,
But will never win by half
The praise that modesty's won.

"Who wrote that?" Doc Stuart asked.

"Robert Burns."

"I don't believe it. I never saw it in Burns."

I had my copy of Burns studied in college and the next day handed it to the salty old Scot with the page open on the quatrain. He wasn't the kind to think he knew it all, but was taken aback.

As most reading people in the English-speaking world, especially in the South, knew during the last century and as they passed on the knowledge to my generation, Sir Walter Scott wrote his first novel under the name of Waverley. "Nobody knew who Waverley was," Doctor Stuart told me, "until one night at our house [in Scotland] the talk after dinner turned on *Waverley*. Everybody had read it. Somebody pointed out an anachronism in the novel. Walter Scott had been listening and not saying anything until at this point he forgot himself and exclaimed, 'I meant to look up more history on that point.' After that everybody knew who Waverley was." That was Doc Stuart's story. Anybody who wants to check on him can look into Lockhart's life of Scott, which I did not read until 1917. It remains one of the most fascinating biographies of my reading career. I should not care to reread *Ivanhoe*, but, as Lockhart said, Scott the man was greater, more ample, than the writer.

Not long after I left Alpine the death of a baby there was attributed to Doc Stuart's mistake in filling a doctor's prescription. He had all along been mixing drugs contrary to law. His life as a pharmacist was ended. I never learned how he died.

When I left Alpine in the summer of 1911 my career as teacher in public schools ended, though I was still fumbling around in the dark. I threw away a year and a half as teacher (for a few months) in the Preparatory School — long since dropped — of Southwestern University at Georgetown, then as secretary to the president. The next time I got back to Alpine, along in the 20s, I was teaching English at the University of Texas and was writing — for joy and for money.

I had known John Young, real estate dealer — he could never have graduated into a "realtor" — in Alpine, but had never actually conversed with him. He now wanted to talk about my collaborating on his reminiscences. He had been mavericker, brush-popper, trail-driver, hunter for the Lost Nigger Mine; and he owned "a mountain of marble" down in the Big Bend country. His ambition was to make enough money off the book to build a marble hotel in San Antonio, where the cow people of southwest Texas would be at home. The outcome of our association was my first trade book, published in 1929, *A Vaquero of the Brush Country*. It did not fully satisfy Mr. Young, for I put into it a great deal of background related to but apart from his experiences. I made him more a figure of the earth than the hero of his own imaginings. Without my knowledge of the fact — for I have never been analytical of self — I was moving toward the point of view that everything is kin to everything else. *A Vaquero of the Brush Country* is still in print — as are most of my books — but the royalties on it were never enough to build the marble hotel.

Had I not gone to Alpine to teach school I should hardly have written *A Vaquero of the Brush Country*, but most assuredly I would have written. *Coronado's Children*, my next book (1930), owes the full story of "The Lost Nigger Mine," one of its best chapters, to Alpine beginnings.

A character of the town during my year there was Allen Palmer. He had been one of Quantrill's men during the Civil War, was tall, slender, erect, proud, reserved. On a summer trip to Alpine shortly before *A Vaquero* got published, I was in John Young's real estate office leading him out on something when Allen Palmer entered. I deduced from the conversation that "the vaquero," as John Young later liked to call himself, though the title to the book was mine, had rented a cottage to the Quantrill veteran. At that time many consumptives went West to live in a high, dry climate, and Alpine had its quota of them.

"Well, Allen," Mr. Young asked, "are you ready to move in?"

"Yes," he replied, "the old lady and I went there this morning and fornicated all over the house."

The relation of fumigating to fornicating may not be logical, but neither John Young nor I cracked a smile. His humor was more bucolic than mine. I left some of it out of the book — as I have left love and all that out of this sketch of Alpine experiences.

CHAPTER TWELVE

Columbia University in the City of New York

I HAD decided to teach English beyond high school level, and with this purpose in mind, early in January, 1913, set out for Columbia University in New York to take a Master's degree. Actually, I wasn't much concerned with my career. I had only a vague, dim conception of what was involved in university or college teaching. I knew that it took a whole year to get a Master's degree. I planned to use at least a year and a half. I was young enough not to have any idea that time would ever run out.

I had saved a little money — I don't know how much. After a while I wrote my father to sell a few cattle I had and send me the money. I suppose that later on he added something to what I needed.

I went by train, the only way to travel from Georgetown, Texas, to New York. I don't remember how I got out to Columbia University from the Grand Central Railroad Station. It may have been by the subway. That came to be the only means of transportation in New York that I used.

I enrolled in Columbia University and had a room in Livingston Hall, a men's dormitory. I stayed there until about June of 1914. New York gave me more than the university gave me. For a while I kept a kind of diary, but after looking it over a few years ago, I was so disgusted with the sentimentality in it that I destroyed it.

Soon after arriving in New York I went to the Metropolitan Museum of Art and thereafter went many a time on Saturday or Sunday. One could go to the Metropolitan in the forenoon, procure a substantial lunch there at a small price, and stay all afternoon. One of the pictures I observed and went back to frequently was of purple-colored snow in the woods. New York and the country around it were at that time covered with snow. It all looked white to me except where darkened with dirt, smoke, and coal dust. One sunny winter day when I went across the Hudson River as I often did to be alone in the country, I saw snow under trees that had a purple tint. The cast of light made the coloring. I had not yet read in Oscar Wilde that nature follows art, but I had learned that art and literature open one's eyes to realities.

The subway station for Columbia University was at 116th Street. One could go up to 125th Street and get a ferry across the Hudson River to the Palisades in New Jersey. One could walk in the woods, feeling he was in the country far from the clanging city, clear down to Hackensack, New Jersey. All that land is in pavement and houses now.

One of the first places I went to see downtown in New York was Broadway at Times Square. Many of the theaters then, as now, were in the region, and I went to them two or three times a week. I paid less than a dollar for a ticket in the galleries. As I look back, I am sure that I received more from New York theaters than from Columbia professors.

I had read Shakespeare's plays in college, but only now in the theater did they begin to accumulate connotations. Marlowe and Southern, names still high in the world of actors and actresses, were playing a long repertoire of Shakespearean plays. Miss Marlowe was getting along in years, but her Juliet was as fresh and lovely as any April flower and more tragic than Ophelia in *Hamlet.* Three times I went to hear Forbes-Robertson play *Hamlet.* He made the man Hamlet as unaged as the play itself is ageless. After I came to Austin to teach in the University of Texas, Forbes-Robertson played *Hamlet* in the Hancock Opera House. I went to see him again. I never saw him off the stage, would not have had the effrontery to speak to him anywhere.

After I came away from Forbes-Robertson's *Hamlet* in New York the gravediggers, the players within the play, the ghost of Hamlet's father, the platitudinous but profound Polonius, his unwise son, Hamlet's mother, Hamlet's friend Horatio, and above all Hamlet himself would for a long while remain more real to me than the throngs in the streets, the people going into restaurants to eat, the policemen on horseback, horse cabs among automobile cabs, streams of people going in and out of subway trains, night-time walkers across the campus of Columbia University, students I saw at breakfast, students I saw in lecture rooms, professors I heard lecturing. I wanted a skull even though I could not expect the particular skull picked up by a gravedigger in the play:

> Alas, poor Yorick! I knew him, Horatio: a fellow of infinite jest, of most excellent fancy; he hath borne me on his back a thousand times. Where be your jibes now? Your gambols? Your songs? Your flashes of merriment, that were wont to set the table on a roar?

Scores of times I have taught *Hamlet*, *Romeo and Juliet*, *Othello*, *King Lear*, plays dominated by Falstaff, and other Shakespearean plays to classes of college sophomores. Never once has anything in Shakespeare palled on me. Life has provided me many good things to be thankful for. Foremost among them Shakespeare will remain to the end.

Madame Pavlova made a deeper impression on me in ballet than most actors and actresses I saw on the stage. Lady Gregory brought the Abbey Theater cast from Dublin. I was present the night they started playing and heard Senator Cochran, an Irishman, make a speech. There had been a riot in Dublin over the production of Synge's *Riders to the Sea*, a somewhat satiric play on Irish nature. A riot was expected in New York, but it didn't amount to anything. The best known Irish accomplishment in New York was Tammany Hall.

One of the noted characters of the city was Emma Goldman. I have heard her referred to as "Red Emma," but at that time communism was of little consequence on either side of the Atlantic Ocean. She would make speeches evincing enormous vitality. I remember her talking about the "solidarity of labor." Labor unions at that time were considered by some to be as un-American as the House Un-American Activities Committee proved itself to be in the time of McCarthyism. I didn't get any ideas from Emma Goldman — only glimpses of another world and a feeling of vitality. In those days I had few ideas about anything, but I can't remember when I was not on the side of rebels. Columbia University gave me nothing of rebel ideas. The country is always needing rebels in thought.

One day I visited the New York Stock Exchange and was excited by the extreme excitement and energy of brokers on the floor below me, buying and selling stocks. I didn't know any more about stocks than I know now about atomic power. Not long after I viewed the brokers and their wild energy I went to Wall Street on a Sunday morning. It was as silent and as deserted of traffic as the woods in New Jersey.

I don't remember whether it was a nickel or a dime that one paid in ordinary saloons downtown for a glass of beer that entitled him to a sandwich or two at the counter. This was the cheapest way to eat. I took most of my meals at the University Commons. In time several of us got to going to an upstairs restaurant across Amsterdam Avenue from Livingston Hall.

Among my eating companions I remember Harvey Hatcher

Hughes of North Carolina. He was a monitor for Professor Brander Matthews, under whom I took more than one course. Hughes kept class records and also, I understood, graded our themes and examination papers. He was writing a play, and this play later had a short run on Broadway. He had a room across from mine in Livingston Hall, and I came to know him fairly well. Dick Jones was another table companion. He was taking a Ph.D. at Columbia. His brother Bob Jones, studying economics, as I recall, was often with us. They were sons of the Dr. Jones who once ran an academy for boys at Salado, Texas, and who was a Latin and Greek scholar.

We never had to stand in line at the Amsterdam Avenue restaurant. A table was always waiting for us and a particular waitress was always ready to serve us. She said to call her Sally, but I can't think that was her original name. She had a Swedish look and a Swedish build and was the personification of good nature. I came to notice that on a bill or check she would take about ten per cent off the menu price. The standard tip was ten per cent; her deduction allowed us to pay the tip without digging up anything extra. The cashier seemed to be the manager, and I noticed once or twice that he scrutinized the check, but he never questioned any of us. One evening at supper Sally told us she was going to be married. We decided to give her a wedding present. I was put in charge of the money and bought a cut glass tray, a pitcher and some glasses. The supper at which we presented this glassware to Sally was as much an event for us as it could have been for her. The dishonesty in which she led us didn't bother us and never has bothered me. We missed her after she married and went away. I remember her far better than I remember most of the students with whom I was associated.

The Columbia student who made the strongest impression on my imagination was a man, also of Livingston Hall, well up in his forties, I judged — a veritable ancient to most of us.

Everybody knew him by sight and by legend. He was a sport in dress and often went out from the lobby swinging a gold-headed cane. According to established rumor, he was the inheritor of a will providing that he receive annually five thousand dollars — real money in those days — so long as he advanced his education by studying in Columbia University. He had been enrolled for more than twenty years. He took as few courses as the regulations allowed and had to pass a certain number of them in order not to flunk out. He had splattered around in various fields. He always looked to be satisfied with life and was said to have no prospect of ever graduating from the will that benefited him.

When I went to Columbia my mind needed discipline. It was not seeking discipline, however, and therefore got only a very limited amount of it, though it did drink in a lot of life both in and outside of books. I received credit for a course in Anglo-Saxon without mastering anything of the language. I failed a course in Renaissance literature because I could not write an examination essay on "Platonism in the Renaissance Age." Platonism did not interest me, but at least three books I read in the course became a part of me: (1) the autobiography of Benvenuto Cellini, who was drunk with life; (2) Rabelais, who was drunker and less guarded; (3) Margaret of Navarre's *Heptameron*, some of the stories in which appeal to me as being more vivid and naughtier than stories in the more famous *Decameron* of Boccaccio.

The liveliest, wittiest and most famous professor of English in Columbia University was Brander Matthews. He was a playwright, essayist, and critic, and, I gathered, moved in the most sophisticated circles of literary people, actors, and artists. He taught courses in Shakespeare, at least two of which I took, but he had no interest in the Ph.D. kind of learning. Some of his classes were widely attended, and in the first one I took I found what I had in Texas been warned to expect. That was the presence of Negroes, both men and women. I soon came to regard them in place, as much so as I regarded a few nuns in the same class, or as I had grown up regarding Mexican vaqueros in a cow camp. This was the beginning of my conversion to the idea that Negroes have as much right to an education as anybody else.

In his class talks — hardly formal lectures — Brander Matthews was a fertile teller of anecdotes. Harvey Hatcher Hughes one day said to me: "Brander" — a familiar name that a good many people gave Professor Matthews to his back — "is going to Baltimore to deliver a lecture to a big gathering. He wants to sprinkle in a few of his anecdotes and can't think of those he has been telling in your course. I notice you keep notes. Maybe you can supply an anecdote or two."

"I might," I said.

I remember two that I called up. I have no idea whether Brander Matthews told them in Baltimore or what connection either had with Shakespeare.

One anecdote was of two brothers often seen at conversation parties. One of them was noted for witty remarks and the telling of character anecdotes. After Brander Matthews had encountered these brothers a few times and heard the bright one brighten, he began noticing that the obscure brother frequently in a quiet way gave openings or leads to the bright talk. Brander heard the same lead repeated and then repetition of the same bright talk. His conclusion was "repartee is repertoire."

Then there was the story of Henry Watterson, noted journalist and public speaker of the last century. Watterson had agreed to speak to some national convention of women in Kansas City and wrote a friend living there that he would need "something to drink" on the speaker's stand. This friend understood and took the matter up with the chairman of the speaker's committee.

"Oh, we'll have a pitcher of cold water on the stand," the lady assured him.

"You don't understand Colonel Watterson," the friend told her. "He is old and gets tired and needs refreshment now and then." Saying that he needed whiskey was not in place. "He likes a certain kind of milk. I know. We always have it for him in our house. I'll bring it myself in a silver pitcher that he favors."

The lady agreed. The friend brought the pitcher, tall and cold with ice, for the speaker and saw it placed, with a large silver cup, on the speaker's stand. Colonel Watterson began talking in the brilliant style for which he was noted, but before long his voice sank and he seemed to be tiring. He took a look into the contents of the pitcher, but made no move to pour. Indeed, his face expressed distaste. Before long it expressed a marked weariness.

Now Colonel Watterson paused, deliberately poured from silver pitcher into silver cup, instinctively sniffed it, drank, paused again, visibly brightening. He repoured, drank the cup empty, set it down, and exclaimed, "My God, what a cow!" The milk was spiked with some of the best whiskey that ever came out of Kentucky.

Another professor of English at Columbia University whom I remember was W. P. (William Porterfield) Trent but I don't remember anything he said. He authored a history of Southern literature, with extracts. I own it, but there is nothing in it for me now. A good part of the Southern literature represented in the book was written at a time when ideas contrary to slavery were as forbidden to Southern writers as positive ideas on civil rights are now foreign to any daily newspaper in Jackson, Mississippi.

Professor Trent had a manner of seeming to try to enlarge his stature by a stand-off attitude toward his students — toward me at least. One day while I was standing in his office waiting to speak to him while he attended to another student, I picked up from a table a collection of short stories edited by Brander Matthews. When he turned to me, I remarked that I had not known of this book. He replied nothing, as if to ask, "What now is your business with me?"

It was under him, however, that I read Boswell's *The Life of Samuel Johnson*. I bought a two-volume set, marked many passages, and at the end wrote: "I regret there are no more pages." It was the seventeenth day of August, 1913. I have reread passages here and there many times. It is the best biography ever written of any man. Like rain on grass in ranch country, it never fails to refresh and invigorate me.

CHAPTER THIRTEEN

Along Lake George

Written in 1913 as a "Log Book"

THE trip up the Hudson from New York City was divine, despite the fact that a tedious old advocate of Wall Street — a publisher of a trade journal — was with me all the way. Good God, how few people there are that do not bore me, and how I must bore them! Mr. Delano — that is his name — wants me to stop with him tomorrow at Saratoga — but if I know my heart I shall be sleeping tomorrow night under the heavens.

Albany I have not seen yet, since it was dark when we got here. But I appreciate the quatrain done in marble over the old Dutch fireplace of Keller's Hostelry across the street:

> *Who'er has travelled life's dull round,*
> *Where'er his stages may have been,*
> *May sigh to think he still has found*
> *His warmest welcome at an inn.*

Chauncey Depew is etched beneath!

On the way up the River old Mr. Delano started the subject of William Jennings Bryan. I was drinking in the river and wanted to let my thoughts soften and float away and away even beyond the gossamer blue veils that wrapped the distant Catskills in their gentleness, but courtesy demanded that I argue, though I admitted that I knew nothing and cared less about the currency problem. At night the old man took up his subject again, and I kept him up and made him so angry that he swore he "knew damned well now" that I knew nothing about this or any other politics. I prayed God fervently that I might never hear more of any of it.

Next morning I rose early and knew from the air that I was not in New York. After a walk and a breakfast I mounted State Street to see the capitol. The most satisfactory thing I found about it was that it is not so noble as the Texas one. It is built in the style of the French Renaissance, and E. A. Freeman thought it the château of some old marquis. Oh, it is rich and be-spired and be-frescoed and decorated, but it has not the lordly, the Calhoun-like dignity, the grandeur of the Austin pile. The senate chamber is wealth of work and brass, but would be more fit for a king's banquet hall. There is not a single monument on the grounds, and the approach from State Street, which might be made very stately and sweeping, is through an unkept lawn.

Leaving Albany, "Old Currency" and I took the trolley for Saratoga, forty miles away. The fare was fifty-five cents. It is a beautiful route, past apple trees with ripening fruit, over the Mohawk River, by a few little secure ponds and into the trees of Saratoga Village.

At Saratoga everybody bets on the races and nearly everybody drinks the water. There is a hotel large enough to accommodate a political party, with a court roomy enough to hold a convention in. I should like to go there for a week after having been in the country a year. As it was raining all afternoon and evening, I had to listen to Old Currency grind out his dictums — already twice heard — to two New York acquaintances we had made. I slept in the mess room of the YMCA for forty cents and had the most bevalleyed and bemountained bed I have ever had.

"It is my first night in Saratoga," I said to an old paralytic whose bed was near mine.

"I wish it were my first night," sighed he. "For forty years I have come, but I think the waters are helping me *this* year."

At eight o'clock Saturday morning I was on the trolley for Lake George, thirty miles away, and what a ride it was! The country was open and green like mine in springtime. The Adirondacks came and disappeared in their blue veils. Occasionally a farmer got off or on, and an old native told me about the North Hudson as we passed over it at Glens Falls. But my mind was following the misty phantoms of the far-away hills. Old Currency was behind and forgotten.

Presently we were in the mountains, we were cutting through them, we were catching glimpses of tarns and brooks, we were rounding a great curve, and we were over Lake George. I forgot to look at the little town at its head. I saw only a sea of shining water curving away around and between cliffs and slopes and little islands and green mountainsides, with a heaven of blue overhead.

At the town of Lake George I took the boat *Horizon* for a voyage all the way down the lake. Many people were on board: some of them had opera glasses to look through; some read the New York papers; some wrapped in great coats took the cabin. Every little while we would stop at a hotel or camp wharf, and it invigorated me to see the health and joy of the people who came down to wave us good morning.

Who said that the scenery of Lake George is not varied? Why, at every angle, at every degree's difference of the sun's height, at every changed distance from the shore's side the hues of water and mountain and heaven changed. There were just enough lazy clouds as light as smoke wreaths to tone the welkin.

Ne'er saw I, never felt, a calm so deep!

At Bodwin I got off, but finding no commissary there, took the branch line of the Delaware and Hudson for Ticonderoga. Ticonderoga is sprawled over and along the Ticonderoga Creek, which runs like a cramped cord through the neck of land joining lakes George and Champlain. It is characterized chiefly by its memorial tablets, by its pulp mills which ruin the flow of the stream and poison the waters, and by the remarkable success it has attained in making one of the most charming spots of earth squalid and unclean. But I think well of Ticonderoga for its host, as I shall tell.

To finish out the evening I made for a mountain in order to get a view of all the country. A native who drove a delivery horse as lean as himself advised me that a mountain six miles off, near Lost Pond, had a fine prospect. No, he had never been there, but he always wanted to go, for he had heard that one could see from it the whole lake almost. One of Barrie's men had always intended to go up to Grub Street, but old age found him still at cobbling; and thus be they long or short journeys — to a hill or to fame — we never take them, though we always intend to. And before long the old delivery horse will be too tired to travel that far and the delivery man will be too feeble.

After circumventing the town I climbed Mt. Defiance and saw, like a toy map with its depressions filled with silver, Champlain before me. I resolved to go to the brink. Plunging out of the forest into the roadside I met a woodmill hand who was going to town. He and his sister were all that were left of the family now; he was about thirty years old. No, he had not been very far down the lake. Fort Henry was just across the neck and I could cross on the railroad bridge.

And across I started, but saw fishing in a pool a fat, red-nosed, neither old nor young man with hair somewhere between yellow and white in color. He would have made a good eighteenth century innkeeper. I remonstrated with him for fishing in such shallow water and he roundly swore that the water was over my head. Had he a boat he could catch a hundred pounds of fish, but a boat cost fifty cents per hour. He told me a fine story about "scale fish" and gloried over how John Allen with thirteen men (eighty-three in fact) had put to flight a whole British army at Fort Ticonderoga, which was what the lumber hand had called Fort Henry. My fisherman had not seen Fort Henry; that was away several miles. When I asked him if I was on Vermont soil he looked reprovingly at me and said, "Thar whur you be." I remarked something about Mont*clam* — never could I remember the name — and he roared out Mont*calm*. Oh, I hated to leave him.

Old Fort Ticonderoga, owned and kept for the public by a patriotic Mr. Pell of New York, is an interesting place with a fine picture of Mont*calm's* death, which the French woman keeper said was "an awful thing." Below the hill are the remains of the *Revenge* — one of Arnold's rigs sunk by the British and raised by Mr. Pell.

I carried a pail of water from the spring for a girl camper, and she thanked me so prettily that all the way back the sunset seemed softer. I fell in with another mill man who told me that his neighbor's three children drowned the day before in the creek below. "They were all he had," he said. As we neared a hut a bevy of dirty, happy children came out shouting "Papa! Papa!"; and he took a little girl in his arms.

I don't remember ever having been so hungry. After a shave and a bath and a supper fit for the gods, while I smoked one of the best pipes I have ever smoked, mine host, Mort Allen, came into the lobby; no one else was there. He was a lumberman by trade, a fisherman by love, and a gentleman by nature. He told me of trips with French Canadian guides into the forests of Canada in dead of winter, of fishing places and of fishing luck, of great forest fires — and when I wished I could see a forest fire, he looked at me so dark that I hastened to add I would not wish for the fire.

The landlord's daughter who waited on the table would have fallen in love with me had I remained longer I am sure — so courteous was I. ("Gentlemen" did not frequent this inn.) With my bag of clothes and a sack of provisions and a roll of blanket I set forth on Sunday morning to make a camp, stopping occasionally to read a tablet "erected by the Ticonderoga Historical Society."

The boy whom I hired to row me around the rock told me how Roger's Slide had gotten its name. Roger, pursued by the Indians to its crest, had hurriedly stripped, rolled his clothes together, started them down the long, almost perpendicular slope and by this ruse escaped. But the boy lived in New York City; so he doubted the tale and said it was all right for a fish-story. I for my part was glad to accept it.

Now the next day I resolved to climb the mountain, not by the long back way but by the side next to my camp. I did climb straight up until I could climb no farther. I found myself on a ledge unable to go up or down. After an hour, two Ticonderoga fishermen came in sight, and they climbed far enough up to throw me a rope. The point, though, is this: the fishermen said the story about the rock was "a damned lie," that the name was given simply out of honor for a brave ranger of Revolutionary times called Roger.

That very night, though, I read in an old ponderous *History of Warren County, N.Y.* by one F. H. Smith that the rock was called Stalapose (meaning "sliding place") by the Indians, and that evil spirits there were supposed to capture the souls of bad warriors on their way to the Happy Hunting

Grounds and, sliding down the awful precipice, drown them in the lake. Henceforth I shall call the rock *Stalapose.*

That evening when in bathing I saw the sunshine on my feet as I stood up to my neck in water. At another place where I could see the bottom I was unable to dive to it.

When the moon was about two hours high, in the language of the barbarous about one o'clock,

> *I awoke and found me here*
> *On the cold hill's side.*

No more sleep that night, but shiverings and tossings and prayers for the sun. At last after two hours of daylight the sun did appear over the hills. I arose damning the whole world and my own schemes in general, but when, after making a fire, I went to wash in the lake and saw the dancing sunbars on the rocks far under the water, my heart became glad and my body fresh.

All the same I went to hunt a farmhouse to board at, and I found it just over the hill a mile away. As I came up through a cornfield, I enquired of the irresponsible-looking being I met, whom I took to be the hired man, where I might find a place to stay. Pointing toward the house, the red top of which I could just see, he directed me to ask "her," and said that if I could not get board there I might get it just "beyeand," where they kept "city people" last year but did not have any now, he "guessed."

As I turned into the open road that led directly in front of the house I decided that I *would* stay there. The comfortable-looking barns, the red brick two-story and attic house with a long red wooden wing extending back, the hammock swinging half in sunshine, half in shade under a great old maple out from one side of the house, the apple trees, the open stable — red, too — just across the road in front of the house, the careless profusion of old wagons and worn-out machinery in a tumbledown shed, the absence of any yard about the house, giving the whole an open and hospitable look, the man and boy hitching up a gray horse in the open stable — all decided me.

I addressed the man. He would see "Ella." The motherly soul, his wife, "guessed" she could take me, if I did not want too many extras. I think I did not look that morning like one who required extras. I settled in with the intention of staying three or four days, and stayed two never-to-be-forgotten weeks.

My first and best friend was Clyde. For a while I thought he was the hired man, then found that he was "his" stepson. Clyde always spoke of Mr. Matteson as "him." He swore like a pirate, yet he was as harmless as a calf. He may have been anywhere from twenty-eight to thirty-five years old, and was in my eyes a personification of Rip Van Winkle when young. I am sure he never hurried or took a quick step all the time I was with him. He gloated to me over the best job he ever had, driving a wagon which was loaded for him and which he could unload without getting out of his seat. It is true that he worked some, but he hunted and fished more and, as he said, each morning found him as eager to go as he was the day before. He had helped kill three bears once and of gentler animals he had slain his tens of thousands. He knew every trail like a dog, every fishing spot in Lake George, every pond for miles around, every blueberry and blackberry patch, every butternut tree, and his heart boiled out tales of hunts and fishings and "sprees" by the hour. Yes, Clyde did like spirituous liquors, and I am sure he liked me much better after the day we walked six miles to the village in the heat and the dust and washed all our troubles away. What a day that was! I remember that I was heartily sorry at getting some friendly letters and cursed myself for having bought a daily newspaper. I would not look through it.

But that day was no better than — not so good as — a dozen others. Most of them were spent with Clyde in his boat on the lake, tramping over the mountains, or fishing in brook or pond. We left in the morning, pockets full of apples, with lunch and frying pan, and never came back till night — to eat like the bears we always half hoped to meet.

One of the best days was the one on which we climbed four miles to Lost Pond, on top of a mountain, and caught all the bass we wanted. A week later we went there early one morning, so clear that on the way up we could see the blue Green Mountains far beyond Champlain, and camped all night, sleeping on sweet balsam by the fire. He who has not at the close of a long lucky day filled his belly with camp-cooked fish and then in lounging happiness smoked a pipe lit with coals has not lived. A pipe lighted from the campfire is as much better than a match-lighted pipe as water drunk from a spring is better than water drawn from a tap. In the parts of those two days that we fished we caught some forty beautiful bass. For weeks afterwards I dreamed in my sleep of the jerk and run and shake of a shining bass. Sometimes it was a race between Clyde and me as to who could pull out one oftener. And even if we struck a hole where the fish would not bite, there was always a fine hope to keep us tingling to the points of our fingers.

We came down the mountain and into the valley while the sun was setting behind us. Something was crying out to "whip-poor-will" in such a ludicrous manner that I had to stop and laugh. We passed a snug little farmhouse where the cows were just coming in, their sides sticking out with the grass they had eaten and their udders full of milk. And I am thinking we were very proud boys when in lantern light we showed our "string" to the folks at home.

Thus the days passed. One morning I helped to mow buckwheat and the old farmer "guessed" I could learn. All of the country people in the Adirondacks "guess." One of Old Currency's jokes is that the answer to the question "Why does a Southerner always *reckon* and a Yankee *guess?*" is this: "Because a Yankee can guess better than a Southerner can reckon."

One evening, in a subdued mood, I walked to the cemetery near the beautiful little Valley View Chapel. There were but a dozen families represented and each had a host of sleeping ones. On a crumbling tombstone I read this epitaph:

> *If there is another world,*
> *She lives in bliss,*
> *If there is none,*
> *She made the best of this.*

I suppose that she did not "make the best of this" if there is another world.

Among the stones towered one so imposing that it was almost ridiculous. It was a great Greek cross, with Greek letters on it, and Mrs. Matteson told me that it had been brought from England. Joseph Cook, I found, had been the wise man and poet of the country. "He was a very learned man, for nobody could understand his poetry but a scholar, I guess," and he had written a song "that was sung in the Brooklyn church." I read his master poem, *Ticonderoga*, in which he had written:

> *From their blood-pools into God's face*
> *Look the dead men and find solace.*

Cook was a preacher. He had opposed accepting money to build the chapel from any man who drank whiskey; yet he himself lived to eat. But with all of his paunch and prudery I think he must have loved nature. One day Clyde and I climbed to an observatory he had built on top of a mountain and found this command:

Here let the honest American sit down, look around, thank God, and take courage!

But on the mountains where I worship I want no man-built observatories.

On the first Sabbath day I wanted to go fishing and Clyde wanted to go fishing, but we were afraid to go. So in the morning I basked in the sunshine and read psalms until I felt wicked when we did steal away to the lake in the afternoon while the old people were at church. We caught some fish but threw them back.

At first the old farmer would pray for me every morning in family prayers after breakfast. But after a night when I bragged long about the wild horses and bellowing steers and lovely animal calls and endless trails of the cactus country of the Southwest, putting in here and there a touch of the bad man and offering to ride for them what they called an unbroken horse, the morning prayers in my behalf ceased. I think the family must have imagined I was a "black man."

A few days later the daughter, engaged to be married, came. She was not beautiful, she was not romantic, she had her destiny fixed; hence I was very circumspect. Yet, when she ventured that it was dangerous for Clyde and me to sleep out in the big woods, I think I must have roused in her a latent longing after the far away and the adventurous. I swore that if I were rich I should have lions and panthers brought to roar me to sleep and that my morning alarm should be the blood-curdling yell of the leopard or the scream of the eagle. Ah, every man should play the braggart once in a while as well as act the savage. The greatest temptation that comes to the teller of tales is to appropriate to himself the adventure of another. The entrails of my horse were never gored out while I lashed the face of a mad longhorn, but those of Juan Basquez's horse were. Must I tell such a tale and have none of the high glory of having been the rider? The javelinas never "treed" me as they did John, nor did I ever sleep on a rattlesnake as old Julián did in the sand one night, nor did I ever really see the lightning play on the tips of the horns and on the manes of the horses; but when the call is made for these tales, must I lose that one night of heroic dominance?

I shall not forget the last Sunday. I felt very holy that day, with the sense of ending things and beautiful things in my soul. Early I walked away up the lake along the broad road through the tall, graceful trees to Camp Mohican. The natives call the potholes on the banks at Camp Mohican "Indian Kettles," and it is pleasant to think that there the Indians ground their corn in the autumn time. The air was just cool enough to make it agreeable to sit by the water's edge on a bald warming rock. I could see everything I wanted to see: Anthony's crooked nose, the woods, the sky, the water. The whole world was quiet. I smoked and thought of my college days when life was fresh and alluring and I had such sweet friends. I wondered where were George — old careless, all-hearted George — and Bertha, and Alice, and Lowe and Will, and I hoped that they were in the same peaceful ecstasy.

Two deserted cottages stood a little back from "The Kettles," which I learned the owners had not occupied of late "because they were so lonely." I thought of the fool who on the way up the Hudson, when asked if he would like to live on one of the mountains, said no, "for it would be too far away from *everything*." It would have been too near God and Beauty and Peace for his mechanical shallowness.

The next day was Monday, my last. The morning came early. After breakfast, with a kind of tremble in his husky voice which I always noticed when he prayed for the absent children, the old farmer asked God that we might all meet again, if not here, in the other world. The simplicity and sincerity of faith in his words touched me deeply, and I wanted to say "Amen." Then the three men left to work with timber. I looked long at the lake, and lay in the hammock and smoked another pipe in the chair by the maple tree. While I waited for the stage I thought of the beautiful little farewell I would make to Mrs. Matteson and Daisy. When the stage came I rushed into the house, tried to tell the mother how I appreciated all, wished Daisy a very beautiful journey through life and an everlasting love for her mother — and we were away.

Occasionally we had to stop at a mailbox by the road. The driver — a mere boy — seemed to know by first name every countryman we met. Two were cutting brush by the road; a few were around their comfortable houses. A shower threatened, then the sun came out, and we lumbered on down into the valley, past the mountains Joseph Cook had denominated his "Three Brothers," over the little wooden bridge spanning Trout Brook, and into the village stirring with a lazy kind of business which always makes me feel that it is good to be doing something.

After idling pleasantly enough for an hour, I took the road for Montcalm's Landing, two miles away, to catch the Lake Champlain boat. As we steamed down the lake, just after midday a sweeping gale blew so as to clear the deck. But with coat buttoned around my throat, the wind in my hair, imagining I was Champlain himself, I sat and stood far forward.

On one side of the lake rise, a little back, the subdued Adirondacks, and sometimes, behind mountains bordering the lake, may be seen the cloudy forms of those far off. On the other side, only occasionally glimpsed, are the Green Mountains, between which and the lake lie broad rolling plains. But the lake is not so picturesque or wildly beautiful as Lake George. There are finer valleys and richer slopes, and pretty farms and winding roads are all along, especially on the Vermont side; but the mountains do not rise sheer out of the lake, the waters are not so translucently pure, and the eye is not startled with so many rapturous surprises. Yet Lake Champlain has more of the dramatic. It is the highway of two nations; its waves roll like those of a sea; it reminds one of the Champlains and Hudsons of the mighty past. To say which lake is after all more beautiful is like trying to decide whether *Macbeth* or *Othello* is more sublime. Whichever you are in is best — of the lakes or the plays. By a flash of imagination you are with Samuel de Champlain on waters never before ploughed, except by the glistening form of a painted redskin or the silent glide of a birch canoe or frantic efforts of a fleeing buck — Champlain pursuing that art "which," he says, "from my early age has won my love and induced me to expose myself almost all my life to the impetuous waves of the ocean, and led me to explore the coasts of a part of America, especially of New France, where I have always desired to see the Lily flourish, and also the only religion, Catholic, Apostolic, and Roman."

At Port Henry, twenty miles down, I landed, and after a single inquiry in that pleasant village of hills and saloons and trees started on my seven-mile walk around the bay to see the ruins and monument on Crown Point. I picked up butternuts. I had an automobile lift. I watched an Indian look over and down the lake and saw in him the pathfinder of the French.

I was in the nick of time to catch the train back to Ticonderoga. When I pulled out my wallet to pay for the ticket it dawned on me that I had not money enough left to get back to New York. But I worried little as I sank into the easy car seat and looked out into the night. Then as I ate ravenously in a little lunch room in Ticonderoga, kept at night by a silly boy whose vulgar companions were raising an uproar, I deliberated. My blanket of the first night was strapped to my knapsack. But I remembered my one night's experience with that blanket and how tired I was for a warm bath and soft bed, and I thought how I should like to see mine host of the big woods

In the Brush Country: with two javelinas (*above*), and a panther (*below*)

C. B. Ruggles, who searched for the Lost Tayopa Mine in Mexico

Old Spanish stirrup found by Ruggles

Ismael, who told the story of Juan Oso, at Piedra Blanca ranch

tales. Besides, I was not broke yet. I had $4.31 and was only 250 miles from the city, a day and two nights away.

At the inn I told Mort Allen of the wonderful fishing in Lost Pond and he told me of more fine hunts in the winter woods. We smoked till late and he begged me to stay just a week more till the law was out when we would go "up the country," where the big deer run. As I heard him talk, I would have given my birthright to have remained and have gone with him. But I could not.

At seven o'clock next morning, my kit over my shoulders, I was on the road to Montcalm's Landing. I found that I had misread the time and that the train would not come until after ten. The walking was glorious, with the sun coming over the hills on my left and pouring its gold over the waters of Champlain's lake. A light wind from the north was bringing down spice of frost, and I welcomed with an inward shout the opportunity of walking to the next station, two miles away, where the train could take me on. Some singing road hands, who evidently took me for a tramp, advised me to keep to the railroad track. It led so near all along the shore that I could hear the lap of the water. An occasional tug was clearing its morning throat. The mountains, on the other side of which I knew Lake George to be, rose sheer on my right. I almost scudded as a beating vitality and the bracing wind took me south. When I had reached the little station I saw that I had yet time to walk to Putnam, five miles farther on, before the train would arrive.

A mile or so out from Putnam a train of freight cars drawn by two monstrous engines came crashing down the grade. As I stood aside one of the firemen waved to me a smile as if to say, "Why aren't you riding?" A few cars ahead of the caboose a great empty car with both doors wide open rumbled by. If I were only in it, how should I ride! The gods are always with me when I travel. As I rounded a big curve I saw ahead the freight train on a siding, waiting for the northbound express to pass. I almost ran; yet I could not help stopping for a minute to examine a hole in the rocks of the bank below that some sort of animal — it must have been a woodchuck — ran into. My car was in such a position with reference to the engines and caboose of the curved train that it was not visible from either. With a bound I threw my pack and self into it. Instinct taught me what corner to stand in to avoid the sight of any passing brakeman. The express thundered by, wheels ground beneath me, and we were moving.

I set that down as the best ride I ever had. By now the Champlain was becoming a little river, dredged to keep it useful as a canal. Whole strings of peaceful barges were below me. We ploughed through cuts in black rocks. Mountains with dark forest trees hung over us. We passed two or three little stations without stopping. I could see everything as I sat on my bag by the door and smoked. The car had been used by other tramps, for the walls were decorated with names and one or two crayon figures not very elegant. *William Ryan*, *Manchester*, *England*, was written in various ways with both pencil and chalk. I would ride thus to Albany, maybe clear to New York — for a little, if the train went on, clear to San Francisco. I prayed that some seasoned vagabond might crawl in to share the car with me and tell of his rides. I wished that I might meet William Ryan himself. He must know a great deal about freight trains that I should like to know. Still I had never fancied Manchester. It smacked too much of factories. I gloated over the money I was saving and counted that I had already ridden far enough that I could pay railroad fare to Troy, eat a "supper" and buy passage for the rest of the way on a steamer. If I could ride a little farther I should have enough to buy a bed for the night.

About eleven o'clock we ran into the yards at Whitehall.

Why, in God's name, should such a smoke-begrimed town be named *White*hall? It reminded me of a town called Divine back in Texas, where I had to stay one hot night in a hotel run by the devil's blackguard. As the train ran along one of its main streets, a few of the citizens gazed at me standing in my doorway. We stopped. By the timetable I knew that it was time for the train I was to be on to pass. I supposed that we would move on after it, and I had no idea of exchanging vehicles. The yards were full of switching trains. A half hour, an hour, an hour and a half passed and still we did not move. A trainman looked in but said nothing. I was growing both bold and restless. I got out to investigate. No engines were attached to our train, though the caboose was still there. Evidently the crew were taking a rest, and I had to reach Troy that evening. I ate for lunch the apple and baker's cakes remaining from my ten cents' worth of breakfast.

At two o'clock I caught a southbound passenger train, on which I rode to Fort Edward. There, after half a dozen inquiries of the natives, I got directions to the old fort, which I found to consist of a fallen tree. I had to wait over two hours for the trolley to take me on down the Hudson Valley, and I came to the conclusion that it was characteristic of all Fort Edwardians, teamsters and all, to stop on the little bridge over the canal to watch whatever barge might be below. I got something to eat in a little lunchroom on wheels. A male cook at a hotel came in to visit the boy proprietor and to him the latter made with a fine air of originality the statement that "in these days money is what talks, my boy." Why he should make such a statement in my presence I could not understand.

The upper valley of the Hudson is a pleasant one, with the low hills beyond, the villages and farms and roads and canals and river filling it. But after we got to Stillwater, an endless street running into Mechanicville, factories and machines had killed all peace and beauty of the land. The sun went down on us along here and jabbering foreign laborers, who seemed not very glad to be going home, filled the car.

It was dark when we got to Troy, about which all I know is that shirts are made there. With $1.91 in my pocket, the idea that a steamship ticket would cost only $1.00 and a large hope that I could somehow get a bed for the remainder, I with the air of a gentleman and a train-robber demanded a ticket.

"Two dollars, please."

Then my pride was hurt for the first time. I had to ask a stranger to "loan" me ten cents. He did so, insisting that I take more, but I refused more with thanks.

That night it came cold and there was no heat in the nearly deserted cabin. Half the time I walked to keep warm, but my mind when not gloating over the day's experiences was filled with pictures of the bath and bed I should have by that time tomorrow. I think I never in my life so much wanted to be really warm and comfortable. As company I had a little dog wrapped in a blanket and the man and woman who nursed him by turns. They had a stateroom upstairs but one always kept the dog company. Then there was a foreign man who was colder than I. The old watchman came in occasionally, but all he knew was that it was very cold out and that the river was low. None of us tried to talk. The clock on the wall was an object of despairing interest.

But at length dawn came — just above West Point. The sun rose a fiery red over the low hills and the steam floated up from the water as I have seen it do from cold lakes when hunting ducks. I began to feel as well as if I had slept all night, and as we came along by the city and into the harbor I felt a great pride and respect. 'Tis a noble view from Yonkers to the Battery in the crisp early morning, with the horns blowing and the sun shining through the steam of engines and boats, and barges and big ships and trains starting out.

CHAPTER FOURTEEN

No Idea Where I Was Going

I CAME to the University of Texas as instructor in English in the fall of 1914. I was twenty-six years old and had just taken an M.A. degree at Columbia University, but the University of Texas seemed as fresh to me, as I look back now, as Southwestern University at Georgetown seemed when I entered it as a freshman in 1906. The enrollment was around twenty-two hundred. It wasn't hard for an instructor to come to know most of the teaching staff; he almost had to know all the instructing force in his own department.

The head of the English Department was Dr. Morgan Callaway, Jr. It is my recollection that he had not had another full professor in the department until the year I arrived. As head (dictator) of the department he had found virtually no underling worthy of promotion to his own rank. He was a genuine scholar and an intellectual disciplinarian, but he didn't believe in instructors' having enough free time or enough money to get worldy-minded. I had correspondence with Dr. Callaway before I left Columbia University.

Shortly after coming back to Texas, in June, I began reporting on the Galveston *Daily Tribune*, an afternoon paper now extinct. After the *Tribune* went to press, I would go swimming and then some of us reporters would get together and eat supper at Valentine's Hole-in-the-Wall, which supplied a good meal for forty cents. My most delightful friend was John Reagan, who reported on the *News*, the morning paper. He was gay and civilized, a plunging reader of world literature, especially the romantic. He collected books on Napoleon. When we parted, he gave me for a keepsake a necktie he had worn and I had it for many years. We wrote to each other occasionally until he died, far too young.

Both Johnnie Reagan and I and for that matter most of the reporters on the two papers spent a good deal of our free time at the public library. It is named the Rosenberg Library in honor of a civilized man who left money to build it. In front of the library is a bronze figure of Henry Rosenberg. Sometimes during my summer in Galveston I would see pigeons light on his head and children clamber up on his knees. The grounds were inviting, and so was the library. In the Metropolitan Museum in New York I had become infatuated with a painting by Jules Lefebvre called "The Girl of Capri." She sits barelegged, bare-headed on a bluff, a fishing net dropped by her side. She is looking out to sea, and you can't know whether she is looking for somebody who will come back or somebody she has never met or somebody she has met and loved who will never come back. Not long after I got to Galveston Johnnie Reagan told me that Lamartine's romance *Graziella* was the source for "The Girl of Capri." I found the book in the Rosenberg Library and read it slowly, for it was in French. That sentimental tale made little impression on my mind and soon faded from memory except that it deepened my unfading memory of the picture. To this day I sometimes look at "The Girl of Capri" hung in my gallery of memories.

No man knows what incidents lie deep in his well of memories. Why I should recollect the following incident I do not know. One afternoon while I was walking on a street near the Tremont Hotel, a man who looked to be able-bodied but who had a whine in his voice accosted me, begging the price of a meal. He said he was very hungry. I gave him a quarter and pointed him to a restaurant where I often ate a meal for that amount. Maybe three or four hours later, in the gathering dusk, I was passing along the same street when the same man accosted me at the same spot with the same plea. I said, "Why, it hasn't been long since I gave you the price of a meal." Without dropping his whine, he said, "Mister, can't you repeat the act?"

I know well enough why I recall another incident of my summer in Galveston. The body of a beautiful young woman was found on the beach but no one knew who she was. My city editor, A. L. Perkins, whom I remember partly for the sprig of blue plumbago he wore fresh each morning in his buttonhole, told me to go to the morgue, where the body was held for identification, and write whatever came to me out of what I heard and saw there. My piece, called "Scenes at the Morgue," was put on the front page. Later, when a group of us went to dinner we overheard two men at the next table talking with favor about "Scenes at the Morgue." Never in the long years since has a book review or any other praise made such music to my ears.

I was drawing only $15 or maybe $18 a week, but was having such a happy time that I wrote Dr. Callaway asking him to relieve me of my agreement to come on to the University of Texas that fall. He wrote back that I had made the agreement and that if I was a real man, I'd stick to it. I stuck to it. During a conversation with Dr. Callaway not long after I started teaching, he informed me that having thought through a subject he had not yet found himself wrong in an opinion. I am glad that I took the route I did take, but Dr. Callaway's avowal of always being right remained with me as an astonishing singularity.

Dr. Callaway was one of the characters of the University. I never pleased him more than one time when I referred to

Thomas Nelson Page's essay on the decay of manners. That was a favorite subject with him — the decay of manners. He generally carried a parasol and a bag of books and papers. He always tipped his hat to an acquaintance or friend even if it were necessary to deposit a part of his burden on the ground in order to have a free hand. Of course, everybody tipped his hat to Dr. Callaway.

Stith Thompson and I came to the University of Texas together as instructors in English. He was getting $1400, and I was getting $1200 — the difference between a Ph.D. from Harvard and, as François Villon put it, "a poor Master of Arts." It was the winter of 1914-1915 that I acquired my knowledge of this "poor M.A." through Robert Louis Stevenson's *A Lodging for a Night*, and I liked him so well that I never became really jealous of Stith Thompson's plutocratic advantage over me through having a higher degree.

He and I were office mates in a big room occupied by two other instructors. We were all conscientious toward freshmen and maintained constant receiving lines for conferences on their themes. Stith knew where he was going, and I had no idea where I was going beyond being in love. I wanted to teach the survey course in English poetry to sophomores so as to help them fall in love more deliciously, but poetry teaching was not permitted to a poor M.A. Stith was teaching poetry, writing a manual for freshman composition and editing Publications Number 1 for the Texas Folklore Society all at the same time.

I had never heard of the newly organized Texas Folklore Society until Stith Thompson asked me to join it and pay one dollar in dues. To tell the truth, I had never heard the word *folklore* until he used it in front of me. I had no more idea of what folklore is than Monsieur Jourdain had of what prose is until his professor told him he had been speaking it for forty years. If Stith Thompson hadn't said *folklore* to me — with not nearly so much emphasis as people say *scat* to a cat — I don't know where I'd be today. And, just think, that part of my education cost but one dollar!

A landmark on the campus at the time was Judge Simpkins, professor of law. He had been in the Confederate Army and wore his white hair and beard long and flowing. I never heard of his saying anything interesting beyond addressing his law students as "My Young Jackasses." Shortly after Judge Simpkins died, Dr. Callaway told me that he was now bereft of somebody to reverence. He said he had reverenced his father and that Judge Simpkins had been a man to reverence at the University — solely on account of his seniority, I deduced. It was evident that Dr. Callaway thought young instructors could do no better than reverence him.

Another character on the campus was Judge Townes, dean of the Law School. He also belonged to Civil War times. He was not flamboyant in the way that Judge Simpkins was; he was firm and kind but in thought belonged to the past century. He didn't believe in public schools. In his opinion nobody should be taxed to educate the children of another man. The words "creeping socialism" had not yet come into use, much less into banality, but Judge Townes considered the public school system too socialistic for individual rights.

One of the University's picturesque characters was T. U. Taylor, dean of the School of Engineering. He wanted to be president of the University as intensely as Henry Clay or Daniel Webster ever wanted to be President of the United States, but never got into that office. He enjoyed coddling and holding up the weaklings of his school. I don't think he was against education in something else than engineering. At any rate, all engineers had to take two years of English, and I was always glad to get a section of them.

I'll never forget the speech T. U. Taylor made right after the United States finally entered World War I. The call had gone out for volunteers. Faculty members were practicing marching squad right with broomsticks to simulate rifles. One can have no idea now how patriotic the country was. A daytime rally was announced to be held under the trees in front of the old Law Building. T. U. Taylor was the main speaker. He began by announcing, "My lips are not fitted to the soft syllables of peace." His main argument for joining the army and helping whip the Huns was wrapped up in a Sam Houston anecdote. He said that while Sam Houston was practicing law after he had been president of the Republic of Texas, any veteran of the Texas army who got into trouble employed him if he could. Sam Houston would put the accused on the stand, ask him his name, ask him when he arrived in Texas. The answer to this question would be a time before April, 1836.

Then Sam Houston would ask the witness, "Where were you on April 21, 1836?"

The answer would be, "I was at the Battle of San Jacinto."

"The defense rests its case," lawyer Sam Houston would then announce to the court, and of course the jury would clear the accused, no matter what the charge.

At the end of his oration T. U. Taylor pulled a little American flag out of his vest pocket and waved it over his head. Most of the able-bodied young men listening to him were already about to join the army. No one could withstand the logic of his argument.

After retiring on account of age, T. U. Taylor wrote three or four slight books, privately printed. *Forty Acres* was the best known, Forty Acres being a name for the original University of Texas campus. Another title is *Jesse Chisholm*, about the man who beat out the principal cattle-driving trail to Kansas. Taylor characterized him as Pioneer, Patriot, Peacemaker, Pathfinder, Prophet, Protector. Why he left out Poet and Pathologist I would not know. His oratorical inclinations were always breaking out. In *The Chisholm Trail and Other*

Routes he included an "Alphabetical Index to The Trail Drivers of Texas," but neglected to explain that *The Trail Drivers of Texas* is the title of a two-volume work and that his index is to a reprint in one volume.

Courses in Education, spelled with a capital E, were regarded as snap courses, but they were so boring to intelligent students that few such were willing to pay the price for that form of snap. The Education people in 1914-1915 listed forty-seven courses, twenty-three of them on the art of teaching, with repetition in nomenclature as well as in content. Nobody could teach in the public schools even then without some courses in Education, but the Education people had not yet got their present stranglehold on the whole public school system. E. C. Barker, professor of history and master of sardonic realism, used to define Education as "the unctuous elaboration of the obvious." He claimed this to be a quotation from somebody else, but in popularizing the definition got credit for originating it. I have quoted him and in turn received credit for originality. Common sense, a sense of humor, imagination, tact, graciousness, and a mastery of the subject — these are the true requisites for a teacher.

Before World War I and for years to come the second-year English course consisted of a survey of English poetry. I always thought this the cream of all English courses. I'd like to teach it again. Now a sophomore can take a course on American novels, or contemporary plays, or something like that and miss the fun, the discipline, and the undying supernals from Chaucer to A. E. Housman. I shall die unscientifically believing with Wordsworth that "poetry is the breath and finer spirit of all knowledge," and that technical "knowhow" is as tawdry as the word itself.

The proper business of English teachers — or teachers of any other literature for that matter — is not to teach pupils to make a living but to lead them to more abundant living even amid the daily round of doings. This assertion implies no hostility to the teaching of trades, techniques, and professional skills. It is a recognition of the potentiality in most human beings for a fuller life. Many times the teacher must groan to herself or himself, "I have piped unto you and ye have not danced." But always there are some who had rather see than remain blind. Always there are reachers for the stars and yearners after the high and lovely.

There was no journalism department in 1914. Then as now the best newspaper writers depended for effect on natural intelligence, cultivation of the art of composing words, and knowledge gained outside of all journalism classes. A big university has to have big buildings, of course. I believe the best teaching I did at the University of Texas was during the post-World War I days when the campus was dotted with frame shacks heated by iron stoves. I taught several classes in those shacks. I doubt that the intellectual content of any journalism instructor has been advanced by moving into a million-dollar building that often makes me think of the old saying about a forty-dollar saddle on a twenty-dollar horse. Journalism, as an agent of learning, is on a par with Education spelled with a capital E. It prevents students, by taking up their time, from studying economics, history, biology, anthropology, languages, English literature, and other subjects that fortify the mind.

Farmer Jim Ferguson was the first governor, I suppose, to put the University much in politics. He talked about the country's going "hog-wild over higher education." When in 1917 he tried to fire an acting president and other men from the University faculty, he was halted by Will Hogg and other ex-students.

So far as getting the University of Texas into politics is concerned, Jim Ferguson was an episode compared with the continuing appointments by later governors of regents on the basis of political partisanship and economic opinion. One Ferguson-appointed regent was a scholar of Latin and Greek who had been master of Salado College (long defunct) in Bell County, Jim Ferguson's home county. Farmer Jim was naïve enough to believe that a university regent might be a scholar and need not necessarily be an oil millionaire or a corporation lawyer.

So far as I know, no philosopher has ever numbered happiness among the "unalienable rights" of man — only "the pursuit of happiness." I remember quoting that phrase once in a letter to the professors of English while I was an underling. I doubt if any one of them got its significance. After I came among them on the so-called Budget Council, responsible for the hiring, firing, and promoting of teachers in the Department, I never heard any consideration given to a man's intellect, wit, love of beauty, urbanity or any other concomitant of what is generally considered a civilized man. The emphasis was always on what he was "producing in the scholarly field," with little emphasis on the quality of production. A teacher's power to communicate to his classes ideas and a passion for literature had virtually no weight with the sanhedrin. I remember the Doctors of Philosophy as unquestioning in their philosophy of life, too timid for skepticism, without imagination, without warmth of thought, sentiment or flesh, everything under control, mastery of facts the supreme virtue of a scholar. I nearly always went away from them, and also from any of the few meetings of the General Faculty that I attended, depressed and remembering Keats's "inhuman dearth of noble natures." Yet I know plenty of professors whom I like and whose company I enjoy. It is the professors who think like academicians instead of like men that give me the fantods.

The year after I came to the University of Texas Uncle Jim Dobie got me to go with him to receive a big string of steers from Bassett Blakely at Liverpool in Brazoria County on the Gulf Coast. Less than ten years later Bassett Blakely furnished the Longhorn cattle for a silent motion picture made from Emerson Hough's novel *North of 36*. It is the only good picture of handling cattle that I have ever seen. I came later to avoid pictures purporting to be of ranch life and work — betrayals of the life. Of course the cowboys in the *North of 36* picture were actors, but somebody had taught them how to handle cattle. I never forgot the lead steer, Old Alamo. He stood representing a vanished breed. The spectator could read the brands on some of the cattle as they grazed or traveled up the Chisholm Trail.

The steers that Uncle Jim bought were not straight longhorns at all. They were bred up. The Bassett Blakely cowhands who loaded them in stock cars at the Liverpool shipping pens were nearly all Negroes. They seemed to me as good at their business as the Mexican vaqueros I was brought up with and as the Anglo-American cowboys I have known. Some farmer came by with a wagonload of watermelons. Uncle Jim bought several, and how those men enjoyed eating them! After the cattle were loaded and the train had pulled out for Fowlerton, Texas, in La Salle County, not far from Uncle Jim Dobie's ranch and leased lands, he said, "We'll go to Houston." He wanted me to buy a few cattle; he said he would sign my note.

In Houston he got in touch with a middle-aged man named Allen, descendant of the original Sam Allen to whom Uncle Jim's father (my grandfather) and a brother named Sterling N. Dobie had sold out their Harris County cattle, range delivery, in 1857. Selling "range delivery" used to mean a guess on the seller's part as to how many cattle wore his brand and another guess on the buyer's part as to how many cattle he could gather. After the price was agreed upon, the buyer went to gathering. Sam Allen gathered a lot more cattle in the

Dobie brothers' brands than they thought they had. I guess they did not lose much money on the trade, for a panic broke out that fall.

Uncle Jim took a look at the cows that Mr. Allen had to sell and advised me to buy. Mr. Allen offered a ten per cent cut. I had been out of cattle trading for a good while and didn't try to make him lower the price. I bought a hundred and thirty or forty cows without taking the cut. Only a few of them had calves. They were shipped to Dinero on the Sausage Railroad (the San Antonio, Uvalde and Gulf), which had been built into Live Oak County after I went off to college and my family moved from the ranch to Beeville. I accompanied the cattle, riding in a caboose, having sent word ahead that I was bringing them. Three or four men on horseback were at the pens with a horse for me. We nooned not more than a mile from the Dinero shipping pens. After we started the cattle on for the ranch, one of them lay down and died. A Mexican said she'd swallowed a *campo mocho* — a devil's horse — while grazing. Nobody knew what to do for her except to skin her after she finished dying.

I leased the Miller pasture of about two thousand acres, just west of and joining the R. J. Dobie ranch, and put the cows in it. Before long I went back to the University of Texas to teach English. The fall was dry. The winter was dry. The coming spring was dry, but the cows made it through somehow. To pay for them I had given a note, signed also by Uncle Jim, to Mr. J. K. Beretta of the National Bank of Commerce in San Antonio. I'd been sending papa a little money to hire men to burn pear for the cows; that is, to singe thorns off the prickly pear cactus.

Everybody was suffering from the drouth. People were selling cattle at greatly reduced prices. They were hunting grass to the east and the north beyond the severe drouth. Through a student of mine I learned of a landowner in the hills west of

Austin who had no cattle and wanted to pasture some. I made a trade with him. I doubt if he could have sold his land at that time for more than two dollars an acre. I doubt that the present owner would take a hundred dollars an acre.

Before I married in September of 1916 I went down to get my cows. The dog days were on. For lack of breezes the windmills could not pump water. Gasoline pumps had recently been invented to hitch onto well rods and pump up water. I remembered pumps worked by a big wheel, working on cogs, pulled around and around, flat on the ground, by a horse or a pair of horses. Papa had one of these pumps on a strong well in the Kessler pasture east of the Nueces River that he for a time leased.

It must have been during a drouth of the 90s that he gathered a herd of big steers from the Kessler pasture to ship. On the way to shipping pens we stopped for the night, vaqueros riding herd on the steers. We were camped near a big mesquite tree. I had made a pallet under it and had found thousands of sugar ants crawling into my bedding when Sid Grover rode up. Sid Grover was for years Uncle Jim's cow boss. He had the reputation of being such an expert brushpopper that without wearing leather leggins and ducking jacket, even without any clothes at all, he could ride through the thorniest thicket in south Texas after the wildest steer that ever tore through the brush and rope it without getting a scratch. This feat, purely imaginary, always seemed too much for me, but Sid Grover was a kind of hero. Now he stopped his horse at the mesquite tree, looked down at me and my pallet, without noticing the little ants, and said, "I wish I didn't have to go on. That bed looks mighty good to me." I did not say, as I strongly felt like saying, "I wish I could go to bed at home."

Getting back to my cows in the drouth of 1916-1917, for a few days I tended a gasoline pump at a windmill in the Miller pasture — no work at all unless something goes wrong with the engine. Spending time around the Miller pasture well, I learned to expect promptly every day about eleven o'clock a certain paisano (roadrunner) coming for a drink of water. Quail and other people came.

I shipped my cows to Austin, where they were unloaded in shipping pens north of the Colorado River. Two or three men I had hired helped me cross the cows through the water, which wasn't high, and they spent the night in Searight's Stockyards just south of the river. I bought some hay for them to eat. One cow got down in the river and died. They were all poor.

The road from Austin to Bee Caves on Barton Creek and on west was just a wagon road, seldom traveled by wagons, and so far as I know not at all at that time by automobiles. We got only four or five miles out of Austin the first day. We spent the second night just west of Barton Creek near Bee Caves. I rented an old field for the cows to graze in. The owner of it grew a little tobacco and gave me a few cured leaves to smoke in my pipe. In that country I saw cattle with the creeps and learned that the grass on the hills lacks minerals and that one had better give plenty of salt to his animals. Minerals mixed with the salt were then unknown. Another day's drive got us to the pasture, somewhere in the region of Hamilton's Pool.

Late the next year some rain fell in the lower country. I remember that the first time I went back to the ranch after shipping my cows I saw lots of grass in the Julia Shipp pasture beside the road. I saw a fat heifer by herself near the fence. My father had had that pasture leased. He told me that he had left a dogie heifer in the pasture too poor to walk. Now she was fat. In the summer of 1917 I told Uncle Jim that the cows were still poor, wouldn't sell for enough to pay the note on them, and that I intended to go into the army. He said to send the cattle to his ranch in La Salle County. I shipped them to Fowlerton.

When I got back from France along in 1919 cattle were

sky high. A good many of mine had died. Uncle Jim had sold what were left for enough money that I had something after paying off my note.

I was with a National Guard outfit in World War I. I wanted the United States to get into the war a long time before it did, just as I wanted it to get into World War II before it did. I could not in those times, just as I cannot now, name anything that I particularly cherish deriving from Germany. There's Heine the poet; he was a Jew. There's great Goethe; he was more severe on the Teutonic temperament than on any other subject. In both World War I and World War II the Germans were trying to destroy the civilizations of France and England. Through the Teutonic Ph.D. system, they long ago dehumanized the humanities in American colleges and universities. I have not lost any sleep over the fact that Russia keeps the Prussians separated from other Teutonic admirers of Bismarck.

When the United States finally declared war on Germany in 1917 — after we had grown richer selling to England and she and France were almost bled to death — I hastened to try to join the army. The army wouldn't take me on account of varicose veins. I had them cut out and got into the second officers' training camp at Leon Springs, Texas. The captain who passed on my application asked what branch of the army I wanted to join.

"The cavalry," I answered.

"Why?"

"Because I want to ride."

"The cavalry is already afoot," he said. "If you want to ride, join the field artillery."

I joined it — and it was on the verge of being mechanized. I'll skip much, including a Swede captain, who had been for years a sergeant in the Regular Army and had got promoted on account of the scarcity of educated, experienced men for officers. He was as ignorant and as crude as a boar hog in a peach orchard and through him I was nearly busted, but a gentleman who outranked him saw me through. I was commissioned a first lieutenant.

My career in the training camp marked the second distinct loss of personality, lapse of power, lack of self-confidence that I had suffered. The first occurred when I entered Columbia University "in the City of New York" — pitiless, to me personless. The condition endured for almost a year until I came to be a powerful figure in a little coterie of unpowerful men. At Leon Springs, in a military life new to me, in which competition was keen, I was pavid and puerile. A certain refined sensiblity kept me apart from my fellows. I could not understand the drill regulations, however assiduously I studied them. I had too long soaked myself in poetry and novels. Subsequently, the natural robustness of my nature asserted itself and without losing sensibility I became a match for the hardiest soldier. By degrees the drill regulations became models of lucidity. I began to enjoy the problems of artillery as much as I had formerly enjoyed a novel. With knowledge came power and self-confidence.

I left Leon Springs with orders to report to the 116th Field Artillery, stationed at Camp Wheeler near Macon, Georgia. It was a part of the 56th Brigade of the 31st Division — National Guard, made up mostly of Alabama, Georgia, and Florida men. Another lieutenant named Dunning, who was to be a chaplain, got orders to go to the same place. We rode the trains together. Lieutenant Colonel Gruber of the Regular Army was in temporary command of the 116th Field Artillery. When we reported to him in his office, he kept us standing at attention for well over an hour. One thing he said I never forgot: "A soldier without pride is not worth a damn." Maybe I had a little pride before; after that my pride in being a soldier never wavered. Lieutenant Colonel Gruber minced no words in characterizing a lot of the National Guard officers as political-minded, ignorant, sloppy and worthless for service. He had been instrumental in benzining more than fifty per cent of the officers from the 116th regiment, and I understood that the other two regiments in the 56th brigade had suffered equal casualties. The benzining was still going on; virtually all National Guard officers left were as scared as a cottontail rabbit dodging a coyote. Lieutenant Colonel Gruber was the hardest, the fairest, and the most admirable soldier I knew during my term in the army. He had been educated at West Point, and he knew; moreover, he had an active mind and had character.

Learning that I liked horses, he put me in charge of horses in Battery A. Before long the captain (my good friend Walter McDonald of Tennessee, a reserve officer like myself) was ordered to Fort Sill, Oklahoma, for special training in field artillery, and I was placed in command of the company. I was terribly ignorant. I made mistakes, two or three shameful ones being due to defects in my nature rather than to ignorance, but I never was scared of my job. We officers never quit studying. At Leon Springs and on with my regiment I gained in mastering firing data more brain power than I have gained in any other one year of my life except while I was teaching American history at Cambridge University during World War II.

I had a fine horse, a bay, part Spanish, that I called Buck after the horse I loved most on the home ranch. I never did have a better time than while I was riding this second Buck alongside our horse-drawn three-inch cannons and ammunition chests over the red lands and wooded hills of Georgia. I don't believe a man on a horse can get a more exhilarating sense of motion than when in full gallop with a whole regiment of well-managed horses hitched to rattling caissons. I learned to love the business of controlling a battery's fire; maneuvering into position against an imaginary foe; drilling the battery to the inspiriting sound of whistles, of beating horsehoofs, of the rumble of caissons and gun carriages; marching; camping out at night — soldiering as if we meant to learn the art of war, and joying in the art.

Oh the infantry, the cavalry
And the blank-blank engineers,
They couldn't whip the artillery
In a hundred thousand years.

Our major, a National Guardsman, was as common as pigtracks, but he was persistent and had occasional streaks of intelligence. He was afraid of his job and was a bully. On one maneuver when we were going into camp formation a little before sundown, he rode up to me and snarlingly asked how I was going to place my "pieces." I had the disposition of them all figured out. I told him.

"You can't do that," he said.

"I can do it," I said. "I know exactly what I'm doing."

"I don't want any more of your lip," he said.

"Then, by God," I said, "if you want to command this battery, take charge."

I rode off a short distance. He muddled things getting the pieces in order. I came back after he'd got through muddling. He never said another word to me on the subject, although he could have charged me with insubordination. Such a charge would have entailed some examination of his own qualities.

He developed into a very good field officer. Though he became friendly toward me and sometimes complimentary, and though he attained superior efficiency, I have never fully forgiven him. He tried to imitate Lieutenant Colonel Gruber, but where Gruber was a flail of just and most powerful invective, Anderson was a vulgar braggart of cheap insults. Had Gruber remained with the regiment, I should have been made a captain, I know.

Lieutenant Colonel Gruber, unhappily for good soldiers, left and a National Guard colonel from Florida took command. We could not understand how he had escaped being busted at an artillery school — probably through political pull. His mouth looked like that of a catfish; he was bench-legged like a bulldog pup. He was cunning without intellectual content — a common characteristic of coyotes and foxes — but I especially like coyotes: their ambitions do not exceed their abilities and they know nothing about depending on pull. This National Guard colonel was so scared of his job that at times his spit dried up. He constantly licked the general's boots. The general was an antiquated Regular Army man who had been retired but called back into service. He was pot-gutted and when he walked he waddled like a fat gander. When our "riding and shooting outfit" went out to practice firing in the field, the colonel never accompanied us. He always stayed around the barracks inspecting kitchens. It might be long after dark when we got back. After a hasty supper, we'd have to go to an officers' meeting. There our colonel would wax severely indignant at spots of grease he had found on a stove in A Battery, dough in the cracks of a table in B Battery, dust under a cot in C's barracks, and so on. He was afraid to go out with the cannon. He didn't know an "over" from a "short." He couldn't have computed the range; he couldn't have computed anything in ballistics. When we were out firing, when we were practicing that for which artillery exists — to shoot — when we were perfecting ourselves as artillerymen, this colonel of ours, who would eventually issue the orders for our advances, our targets, our maneuvers, remained in camp to inspect kitchens! He was in his military element requiring us to stay in camp on Sunday and sing "It's a Long Way to Tipperary," "Some Day I'm Going to Murder the Bugler," "Good Morning, Mr. Zip," etc.

I heard more than one man say that if we ever got into battle in France, this colonel would for certain be reported as dead or mortally wounded. I believe that would have happened. When we got to France he transferred me to his staff. He well knew that I disliked being in his presence, but he probably figured that I would be flattered enough to prove useful; I showed myself so dissatisfied, even surly, that he transferred me back to my battery. Of course, he had his flunkies, but not a single man who could ride and shoot respected him. It was a good thing for him that we didn't get into battle.

National Guard private soldiers and sergeants were as good as any recruits we got through civilian boards, but if the 56th brigade had a single first-rate officer from second lieutenant up who was a National Guardsman, I didn't meet him.

A short time before we were to go overseas, a psychiatrist passed on the enlisted men. McMurtry, the First Sergeant of Battery A, as hard as nails and as dependable as the tides, who said he did not want friends, had told me that a certain yellow-haired, gangling private was an idiot. I took to noticing the man and agreed. The psychiatrist passed him. I asked the psychiatrist to test him again. I think he had hookworms as well as a congenital lack of brains. The psychiatrist tapped him on the knee a few more times with a rubber hammer and pronounced him unfit to go overseas. I didn't think any more of the psychiatrists than I thought of National Guard colonels. The last time I saw Sergeant McMurtry he had lost his chevrons and was picking up garbage in Camp Coetquidan in Brittany. He was a sight better man and soldier than any psychiatrist, chaplain, or National Guard field officer I met on either side of the ocean. Of course, I met comparatively few out of many.

CHAPTER FIFTEEN

How My Life Took Its Turn

If you should ask how I came to write *Coronado's Children*, a book of buried treasure and lost mine stories, a full answer would be about as ramifying as the explanation that Tennyson suggested — but happily did not detail — of the flower in the crannied wall. In a kind of introduction to the book I have gone back about four hundred years to explain Coronado's children themselves and now I'll go as far back as I can in explaining my connection with them.

The Brush Country between the Nueces River and the Rio Grande in southwest Texas, where I was born, is, as age goes in America, an old land, many a dry gully marking the rut made by a Spanish cart and many a title of ownership being derived from some grant for "leagues and labors" issued by the king of Spain. Strips and patches of the region are now in cultivation, but mostly it is still a ranch country, arid and covered with thorned brush and prickly pear, as extraordinary in character as the maquis of Corsica or the Everglades of Florida. This brush hides old, old secrets. A land that is not plowed up or cemented over and that maintains from one generation to another a simple occupation like the pastoral occupation keeps its traditions.

On our ranch,* out three miles from the house — an honest rock house built by Mexican hands and set in a grove of giant liveoak trees — is an ancient site known as Fort Ramirez. People say that Fort Ramirez used to be a Spanish mission. Maybe some padre did baptize wild Indians there; certainly it was the fortified stronghold of a Spanish ranchero. According to the tradition of the country, the Ramirez people were very rich, and, of course, as there were no banks, they kept their gold and silver buried. So when they were massacred by Indians, they left their wealth for some stranger to find. Long before I was born men were digging for it; they are still digging.

For thirty years a half uncle of mine, named Ed Dubose, tried to unearth it, and I suppose it was he who first introduced me to the tales and hopes and adventures of Coronado's children. He and his associates had "plats" to jack loads of silver bullion buried by ruins, on the edge of lakes, in mottes, stretching all the way from San Jacinto battlefield to the ancient church in Santa Fe. They had other charts to lost Spanish mines scattered from the lonesome hills of the San Saba to the Yaqui-guarded canyons of Sonora.

I heard the tales in snatches, and had it not been for the circumstances that arose years later they would probably have lain among many other dead memories. Furthermore, not until I was a mature man did I come to look upon the men who told the tales and participated in them, together with the ground on which they acted and to which they belonged, as being the most vital part of the narratives.

After the war, I went back to my old job as instructor in the University of Texas. Long before this I had ascertained that the love of literature and the ability to impart that love bore no

* In Texas the word *ranch* has not yet been corrupted, as in California, to mean "chicken roost," "potato patch" and all other plots of ground larger than a town lot. Also not all ranchers are cattle kings.

relation whatsoever to the advancement of English teachers in the "scholarly" colleges and universities of America. I'd been overseas and learned a lot. Life at the University seemed pretty tame, but that wasn't the worst. My wife and I were doing worse than starving to death on a government claim. My salary was meager, as all University of Texas salaries were at the time, but I was at the bottom of the ladder with very little prospect of getting higher up until I got a Ph.D. degree, and I did not intend to get one.

Uncle Jim (J. M.) Dobie had been after me several times to go back into the cow business. He was willing to back me. One day along in the spring of 1920 he came to Austin and asked me once more why I didn't go to work for him. He owned 56,000 acres in La Salle County and leased land in La Salle, McMullen, Duval, and Webb counties, altogether a big spread. He had a ranch down in Mexico. He had business interests in San Antonio and elsewhere. He said he wanted a kind of segundo to go around and look after his affairs. I agreed to go with him.

When spring came I resigned my job at the University of Texas and we moved to San Antonio. By this time the cattle market had begun to go down and before long, instead of traipsing over the country looking after varied affairs, I was managing the Olmos ranch in La Salle County. It straddles the Nueces River. We grew about ten acres of sorghum, and that was all the farming we did. We had a cow outfit and another outfit to build tanks and repair fences. Generally I was the only "white" man on the ranch; the hands were all Mexicans. I had never been entirely weaned from ranch life, for I habitually spent several weeks out of each year in the saddle. But as the majordomo of the Rancho de Los Olmos (The Elms), I knew that I had just about reached paradise. On many a half-day's ride I have counted between fifty and one hundred white-tailed deer on the ranch.

One of the Mexicans was named Santos Cortez. He had killed a man "on the other side" during the revolution and got to this side — the Rio Grande dividing the sides, of course. He was a good *pastor* (goat-herder), an indifferent vaquero, a skilled hunter, often assigned to furnish camp with venison and javelina meat, and a lover of talk. Sometimes at night he would come to my room in the ranch house to converse. He wearied, he told me, of talk confined to the sore back of a certain horse, the low water in a certain tank, the distance a certain vaquero had run in the black chaparral out in the San Casimiro pasture before he got a glimpse of the outlaw steer he was trailing, the burning of sacahuiste grass below the Tigre, the dry weather that had been and seemed likely to continue, and other such workaday matters. He craved conversation on higher things. Santos was a kind of freethinker and not at all orthodox in religion. "*El padre tiene huevos como yo*" was one of his heresies. But he believed in ghosts. That's where the intellect of a sophisticate comes in. I myself accept without reservation the ghost in *Hamlet* but reject the Holy Ghost as a metaphysical superstition.

One night after we had branched off on higher subjects, Santos told me of two remarkable experiences he could vouch for on a neighboring ranch. One was his own, the other a friend's. This friend was riding by the site of a long-abandoned Mexican jacal one night when all of a sudden he felt the arms of a skeleton around him and realized that a ghost had dropped down from a tree under which he passed and was mounted behind him. His horse screamed in fright and broke into a run that the rider did nothing to hinder. It was about three miles to the ranch, and that skeleton clung all the way and then at the gate released its hold and disappeared.

"This did not pass with me," Santos said, "but I know it is true. I am going to tell you something that did pass with me. I have never told another. You are next to God with me, and will not laugh." When Santos became earnest in this way, there were always tears in his voice and in his eyes, too.

"*Bueno.* That was a lonesome camp where I kept the goats. Maybe two times, maybe one time, every fifteen days did I see another man. He would bring a little flour and coffee and sugar, frijoles, salt, no more. At night only the coyotes talked, and they did not talk to me. The pastor dog slept with the goats, and I did not have even him for company.

"One night after I had been sound asleep for a while, I awoke drawing my breath in quick pants, like this. There was *un bulto* — a bulk — on my chest so heavy that it was smothering me. I always kept my rifle at my side. I tried to reach for it but could not move a finger. It was like I was tied down with a wet rawhide rope. Tight, man, tight! I could not raise my body to pitch the bulto off. I tried to yell. I had no breath to make a sound, and my mouth it was dry like lime. Look, my tongue would not moisten my lips. I was pinned back flat so that I could not bend my neck to see the bulto there in the dark. *Pues*, what could I do?

"Then I remembered how it is said that thoughts of good will drive away the evil. I began to think of the good God and of the Holy Virgin. I thought hard, and in a little bit of while there was no bulto weighing down on me. I did not hear it run off. I did not see it. It vanished, and I was free. When daylight came and I looked for tracks, I could not find any. It is a thing I cannot explain, nor you either, Meester Frankie, though you are well instructed and have been a master in a big school. These things are not of the earth.

"They are not of the earth even when you see them. One night I was with two other men crossing the Arroyo San Casimiro at the Paso de la Gallina. And there right above the palo verde tree in which the lone *gallina* (chicken) used to roost, we saw a light so bright that it made my eyes go blind. Maybe it was twelve feet high, like a ball. It stayed there a little bit and then slowly, slowly it floated on down the creek. One man, thinking it would lead to gold, wanted to follow it, but it had not called my name. We stood still. It got a little dimmer, and then it just vanished, like a match that ceases to burn."

In the course of time Santos told me many other things.

During the year I spent on Los Olmos ranch, while Santos talked, while Uncle Jim Dobie and other cowmen talked or stayed silent, while the coyotes sang their songs, and the sandhill cranes honked their lonely music, I seemed to be seeing a great painting of something I'd known all my life. I seemed to be listening to a great epic of something that had been commonplace in my youth but now took on meanings. I was familiar with John A. Lomax's *Cowboy Songs and Other Frontier Ballads*. Indeed, I knew John Lomax himself very well. He had paid me $100 a year to write a monthly feature on faculty news for the *Alcalde*, which, as secretary of the Ex-Students' Association, he edited. One day it came to me that I would collect and tell the legendary tales of Texas as Lomax had collected the old-time songs and ballads of Texas and the frontier. I thought that the stories of the range were as interesting as the songs. I considered that if they could be put down so as to show the background out of which they have come, they might have high value.

If it had not been for Uncle Jim and Los Olmos, if it hadn't been for Santos Cortez, the taleteller, I don't know in what direction I might have gone. It was certainly lucky for me that I left the University in 1920 and learned something.

Uncle Jim went broke. The sharp decline of cattle prices beginning in 1920 broke cattlemen as the 1929 plummet broke stockholders. He and I agreed that I should go back to my old job at the University of Texas. There I helped reorganize the Texas Folklore Society, became editor of its publications, and have, since that time, been gathering, sorting and setting down the lore of Texas and the Southwest. My academic work has been erratic and disrupted; the other has not.

I soon became as much interested in the history and legends of the longhorn and mustang as in the traditions of old Sublett's gold in the Guadalupe Mountains. The coyote, the rattlesnake, the mesquite tree and the headless horseman of the Nueces are as interesting to me as the forty-nine jack loads of Spanish silver buried on the Colorado River just a few miles above Austin, where I live. If people are to enjoy their own lives, they must be aware of the significances of their own environments. The mesquite is, objectively, as good and as beautiful as the Grecian acanthus. It is a great deal better for people who live in the mesquite country. We in the Southwest shall be civilized when the roadrunner as well as the nightingale has connotations. Above all, I want to capture with their flavor, their metaphor, and their very genius the people who rode mustangs, trailed longhorns, stuck Spanish daggers (yucca spines) in their flesh to cure rattlesnake bites, and who yet hunt for the Lost Bowie Mine on the San Saba and prospect for Breyfogle's gold in Death Valley.

The qualities most lacking in American literature are flavor and gusto. Flavor and a gusto for life are, nevertheless, dominating qualities in the pioneer stock of America where freed from Puritanical restraint, and the pioneer stock of the Southwest was and yet is pretty free of that restraint. I can't understand why American realists think that in order to be faithful to life they must forever deal with the dull and banal.

Lord Chesterfield observed that he would rather "talk with a captain of foot than with Sir Isaac Newton." For me, the best talk in the world is made up of anecdotes, pictures of highly individualistic characters, tales with "some relish of the saltness of time" in them, about men who "climb for water and dig for food," ride "from hell to breakfast before daylight" — or sit all day long in the shade of a broken-down chuck wagon and smoke "them Mexkin cigarillos." Consequently I avoid as much as possible academicians with their eternal shop talk and drawing-room ornaments. I have sought the company of Mexican goat-herders, lawyers with an eye for characters and a zest for hunting, trail drivers and women who know how to cook frijoles in a black iron pot. I belong to the soil myself and the people of it are my people. I have certainly met many interesting talkers among them — and if they are interesting I don't care what else they are. We hear each other gladly.

In company with one superb storyteller I rode two hundred and fifty miles on a mule across the Sierra Madre. On the trail of the Lost Nigger Mine I took a pack horse and went with a borderer who kept a rusty lizard for a pet down into a rincon of the Big Bend of Texas that is as wild and rough as the Sierra Madre. While I was helping trail a herd of cows to the Gila River in Arizona the boss of the Double Circle outfit told me a fine yarn about one of the many desert lodes of that region.

In 1924 I compiled and edited for the Texas Folklore Society a volume entitled *Legends of Texas*, which contains several dozen legends of lost mines and buried treasures. That collection gave me a reputation among hunters for hidden wealth; they began coming to see me and telling me their stories.

The ordinary man wants to run away from machinery and plough-horse routine. He wants to be pointed to the rainbow's end. He wants to know where there is land not ploughed up, land with secret and strange possibilities of wealth. I have been approached more than once by men who want me to enter with them into a corporation for furnishing maps and data to prospectors. I shall never forget the two men from Kansas, father and son, who came to demonstrate their "minemeter," one of the many machines devised to locate underground minerals, and to get from me more detailed information about the forty-nine jack loads of silver. . . .

I have not told these stories to fool anybody, but I know

Storyteller W. W. Burton

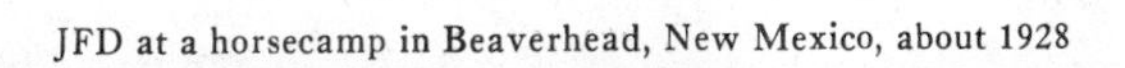

JFD at a horsecamp in Beaverhead, New Mexico, about 1928

Bertha and I

absolutely that I will get responses thick and fast from men who want to go out and dig. If you will read the long chapter on the "Lost San Saba Mine" and the long one on the "Lost Nigger Mine" you will see that these stories do not really come to an end. They cannot come to an end, for the searching and the digging go on.

CHAPTER SIXTEEN

Storytellers I Have Known

"Where do you get your stories?" people sometimes ask me. I look for them, lay for them, listen for them, hunt them, trail them down, swap for them, beg, borrow, and steal them, and value above rubies the person who gives me a good one.

Sunday newspaper article, July 15, 1951

THE first taleteller I recall was a man who got down off a tired canelo horse at our ranch in Live Oak County about sundown one fall evening. He was from up, away up, the Nueces River. In the darkness on the front gallery after supper he got strung out on panthers. One about which he wove a tale would have eaten up a turkey-hunter if the man had not had enough turkeys to feed the screaming, hungry brute, dropping them one by one at intervals on the ground while hastening through the brush to his horse tied at a "bobwire" fence. This panther man, whose name I never did learn, shivered my timbers in a way from which I have never recovered or wished to recover. Many nights out on the front gallery with Papa — Mama inside with the endless work — I listened to an owl in the liveoaks saying, "I cook for myself. Who cooks for you-all?" We listened to the crickets and to the coyotes and to the wind from the Gulf galloping in the treetops and to other components of silence; but on this night only the panther man spoke — to my ears at least.

The next storyteller really to enter my life came about twenty-five years later, after the First World War. I have already told how a goat-herder and hunter named Santos Cortez learned me his lore and changed my life. Listening to his talk, I resolved to collect the traditional tales of Texas. Texas soon got too small for me and other coherences came to supersede man-made geographical lines, and life inherent in tales extended itself. I have been listening for and to tales ever since, though I learned to have little truck with the literalists designated as scientific folklorists.

It was in 1923 that I left Beeville with a small rancher for Duval County on the trail of a legend pertaining to San Caja Mountain — just a long hill. At that time Archie Parr, in the Texas Senate, was known as the "Duke of Duval." His son George has been notorious for years as the inheritor of the Duke's ways. The little rancher I went with was not a good storyteller at all. He was too much of a literalist. Not far from his squat we passed a one-teacher frame schoolhouse inside about a half-acre of blackbrush and catclaw enclosed by three strings of barbed wire. "You might be surprised to know that that fence cost the county a thousand dollars," the little rancher said. I wasn't surprised. That's all he said on the subject.

I remember this helper in my search for stories mainly on account of his bed furnishings. There were not any sheets in the house, and the quilt I slept on had more animalitos on it than any other quilt I ever encountered. Really, though, it was not as bad as a bed I slept on in Karnes County while I was on the trail of a story about ghost riders, a story well told by Henry Yelvington in his *Ghost Lore*. This Karnes County bed didn't have any more sheets than the Duval County bed, but it had the seven-year itch — "just waiting," like the boll weevil, "for a home."

Then there was Ruggles. Late in December, 1927, I almost missed a midnight train to the north out of El Paso while C. B. Ruggles held me enthralled with his story of the Lost Tayopa Mine down in the Sierra Madre of Mexico. Two weeks later I was back in El Paso from a panther hunt in New Mexico, and Ruggles again held me until I barely caught a midnight train to the east. A few weeks later I outfitted with him and we rode with pack mules for ten days across the Sierra Madre — without going through a gate or seeing a wheel, except on a little oxcart that had never been out of the mountain valley where it was made. We were going to fabulous Tayopa, for which Ruggles had been prospecting for six years and which he thought he had finally located near a hamlet in Sonora named Guadalupe de Santa Ana. We were out nearly a month and in all that time Ruggles never palled as a storyteller.

"If Tayopa gives up its gold," I asked him, "what are you going to do?"

"I'm going to find La Gloria Pan."

The Gloria Pan, in Durango or somewhere else, is another of the legendary lost mines of the Sierra Madre. I wrote the story of Tayopa for a magazine and finally put it into a book, *Apache Gold and Yaqui Silver*. Four or five years after I rode the trail to it, I heard from Ruggles in Oklahoma. He was married and just back from Alaska, where he had had extraordinary experiences. He was expecting to have more. Then I lost track of him. I knew that Tayopa had not worked out. Over the years I have heard from various men who have "known" where it is, always at another location from that made by Ruggles.

One Sunday morning in a hotel room in Tucson, my telephone rang. "This is Mrs. C. B. Ruggles," the voice said.

"C. B. and I read in the paper that you are to make a talk at the University of Arizona. We have come up from Arivaca to see you."

Twenty-five years had passed since I had seen him, but Ruggles was himself, seventy-three years old now. He had two mining claims staked out near Arivaca, not far from the Arizona-Sonora line — and they would pay when the price of gold went up. Meanwhile he would be setting off soon for something unbelievably rich. This is the story he told, for he did not disappoint me.

Years ago on an expedition down into the Ocampo country of Chihuahua he took along an El Paso mining engineer named Noble. Each had his own mount and pack mule but they had in common a mozo — the servant, guide, part cook and altogether handy man so necessary for travel in the Sierra Madre.

In that country every trail goes down a canyon, up a canyon, over a mountain to another canyon. One day Ruggles and Noble stopped in a canyon at the mouth of a side-canyon, and while they were halted Ruggles walked two or three hundred yards up this side-canyon until he came to a waterfall over a ledge. There was not much water in the stream; beneath the ledge was a shallow pool. In it Ruggles saw something that looked like an enormous blue egg. It was too big to have been laid by any bird on earth. The blue was almost indigo. There it was in the shallow water. He got down near it and stooped to pick it up. He could not budge it. The underpart was covered with slime that made a hand-hold difficult. He crossed his legs, got a firmer hold and still could not raise the "egg."

Looking about, he saw a large ball of the same color. He picked it up but was astounded at the weight. It was solid something. Then he picked up a smaller ball. The balls, manifestly, were not rocks. He knew that they had come from some formation nearby. Examining the ledge more closely, he saw that it was made of gneiss attached to a vein of the blue substance. He tried to break off some of the blue substance but could not. He followed the vein for maybe a quarter of a mile up one side of the canyon and saw that it lay exposed up the other side. Then he took the two balls and carried them to camp.

He showed them to the mining engineer, Noble.

"I don't know what it is," Noble said, "but it is worthless. I know that." And he threw the larger ball, which he had taken in his hands, down.

Ruggles picked it up and put it in his morral hanging to the horn of his saddle. He put the smaller ball in a saddle pocket. Noble remonstrated with him for carrying so much weight, though the horse that carried it belonged to Ruggles. On the way out of the canyon he kept harping on the weight until, finally, Ruggles discarded the large ball but kept the small one.

He had it when they got back to El Paso. Whether the heavy stuff was worthless or not, he wanted to know what it was. He knew an assayer named Millar, who had an office downtown but taught in the College of Mines. He figured that Millar would be at his office about eight o'clock in the morning before going to the college.

A little before eight he reached the office. And there Noble was.

"You've brought your little blue ball, I guess," Noble taunted.

Talking to the assayer in private could not be very well managed. Ruggles handed him the small ball.

"I don't know what it is," the assayer said, "but if you will let me, I will take it with me up to the College of Mines and find out. You won't mind if we cut off a slice for assaying?"

Ruggles did not mind. About three o'clock that afternoon he was back at the office.

"Nobody," the assayer said, "ever saw anything like this. It assays ninety-eight and nine-tenths per cent pure silver. I can't imagine what sort of formation it is out of. That color is unknown to silver."

Ruggles got back what was left of the ball. As he stepped out onto the street another man associated with the College of Mines accosted him. He had just been fired, but Ruggles did not know it. The assayer had shown him the blue ball, and now he asked to take it for further examination. Ruggles let him have it — and that night he left for South America.

"But, Ruggles," I said at this point of his narrative, "prospectors have been all over the Sierra Madre for hundreds of years. Why wouldn't some of them have discovered long ago such an exposed vein of pure silver?"

"They were just like Noble," Ruggles replied. "They saw it and did not recognize it. And it's still there, where it's been for thousands of years. There's a good automobile road into Ocampo now. All a man needs is a jeep, a crowbar and a metal saw. A hunk of that blue stuff no bigger than an old-time case of canned tomatoes would make a jeepload. There'll be no milling involved. The stuff can be taken straight to the mint at Chihuahua City. Ninety-eight and nine-tenths per cent pure silver!"

Two or three years before I saw him in Tucson, Ruggles made a trip into Chihuahua to bring out some of the blue silver. When he got to the canyon where it is located, he found eight or ten feet of dashing water. The rainy season was on. He stayed for a week or so waiting for the water to run down, but rains kept adding to it. His time was limited; he had to return to Arizona.

While he was telling of his plans to go back again, he said that he might take a modern metal detector, go to the church at Guadalupe de Santa Ana in Sonora — his location for

Tayopa — and find all the ancient treasures supposed to be buried under it.

"But, Ruggles," I said, "why fool with unknown treasures when that great vein of silver, ninety-eight and nine-tenths per cent pure, is there for the taking?"

"I guess you are right," he said. "Come and go with me."

In the summer of 1933, I went down to Saltillo with Henry Nash Smith, of *Virgin Land* fame, now at the University of California. From Saltillo we rode on a short train over a jerk-water railroad to the end of it and got burros to take us to a hacienda in Zacatecas called Los Cedros — the only time I ever rode a burro on a pack trip. The administrador of the hacienda was a good storyteller. He helped a person soak up life. When the Madero Revolution began in 1910, Los Cedros had an extensive vineyard, but every time the Carranzistas came they sacked the winecellar, and every time the Villistas came they sacked it again, and finally the owner ordered all the grapevines uprooted so he wouldn't have any wine, and that's the way it was when we were there.

We left this hacienda on good horses, with a good mozo, and took nearly a day to travel to an outpost to which the administrador had sent word that hospitality be extended to us — as it certainly was. The caporal of the outpost insisted on our sleeping inside. The house was beautifully whitewashed, but at that time over great parts of the outlands of Mexico any traveler took his bedding. I've been to *posadas* (inns) where I was expected to use my own bedding. Henry Smith and I each had a bedstead on which to spread our bedrolls. Our mozo lay on the floor with his head just inside the door, to guard us. No sooner was our candle blown out than I began to feel something, something conducting itself in a vulgarly familiar manner. The familiars were not the fleas in one of Roy Bedichek's stories. A cowboy said he didn't mind what the fleas ate so much as what they tromped out. These weren't fleas.

"Henry," I asked, "do you feel anything?"

"I certainly do," he replied. "It bites, and I don't know what it is."

"Well," I said, "I do." I lit a match and saw bedbugs by the hundreds scurrying up the whitewashed walls and over my tarpaulin.

I said to the mozo, "We're going to get out of here."

The moon was full and we took our beds off about a hundred yards from the house and spread them down on the ground, where we got rid of what we could see on the sheets and tarpaulins.

You're not going to get tales that linger in the imagination except from people who have time to linger, time to stand and stare at cows or anything else that comes along. In my experience, the best taletellers did not spend hours a day in a bathroom scrubbing themselves. The first time that Bertha Dobie and I were in Saltillo at the old Saenz Hotel there were no tourists in the town, and the cook served frijoles fritos for breakfast, plain frijoles for dinner, and nacionales for supper. Our waiter had time to tell a story about a coyote and a cricket — a story that years later I put into my coyote book. Imagine a waiter in a wholesale eating place having enough time to tell you a long cuento and to pass the time of day besides that. The diners were so sparse in this hotel of repose that two of them, entire strangers, upon finishing their meal and passing near our table on the way out, murmured politely, "*Buen provecho!*" (May it, the food, benefit you!). Tales belong with such courtesy and such leisure.

The last time we were in Saltillo, which was in 1954 during the big drouth, we stayed again at the Saenz Hotel, all rebuilt, modernized, bustling with business. In front of it the afternoon we arrived, I was accosted by a young man who said he was a guide, and would I accept his services? "No," I said, "I don't want a guide. I want a story. I've been guided too much already."

"What do you want a story about?" he asked.

"It doesn't make any difference what — about a rattlesnake, a coyote, a woman without any head who keeps crying, a bear — whatever you wish."

"Oh," he said, "my grandfather has a story that's true about a bear."

"Well," I said, "guide me to your grandfather."

He said, "*Mañana.*"

"You'll find me here at this hotel *mañana*," I said.

Late the next day we met on a street and I asked, "Why did you not come to take me to your grandfather?"

"My grandfather's sick and can't see you," he replied.

"How am I going to learn that story about a bear?"

"I know it. I'll tell it to you."

"When?"

"I've got some people to guide now. *Mañana.*"

The next day when we met I gave him five pesos and said, "I want to hear that story about the bear."

He said, "*Con mucho gusto.*"

We went into a cantina where there were chairs at an empty table, peace, and beer. There he told me a fine story about a bear that kidnapped a bride and took her off and made her his own mate.

This reminds me of one of the best stories I ever heard anywhere, and of a philosophy about stories. Luck is being ready for the chance. I've had lots of chances, have missed lots of them, but not all. In hearing stories much depends on chance — as in falling in love and in getting married. I believe, however, that ninety per cent of what are usually called "lucky finds" accrue to people who have made preparations and have the ability to recognize and catch hold of a find when it is within reach.

In the fall of 1932 I was with pack mules and mozo twisting around, through, and across the mountains of northern Mexico to the west — always to the west — just looking, listening, and living the most independent form of life I have known. Except for a few fences and ranchos, the country was all open and unrestricted by man — a country immense, immense. It seemed to belong to me as much as to anybody else. In the high Sierra Madre itself there were no fences at all excepting poles around little corn patches, no ranches, only *rancherías* (settlements) of poor — but always generous — squatters. Some of these squatters instead of fencing corn patches guarded them in season against bears.

One morning I saw a small bear running up the side of a mountain. I was not ready for the chance to shoot, despite the fact that I always carried my .30-.30 in a scabbard attached to my saddle. My saddle mule was bent on going the opposite direction. That afternoon we came to a perfect place to camp: wood, water, grass, scenery, all outdoors to hunt in if one wanted to hunt. I had a strong impulse to linger, but had set out to reach the Colorado ranch that night. I was making for high country and left next morning for the Piedra Blanca ranch at the foot of the Del Carmen Mountains. This was in Coahuila. It was the time of the year for cold nights and hot days. I rode ahead across a greasewood plain, breathing the dust raised by my mule. Late in the day I came to the first watering — well, windmill, troughs — at a place called Los Huérfanos (The Orphans) on account of two sharply defined hills, the Del Carmen range looming over them. The shack at Los Huérfanos was deserted. Three or four horses with scarred backs were near the troughs. My mule was absolutely played out. I drove the horses into the pen, roped the freshest-looking, saddled him, and led my mule on for the Piedra

Blanca. I knew I was in the Piedra Blanca range. After mozo and pack mules arrived two hours later, we made camp but ate with the Piedra Blanca vaqueros.

A superannuated American who had been with Frederic Remington in Mexico was very hospitable, locating me in a room with two beds. The house was small. After supper he disappeared, and I went out to the kitchen, with thatched roof and walls of tightly wattled poles, apart from the house. A good fire was burning on a platform of clay and rocks in the center of the kitchen (or roofed corral) and against the walls pine logs that had been dragged down from the mountain served as benches. Four or five vaqueros sat on them.

The cook, a powerful man named Ismael, was washing dishes. He was puro Indio, pure quill, as black as Othello. I guessed that instead of shaving he just pulled now and then a few stray hairs out of his face. Tonight he had a fresh audience, and from something I had said or from the way I looked he knew he had an eager listener. Almost at once he launched into a long story, a true epic, of Juan Oso (John Bear), the son of a he-bear and a Christian woman. The story split off into and incorporated several fairy tales and parts of other hero tales. I later put the Juan Oso part into *Tongues of the Monte*. It was midnight when we went to bed.

I had hardly more than gone to sleep when a voice very far from gentle roused me. The owner of the Piedra Blanca ranch, from Del Rio, was standing over me. He had brought a beef-buyer from Kansas; both had their wives and had to sleep in the house. I got up, got out with all my personal belongings, unrolled my bedroll in my own camp, and was perfectly contented. When you become at home with pack mule and camp you find yourself gloriously liberated from things — things — things.

The next morning when I got up, the beef men were gone, but the wives were there. They seemed to expect me to entertain them, and when I told them the story of the half-breed bear-man, thus fixing it better in my memory and learning how it could be improved in spots, they were manifestly shocked.

A thousand times I have reflected on swart Ismael there in the corral kitchen at Piedra Blanca as about the most picturesque, abounding, plenteous storyteller I have encountered, a kind of Alexandre Dumas in energy of creation, anything but "mute," however illiterate, and glorying in his own output. Many times also I have reflected: what if I had stayed at that fine camping place a day and a half back and had arrived at the Piedra Blanca after the money-hungry owners and their respectable wives were already established there? I should have eaten with them, been obliged to share their domestic dullness, never have heard Ismael at all, never learned about Juan Oso. Of course, after I heard this bear-man story, I began to hear variants, just as after acquiring a new word one begins noticing its use in all sorts of places.

I tell you a tale tonight which a seaman told to me
With eyes that gleamed in the lanthorn light and
a voice as low as the sea.

Maybe I never heard but one taleteller who had a voice in which was the sound of the sea. Late in 1940, before the United States had joined against Hitler and his Germans, I was in Montana hunting bear stories. I headquartered on the ranch of my old friend Marcus Snyder, who wasn't a Texan but a Texian. He and all his people were out of the old rock. He wasn't much of a storyteller, but he was muy amigo with Chief Yellow Tail of the Crow Indians. Chief Yellow Tail wasn't much of a storyteller either, but he knew well the leading storyteller of his tribe. In fact, he knew several storytellers. Yellow Tail got me an able and understanding interpreter named Shiveley, a half-breed, and for several days I listened to ancient Crows tell stories about bears.

One of them I remember more vividly than I remember even his best tale. He was tall, spare, maybe six-feet-two, dark, saturnine in countenance, decayed in frame, but majestical in representing the mighty past of his people. We were sitting where we could look out at approaching winter, getting colder every day, snow coming down. Some days I would ride out on Marcus Snyder's ranch and watch the rabbits turn white. Every day they'd be a little whiter, and after a while what looked like jackrabbits to begin with were snow rabbits. This ancient Crow sat where he and I could both contemplate with our eyes the Big Horn Mountains. Sometimes we sat there for whiles without breaking the silence. I told him that I did not want just a bear story. I wanted a story of a bear hero, as there are men heroes. He told about a bear named Looks Both Ways. This bear had killed a woman, and the warriors had gathered to go against him. He rose up in a thicket of wild chokeberries to meet them, and he made signs, taking the bravery away from each enemy heart and putting it into his own heart. They could not defeat him, although they were mighty warriors. I shall never forget the mountain-and-sea-combined sounds of that old Crow's voice, or his dignity as he told on in harmony with the vastness and the silence of the Big Horn Mountains.

On this fruitful expedition to Montana I went from the Crow Indians to the Lame Deer Cheyenne reservation, where I was taken for an importer of peyote but got another good bear story. Then I went to Great Falls. As soon as I had parked my car, I made a beeline for the Mint Saloon to see the Charles M. Russell pictures. Almost at once I became muy amigo with Sid Willis, owner of the Mint, and, according to him, at one time a boon companion with Charlie Russell. He told me some Russell stories that belong in another place. One slash of realism may never get printed. Sid advised me not to pay out good money on a hotel but to go upstairs in a house across the street where I could find a room at a very reasonable rate.

Staying at the same place was an old cowpuncher named Bob Kennon who had known Charlie Russell and whom Sid Willis designated as my guide and guardian. We drove up to the Canadian line, where it was cold enough to freeze the horns off a brass billygoat and where, because the system craved it, plain meat tasted like something the gods had ordered. I found another interpreter and learned two or three more bear tales from the Blackfoot Indians. While Bob Kennon and I were holed up in a little hotel in the town of Browning he told me the story of a noted lobo wolf named Snowdrift. When we got back to Great Falls, he came into my room and retold the story slowly while I took it down in longhand. Eight or ten years went by before I referred to it. Then, upon request of an outdoor magazine for something, I wrote it out and got a $500 check for it. I'll die feeling mean because I did not at once make a search for Bob Kennon and share with him. I regard the Snowdrift story as one of the best I've written on any subject. How casual the chances for good stories seem!

To approach Nat Straw logically I must go away back in time. When *Coronado's Children* came out in 1931 as a Literary Guild book, the promoters held something of a blowout in New York. At one function an editor of *Vanity Fair* commissioned me to write two pieces. I titled one piece "Golden Liars of the Golden West" — mostly a concatenation of yarns. One of them I had heard told by a hunter of mountain lions on the Double Circle Ranch in Arizona. He credited it to Nat Straw. It's a bear story. As I know now but didn't know then, it is a folktale that has traveled from one host to another.

Nat Straw had tamed a grizzly to ride and one day rode him up the mountain just for exercise, or maybe to enjoy the scenery. He didn't take a gun with him, and so couldn't shoot when he came upon another bear away up in the tall timber. This second bear wasn't a bit shy and his bear wasn't either, and so Nat Straw dismounted and let him fight. He rode without saddle or bridle. The two bears fought and they fit, and Nat got scared that his bear was getting the worst of it. Easing up to the bears, he grabbed one by the ear, straddled him, and headed him down the mountain. About halfway down he became unable to guide the animal and in pulling its ears noticed that one of them was notched — not his bear at all.

At the time that *Vanity Fair* published "Golden Liars of the Golden West," with Nat Straw leading all the rest, a friend of mine named Clarence Insall was covering lots of country gathering walnut roots to ship to France so they could be made into briar pipes and shipped back to the United States for us smokers. He knew Nat Straw and, expecting to see him on the Gila River, took him a copy of the magazine making vain use of his name. After reading the piece, Nat Straw told the walnut-root hunter to tell me that he certainly was not the only liar in the West.

Maybe seven years later, I was in New Mexico trailing down the Lost Adams Diggings, one of the happiest trails I was ever on. After having received, high up in the Mogollones, among the mountaintops, authentic tidings of things both visible and invisible, I went to Santa Fe on the road to Texas. Here I ran into two old friends, Stokely Ligon, naturalist, and Dub Evans, rancher and lion-hunter. When I told them what I'd been doing, they said, "The idea of being on the trail of the Lost Adams Diggings and not seeing Nat Straw! Why, Nat Straw took up with a Navajo squaw so he could learn the tribal secrets of the Adams gold. You've simply got to see him before you leave New Mexico. He has more lore on the Adams Diggings than any other man in the country."

I found Nat Straw on the Gila River above Silver City, living with a young couple. Out a short distance from their house I camped under the biggest cottonwood tree I've ever seen. Nat had quit yarning, he said, and had lost all interest in the Adams Diggings. He said that at the time he lost interest he wrote high up on an aspen: "The Adams Diggings is a shadowy naught that lies in the valley of fanciful thought." Yet he had experienced some fine stories before he came to that poetical conclusion. While he was telling all he knew and a little that he didn't know about the Adams Diggings, he kept bringing in bears, bears, bears. Frequently I had to pull him off bears back to gold.

After I had pumped him dry on the main subject I encouraged him to head out on bears. When he got wound up on Old Susie, the last famous grizzly killed in New Mexico, I said, "Mr. Straw, I can sell your bear stories to the *Saturday Evening Post*. I'll give you twenty per cent of the check."

I spent another day with him getting bear stories and on the road to Austin composed the piece in my mind; it was rising like yeast and composed itself. Within two or three weeks Wesley Stout of the *Post* had written as warm a reception as anything of mine sent to an editor ever aroused. Maybe this was the happiest experience I have had with a storyteller that I hadn't been looking for. If you are ready, you'll meet them when you're looking for them, and you'll meet them when you're not looking for them. They show up as deer show up to a deer-hunter.

On the way to England in 1945 to teach in the GI University at Shrivenham I was delayed a few days in New York. About sundown one evening while I was walking from 42nd Street up a short block to the Biltmore Hotel on 43rd Street next to the Grand Central Station and only a block from the Air Terminal, the street not crowded at all, I saw a Negro man looking mighty happy. Maybe thirty-eight years old, slenderish, wearing a smile and a little hat, he came tripping my way.

Under one arm was a bottle-shaped package. There could be no doubt that he had been keeping company with a bottle. His smiling face shone with joy. Every now and then his feet were flashing cuts of the Pigeon Wing, or maybe it was the Double Shuffle. Then he would let out a very low and not at all peace-disturbing shout of joy.

I stopped, fascinated. Other pedestrians paused, then passed. I moved toward the corner, and the joyful one capered my way. A young Negro passed him, turned his head slightly and without coming to a halt gave him a warning. The celebrator raised his voice, his spirits rising with it. "He's back from France, and thinks he'll tell us folks how to act."

He came to me talking. "Yes, I've danced in high places. Boss Man said he wanted me to dance. I said I'd dance if he paid me top money. Boss Man said he'd pay me top money if I could tell a bigger lie than anybody in Europe. This is what I told him:

"One time there was a planter had twenty-eight hundred acres black bottom land, and he planted it all in corn, every acre of it. The rains came right, and the crop turned out fine. He gathered it and next year planted another crop, and it was fine. He went on that way for eight years, and gathered all that corn off them twenty-eight hundred acres, and he never sold a sack of it, just kept it. He was laying it all up.

"He built what we call a crib. It was two miles and eight square feet this way and two miles and eight square feet that way, then two miles and eight square feet over yonder way, and two miles and eight square feet the other way. It had a cement floor so weevils couldn't come up. It had a concrete wall all around one hundred feet high, and it had a roof all over it. And when the planter got all that corn for eight years off his twenty-eight hundred acres in the crib, it was chock full. He locked it up and said he didn't need no more corn.

"There was just one hole in that wall, and it was a little hole to let air in. And then along came the seven-year locusts. One of them spied the hole and he flew in. Locusts like corn, you know. This seven-year locust, he stayed there seven years, and then he flew out with a grain of corn. Another locust was waiting to take his place, and he flew in and he stayed seven years, and then he took out another grain.

" 'It wasn't the same locust?' Boss Man asked me.

" 'No, 'twan't same locust. It was 'nother one.'

"Then Number Three locust, he flew in and stayed seven years and took out his grain of corn. Number Four, he was ready, and he sizzled in and he stayed seven years.

" 'Looky here,' Boss Man says, 'you going to keep them locusts flying in there one at a time and staying seven years till they get every grain carried out of this big crib?'

" 'That's just what them locusts have to do, Boss Man,' I says.

" 'Well,' he says, 'you done told a bigger lie than any of them people from Europe can tell.' "

Here a man who had paused a minute or so to listen to this New York sidewalk variation of one of the *Arabian Nights* tales warned the entertainer that his package was about to slip from under his arm.

"It don't make no difference if it does break," the shining one said. "I got plenty of money, just plenty."

And he skipped away and out of sight.

"The best adventures are not those we go to seek."

Some of the most memorable storytellers I have encountered were, like this dancing Negro on a New York street at the end of the day, but ships that pass in the night. Two I'm thinking of gave me only a single sample each of their powers.

Away back in the 1930s when I used to go panther and

wildcat hunting with Bob Snow, game warden with the Texas Game and Fish Department and exponent of the border country, he spoke frequently of the storytelling abilities of his friend Saturnino Cantú away down in the lower Rio Grande Valley. One fall day my wife Bertha and I were in the vicinity of Raymondville, where Bob Snow's brother Luther reigned as sheriff and where Bob was lingering a little while. They had us for a fine supper of white-winged doves. I'd been prodding Bob on the storyteller. It must have been more than an hour after dark when we finished eating. "Now we'll go hear Saturnino," Bob said.

"He's asleep by now," I countered.

"We'll wake him up."

Then Bob drove us a few miles over a dirt road to a jacal with a field in front of it and with thickets of mesquite and other brush surrounding the other three sides. The cabin was in darkness, but Bob, with his loud, cheery voice, soon aroused Saturnino. He came out in the starlight buttoning his shirt.

After a swift introduction in Spanish, Bob said to Saturnino Cantú, "This gentleman likes stories. I have been telling him what a fine storyteller you are. Please do us the favor to tell a story."

"With pleasure," Saturnino responded, "but what shall I tell a story about?"

"About anything you please," Bob instructed.

By now Saturnino was wide awake. He didn't hesitate for a minute. He was a professional troubadour in his way. He did not have to be reminded by something of something else. He struck out at once into an ancient story, probably brought by the Moors to Spain and then taken by the Spaniards from Spain to Mexico, of "the two companions." He told on like an accordion, giving out notes while both inhaling and exhaling. His voice was musical, rising and falling in the manner of many old-time Mexicans. We sat in the car while he stood there in the starlight and told on and on the picaresque traditional tale of two rascals exceedingly fertile in their creative lying. I put the story in the yearbook published by the Texas Folklore Society in 1944, *From Hell to Breakfast*. As I look back, the ebullient liars of the tale do not seem nearly so interesting to me now as the storyteller named Saturnino.

During World War II while the patriots of what is now West Germany and also East Germany bombed London almost nightly, I was living with the dons in Emmanuel College, Cambridge, as visiting professor of American history. There's nothing in America like the colleges of the old English universities. Every night, almost, some man from far away who had been at Emmanuel came to High Table for dinner. After dinner we always repaired to the Common Room for talk with wine and then with coffee and tobacco. A man might linger there a good while or he might rush away to work or to some other pleasure.

On the night I'm thinking of, I lingered. The guest was a taut, slender man somewhat short of forty, back from India or Afghanistan or Egypt or some other country that I cannot be sure of. He wasn't saying much, but everything he said went home to me, and before long only we were left in front of the grate in which coal burned cheerfully. There was a little wine left in the decanter, for Page, the butler, had not taken it away. I've forgotten this man's name. Worst of all, I've forgotten the story he told. It was a kind of fable with biting irony on life, something akin to the seven ages of man in Shakespeare or the ages of man in the folktale that does not get into respectable print. After I was alone, I wrote the story down. I sent it back to Texas for printing in a few newspapers for which I've written a Sunday column for many years. I've been unable to find it either in my files or in any newspaper. I guess it never got across the Atlantic.

Many, many times I've remembered that Englishman sitting there by the coal fire telling this ancient tale of withering irony. I imagine he had many other such tales, for a person who loves stories learns many, and if he can tell one, he's bound to tell others.

I remember a few storytellers, not the very best, because they entered into my life in a way to change it. *Legends of Texas* was in the past, and I was gathering, gathering tales of lost mines and buried treasures to be woven into *Coronado's Children.* A bright student in a very bright class of mine at the University of Texas was named Leeper Gay, brother to a successful and respectable lawyer — but Leeper never intended to be either successful or respectable. A theme he wrote me was about a man looking for the Lost San Saba Mine. Then he introduced me to Wes Burton.

Wes must have been toward fifty years old at the time and lived with his parents in South Austin, across the Colorado River from the main areas of culture and self-righteousness. His father, who had been a Confederate soldier and a trail driver, had a bully story on the origin of that sad ballad "When Work's All Done This Fall." His sister Pinkie, corpulent and blind, played an organ and sang ballads going back to the eighteenth century and beyond. What with singing and with taletelling, sometimes it would be two o'clock in the morning before I got home from a visit to the Burtons.

They had a ghost in the yard, had seen him on several occasions. He belonged to a man who had been killed in the kitchen, and Mrs. Burton said they couldn't scrub his blood out of the floor. They tried to show "the damned spots" to me, but I couldn't see them.

Wes was a blacksmith turned mechanic; he would work a few months and get money enough to stake himself and some fellow-dreamer for a long hunt for what he called Los Almagres Mine — another name for the Lost San Saba, or Lost

Bowie. One time he brought in some kind of ore that he was melting in an iron pot over a wood fire out in the yard when I got to the Burton house. He had extracted about a tablespoonful of it and didn't know what it was. He knew very well it wasn't silver.

"Wes," I said, "I'll just take it over to the University and get the geology department to analyze it. It won't cost you anything."

"That's fine," he agreed.

After staying and enjoying myself for maybe two hours, I said, "Well, I'll take that ore now."

"No," Wes said, "I don't believe I'll let you take it." Then he added, "Them fellers over there would just bumfuzzle me with their assaying business."

To quote Henry Ford, "I don't like to read books. They mess up my mind."

The first word I had from Bill Cole of Valentine, Texas, was in 1924. Newspapers over the state had been generous in helping me stir up interest in legendary tales. After reading a sample I had sent to an El Paso paper, Bill Cole wrote me to ask how much he would have to pay the United States Government when he lifted out twenty-five mule-loads of Monterrey loot buried at El Muerto Springs in Jeff Davis County. He knew that the stuff was there and that he was going to lift it out before the coming summer rains set in — if they came. His sole uncertainty was on how much he would have to fork over to Uncle Sam.

One of his early letters — slightly trimmed, with a few punctuation marks and capital letters applied for the sake of clarity — will say more about the man's mind than I can say.

Kind Sir. In 1917 the state stoped my business, pool hall and siegar stand. I went after 3 different bunches of burried stuff, an I will say without braging that I am the chieff finder of texas up to date. [This simply means that he had found lots of places to dig.] You nodout have heard of the 2 sets of crosses and 2 springs near Davis peak at location of old stage stand where there is 25 mules loads under a big flat rock sealed up with concreet made up with Blood. I thought that was to many mules but it is all true. They made up the concreet with granite gravel an a white lime formation an stuck it to gather with antelope Blood. The stuff had to be blowed with dinimite.

I want to know when an who got a patton on 320 acr in Block 360, sec. 21, Jeffdavis Co. If you get a chance to get that information for me you will get paid for your trouble. Capt Fox knowes me. I think he is on the poliece force at Brownesvill. When ever a man dont think them oldtimers did not bring gold an silver a cross [the Rio Grande] by mule train he is badly mistaken, there is 105 mule loads in pinto canion, precidio Co. there is a bunch in marves [Maravillas] canion in Brewster Co.

I have a map to the pinto canion stuff if you will come out here about next may or June wee will try them both a whirl. I will be done with my Jeffdavis Co stuff an I will furnish all the expence money we will need. I know that sounds like B S but its a fact. The old time mexicans know it but there priest tells them not to work after burried treasure. I had to do all my work myself — could not hire them at $4.00 per day.

hoping to hear from you
W. E. Cole
Valentine, Tex

There is no occasion for retelling here the story of the Monterrey loot. I dwell on Bill Cole's satisfaction with the evidence. "While I was digging through the concreet made out of antelope Blood and granite gravel," he wrote, "flies would blow my clothes whenever I came to the surface. When I told this to anybody in Valentine they would look at me as if they thought I was crazy. They've had a chance to help raise money to dig on down but they don't take it. They don't know what the evidence is."

In the summer of 1926 while on a ranch out from Sierra Blanca, I sent Bill Cole a telegram saying that if he was to be in town on the following Saturday, I'd see him. He telegraphed, "I'll be here." Perhaps he was looking for me to come by car. I took the Southern Pacific train and got off at Valentine late in the afternoon. While the train was pulling out, I spotted the combination telegraph operator and passenger and freight agent. He wore those funereal black covers over shirt sleeves from wrist to above elbow that telegraph operators used to wear. His complexion was sallow and his eyes were dim; he was chewing tobacco.

"Could you tell me where to find Bill Cole?" I asked him.

He grunted, made a motion, and walked up the platform maybe forty feet, I following. Then he stopped and spat on the ground and said, "You see them whittlin's?" I saw them. "Jest follow them whittlin's," he said, "and you'll come to Bill Cole's house." Valentine was and is a small village. It wasn't hard for me to find the house.

Bill Cole, about fifty-five years old, was there reposing behind his black handle-bar moustache. His hair was as black as his moustache, his black eyes flashing whenever he spoke with any feeling. He had deliberate ways but was emphatic in his views, and he was very hospitable. His mother kept a roominghouse for railroad men, feeding them at times. She had a room for me. I appreciated her cooking. I stayed two days and nights getting the story of the Monterrey loot and going out to the El Muerto location where Bill had been digging for years and was to keep on digging — at his leisure — for the remaining thirty years of his life.

He was always bothered by water seeping into the shaft. He couldn't raise enough money to get strong enough pumps to pump it out. His crowbar got stuck in silver two or three times, he claimed, but he never could pry any silver out. To use the words of a Bill Cole letter, "I can make afidivid that I seen refined gold an silver in that hole in two different places. The last time in the botum it showed on my crowbar plain."

My book with the story of the Monterrey loot was published in 1931. After that I heard from Bill only occasionally. One time while driving through Valentine, distingushed by extra ample shipping pens, I saw a charcoal sign on a vacant building beside the road: *Bill Cole Champion Burried Treasure Hunter.* He felt, I think, that I had not taken him seriously enough in the book I sent him. As in the song of Frankie and Johnnie, "I meant no harm."

After ten or eleven years had gone by I was on the Southern Pacific going to El Paso. As usual, the train stopped at Valentine for the engine to take on water. I thought Bill might be down to see the train pass and walked forward to where some baggage trucks stood on the platform. Bill was sitting on one of them, slumped over, whittling.

"Hello, Bill," I said.

He looked up and said, "I'm in water now."

"Why, you were in water when I saw you fifteen years ago," I said.

He looked as wise as a treeful of hoot owls, and commented, "There are wimmin and wimmin, and there are waters and waters."

"You mean you're in the right water now?" I asked.

He looked at me as if to say, "You are a damned fool for asking a question with such an obvious answer." The conductor called all aboard, and that was the last I heard Bill say on the Monterrey loot.

In 1948 a man working for the State Department in Washington wrote me that he and his son George had been to California and had returned East through Valentine, Texas, in order to visit Bill Cole. That was George's idea, conceived by Bill Cole's hunt for the Monterrey loot as told in *Coronado's Children.* Sixteen years old, George did not want to go to school any more; his parents hoped he would be led into the respectable path of either geologist or mining engineer. The

State Department man wanted to know whether I thought Bill Cole would be a proper mentor for George. Before I could make up my mind on what to say, George's mother wrote me in great concern also. I inferred that she did not know her husband had written. She said Bill Cole had offered to board George and pay him $2 a day to dig. What did I think of Bill Cole as a beginning teacher in mining?

I never have felt as sufficient as Dorothy Dix, or a father confessor, or Dear Abby in advising people how to conduct their private lives. On the other hand, I never have felt so insufficient that I wanted to turn my life over to some myth, some Billy Graham form of sensationalist, some ecclesiastical corporation. The Department of State man had seen Bill Cole and talked with him; he had a better chance than I at knowing his son George. I left it to the pair to make up their own minds. So far as I know, George did not enroll in Bill Cole's school of mining. Of course, he could have done a lot worse. He could have enrolled in some School of Education.

The last letter I had from Bill Cole, written in March 1947, concludes thus, most of the punctuation marks being added:

> Since I seen you, instead of one location out where I was at work, there is 5. I have done work on all 5 — enough to satisfy me that I am right, but have not finished any one place. If you come out this way this summer stop an see me, if you get here at night and I am gone get a kee from Conring and take my room — the east front room, there will be a bed in there, then next morning come on out to the mountains — you know the way.

In the summer of 1958 an intelligent and able young man of Austin named Ed Wallace, who had prospected in the Chinati Mountains and elsewhere out from Valentine, came to see me. He had been with Bill Cole a good deal before Cole died in 1957 at the age of eighty-six. Bill, he said, had maintained a wholesome unconcern for his soul until he died, had carried himself erect as of old, and always had money enough to drink good whiskey and eat good meat regularly. He enjoyed sharing both with somebody he liked. He evidently liked Ed Wallace, who had come across him first in the mountains.

Bill had not confined his digging to the mountains. He dug two big holes in his own front yard and tore down the gallery — some call it porch — to the house in order to dig under it. This was after his mother, old, old, had died. He was following "sure leads." His crowbar had got hung in what Bill pronounced "bullion" in one of the holes in the yard. It took a block and tackle to pull the crowbar loose.

Of all the storytellers who imparted something out of themselves to me, Railroad Smith alone revealed a plan for stringing together stories that he either told or left half-told. Back in the days when the University of Texas campus consisted of forty acres and no skyscraper, R. R. Smith used to "come home," as he put it, once in a while to talk. He could talk through the day and talk through the night. He was long beyond the longest of art. His figure was as elongated as that of Abraham Lincoln and his countenance was as tristful as that of Don Quixote, though he had a strong laugh in his belly. He had a long-drawn-out voice that was lingeringly pleasant to hear; his eyes could see a long way into space and also into people. He belonged to the liveoaks, mesquites, prickly pear, ranch manners, dry weather, homemade ethics, and take-your-time psychology of Atascosa County, which is down in the Brush Country.

He was a lawyer — mainly a criminal lawyer — belonging to times antedating the corporation practice of retaining most of the good lawyers of the country. He was proficient in selecting juries and also in swaying them with voice and words; he studied humanity more perhaps than he studied law books. He lived on a few acres including a calf pasture out from Jourdanton. He called his place Goat Hill and his friends called him the Philosopher of Goat Hill. A few people knew that his first name was Ralph, but everybody called him Railroad. He had read a good deal of history and poetry. He admired Jim Hogg — the one statesman, a liberal, that Texas had had for governor since Sam Houston — and he had a genius for letting things soak into him while he rested in the shade.

The bent of some of his ideas may be deduced from a pamphlet that he published in 1925. The title page reads: "A Little Preachment and a Short Epistle to the Bigots of Texas, by Brother Railroad Smith. For sale to Students of the University of Inquiring Minds and to Ex-Students of the University of Texas at 25 Cents the Copy, Prepaid." The time may come when this will be as much a "collector's item" — often a term for something nobody wants to read — as a pamphlet written by some ignoramus on some criminal of six-shooter notoriety. However, I myself do not expect to see the cult of violence surrender to cultivation of the civilized.

One of my long talks with, or, more accurately, listenings to, Railroad Smith was about the time "A Little Preachment" came out. I don't remember where we started, but midnight and then two o'clock found us sitting on the sidewalk at the corner of 23rd and Guadalupe streets in front of the University of Texas. One of Railroad's ideas was to write down a collection of old-time Texas stories. They were to be told in a blacksmith shop by a blacksmith sharpening an ax on a grindstone. This blacksmith would pour water on the grindstone to keep it from making the steel too hot and taking away its temper. While he talked on, holding the ax in his hand, the water would evaporate. Meantime, telling on, he would be running his thumb over the ax-blade, testing its sharpness or dullness. He would spend the whole day watering the grindstone and testing the ax without grinding it at all, but in the end he would have told enough stories to fill the hopper of a corn-grinder waiting to be repaired.

Among the stories that Railroad Smith told me that night and on other occasions was one of two oxen that, after being driven to South Texas by an early settler, got loose and made their way back east of the Mississippi River. I put those oxen into *The Longhorns*. He told me the stories of John Booth's ride of vengeance and of Gregorio Cortez on his little brown mare, both of which I put into a long piece first called "The Saga of the Saddle" and then "Riders of the Stars." After appearing in several places, these rides were finally lodged in *The Mustangs*. I am not sure, but I think Railroad Smith had defended Gregorio Cortez. Anyhow, he visited Gregorio in the penitentiary in Huntsville, where the convict gave him the details of his ride. It takes details and details to make a story, and Railroad Smith's memory held details as securely as the vise in the blacksmith's shop held the handle of a branding iron. Even better than his memory was his ability as creator to supply details. "Disremembering" may at times contribute more to art than remembering.

Storytellers, storytellers. They string out in my memory like a long, long recua of pack mules, each of a different brand, different color, and different disposition, twisting through the mountains, going down in the canyons, climbing up over the cumbres, trailing across plains of fine grass to an unreachable beyond. Compared with the ideals of slickness, noise, and religiosity they seem almost mythological characters, but they were more real than facts, all of them belonging to times when folks had to amuse themselves, before machines to furnish amusement had been invented. There was John Rigby of Beeville, who had bossed herds of longhorns up the trail to Wyoming, and who for years was brand inspector for the Texas and Southwestern Cattle Raisers Association. I judge that he made up a good deal of the story of Old Sancho, the steer that came back to Esperanza Creek in Frio County, Texas, after being trailed clear to Wyoming. I myself did some constructive work on the story. My publishing it and other stories from John Rigby made him an object of derision among certain masculine vulgarians of the town. He did not end life with the joy deserved by a wonderful storyteller. He did not belong among ignorant literalists.

One afternoon I started from Albuquerque to Santa Fe, expecting to spend an hour with my old friend Jack (N. Howard) Thorp at Alameda, a few miles out on the road. When night came Jack was still telling, and I was still hearing on. We had supper and he kept telling. I was welcomed to stay all night, but there wasn't an extra bed. In those days I always carried a bedroll. Jack made coffee before daylight, and kept on talking. I put a very fine mustang story of his in my mustang book. Some of his superb stories are in his posthumous book *Pardner of the Wind*, but some of his best never got into any book. It takes the right chemical mixture to bring any talker, any storyteller, alive. Jack and I were finely suited to each other and each knew it.

One of the most abundant tellers of rattlesnake lore I have ever listened to was Dr. Syfert of the Cusihuiriachic Mine in Chihuahua. He had seen with his own eyes, heard with his own ears. I never knew Captain Frank Hamer of the Texas Rangers so well as I wanted to know him. One night in the latter part of his life at a dinner out on a ranch, before we had eaten but not before we had drunken, he unloosed his word hoard on the creatures of the Southwest as he had observed them while riding for years on a horse and sleeping on the ground. That night he made me realize what a delightful, although not historically or biologically accurate, observer he could be in narration. Any good talker, no matter how many nonfacts he employs, is better than the encyclopedia.

I never heard a really good talker who could not narrate. I suppose Roy Bedichek was the most excellent civilized narrator I've known. He seldom told folktales. He excelled in sketches of people and in narratives of incidents out of his own life, weaving in enrichments from the classics and also from barbers, cedar-cutters, farmers, freighters, cowboys, and other men of the earth who had never read a classic and very little of anything else, infusing humor and humanity into the whole.

John Lomax could not be surpassed in stories of human beings connected with his own wide experiences. Many of Carl Sandburg's best stories do not grow out of his own experiences but out of what he's heard and read; perhaps Abraham Lincoln gave him something in the art of applying a story. Will Burges, lawyer of El Paso, is gone now. In his gusto for life he was one of the best eaters I've ever seen eat and one of the best talkers I've ever heard talk. He never let his eating interfere with his talking or his talking interfere with his eating. All he needed to turn a feast of beef into a flow of soul was a good listener. I tried more than once to get him to put down some of his stories. He would merely laugh and say, "O that mine enemy had written a book." His lack of ambition to make literary use of what he knew made his talk better, I suppose. Dr. Samuel Johnson became the great talker after he had ceased to write much.

Walter Webb, the thinker, did not weave narratives into his histories nearly to the extent that he wove them into his talk. He lived, observed and remembered. The wells of narrative and characterization were in artesian flow with him. I can truly say that I've enjoyed reading Herodotus more than any other historian. Herodotus never allows fact to get in the way of narration — or truth — or rhetorical laws of coherence to dam the flow. He is one of the great storytellers of all ages. When Evetts Haley cuts loose from documented facts, he's the same kind of storyteller that Herodotus was, perhaps now with more irony.

What's the use of going on? It's pictures and stories that count — not allusions.

I do not believe that any young man of parts could today set out to find storytellers and meet them on every hand as I met them between the World Wars. Instead of entertaining each other with tribal lays now, tribesmen listen to radio and look at television. I suspect that the percentage of good storytellers among the sophisticated who spurn sponsored amusements along with canned advertisements is higher than among the unsophisticated who can afford television and radio. Slick stuff may promote sterile wisecracks but will never engender characters and stories.

When Chaucer comes with his tales and John Aubrey with his character anecdotes, ideas and causes fade away. All of Samuel Taylor Coleridge's metaphysical theories, spun out of philosophy-befogged intellect, are forgotten; his sure passport to immortality is that tale called "The Rime of the Ancient Mariner." I have an enormous respect for thought. I surrender all to a storyteller — if he's good enough. It's the despair of a writing man who has known the best of storytellers that he cannot translate their oral savor into print.

INDEX